Annual Editions:
Comparative Politics
32/e

Edited by Caroline Westerhof
CA National University for Advanced Studies

http://create.mcgraw-hill.com

ISBN-10: 1259224961   ISBN-13: 9781259224966

Contents

Preface

In publishing ANNUAL EDITIONS we recognize the enormous role played by the magazines, newspapers, and journals of the public press in providing current, first-rate educational information in a broad spectrum of interest areas. Many of these articles are appropriate for students, researchers, and professionals seeking accurate, current material to help bridge the gap between principles and theories and the real world. These articles, however, become more useful for study when those of lasting value are carefully collected, organized, indexed, and reproduced in a low-cost format, which provides easy and permanent access when the material is needed. That is the role played by ANNUAL EDITIONS.

Comparative politics focuses on the empirical study of political behaviors, institutions, actors, legitimate and illegitimate regulations and rules to facilitate explanations, predictions, and theory-building. This book sets as its task the presentation of information based on systematic study of such behaviors, institutions, and rules.

The volume is organized to emphasize political behaviors, institutions, actors, and rules from a comparative perspective. Current comparative political texts make similar arguments regarding the need for such a focus. This is a comparative study, which may or may not be specifically regional or country specific.

Annual Editions: Comparative Politics, 32/e develops, where possible, comparative relationships about how people and governments behave and interact politically. Such is determined by rules, institutions, and actors that are in place across a range of countries and political systems. Systematic generalizations that address the questions of "why, what, and how" regarding political behaviors and institutions apply across countries and political systems. We do not dispute that country-relevant information contextualizes behavior and interactions. Rather, we consider it necessary to clarify the generalizations that provide baseline knowledge regarding "why, what, and how" of political behaviors and institutions. With this baseline in place, particularities that are observed become even more interesting or unusual and are more easily understood.

We address the relevant political questions of "why, what, and how" regarding political behaviors, actors, and within institutions. Students are introduced to debates, questions, and circumstances that create the issues involved within the diversity of the global arena; such data is drawn from the news, public press, current governmental readings, and referred journals across different nation-states.

Each of the readings has Learning Outcomes, Critical Thinking questions, and Internet References to help facilitate the student's learning and understanding of the topics. This academic structure ensures that students see how the discipline and issues connect with other nation-states and are involved in the practicum of world politics, whether in individual countries, in multinational relationships, or within world organizations.

We become aware of the ever-changing footsteps, military and civilian, involved in globalization. There are the political changes going on in the Arab states, in the Middle East, in Burma, the instability of older democracies

such as India, the economic and political crises in the African countries. Such data underscores the crucial importance of knowledge regarding foreign governments and societies. In the global society and within the world economic issues, poor or weak governments, institutions, and changing actors have direct consequences on our lives.

Comparative politics is a dynamic subfield in political science. It reveals how other academic and social disciplines study governments and politics, showcasing the significance of the comparative political science approach.

We approach democratic theory, its ramifications and varied interpretations, emphasizing the nature of comparative politics. It is a theoretically driven enterprise, with its requisite debates, tests, and counter-arguments raised and evaluated over time.

The reality of discussions on democratic theory highlights the relevance of citizen participation and addresses why and how citizen participation is organized and in what forms. The emphasis is on the particularities of interest groups and political parties, advocacy groups, and pressure politics as outlets of political behavior that, if repressed or ignored, may lead people to find "less democratic ways" to participate.

The political discipline of the social sciences must consider the actors and the institutions of government in addressing questions regarding the roles they play in the political process, how they affect political behaviors, and, perhaps most importantly, how their successes or failures are evaluated.

The executive, in the study of comparative politics, plays the leadership role of accountability and responsiveness to the public. How that role is handled in both democratic and autocratic systems of government determines the nation-states' responses to world issues.

Accountability in the nation's legislature may increase citizen participation if it is within a democratic system. It can be implemented as the mouthpiece of the autocratic leader. Given the importance of representation aspect, some nation-states may seek to improve participation of minorities, including women, and to understand how electoral systems may hinder or improve that representation.

The unelected bureaucrats and members of the government include the judiciary, military, civil servants, and others who are involved in policymaking. Is there resentment against unelected officials, even in democratic governments? In fact, it was recently noted that many, at times, find the political activism of United States Supreme Court decisions to be distasteful, and believe that such "judicial policy-making" should be left to the elected political actors.

How do institutional changes occur? By election, by military coups, and other means? Institutional actions and political behaviors are reciprocal.

The transitions in the Middle East certainly reveal that our thinking about how transitions occur need to be revisited. Domestic demand and new pressures are essential for initiating institutional changes; however, it is not culture but, rather, tolerance and equality that fuel the strengthening of democracy. Equally important, are ways that authoritarian governments circumvent this push for democratic accountability and responsiveness. Autocratic leaders, sooner or later, recognize that the world scene views accountability, responsiveness, representation, and civic participation as crucial, even under a dictatorial regime.

What do we need to know in order to project how the political arenas on the global scene will develop? It is important to understand foreign political institutions and policy processes. Whether we look at Asia and the eastern part of the world or Europe, the Middle East, or the Americas, can we uncover the predispositions of what regions will embrace the transition to democracy, and what regions will be controlled by authoritarianism, a reminder of how important it is to understand foreign political institutions and policy-processes?

There are several individuals to thank for this current volume. Thanks go to the editorial staff at McGraw-Hill, particularly Jill Meloy, Senior Developmental Editor, for clear and insightful advice, support, and gentle reminders of deadlines. Also, thanks to the many colleagues at the Australian National University and the University of Kansas, whose support, advice, and critiques are gratefully recognized. The responses of the advisory board members in critiquing and suggesting selections in this edition are instrumental; we are indebted to their painstaking efforts and commitment to see an improved, accessible, and academically rigorous edition. Finally, thanks to the readers, whose comments helped with the selection of readings. We hope that you will continue to help improve future editions by keeping us informed of your reactions and suggestions for change.

Caroline Westerhof
Editor

Editor

Caroline Shaffer Westerhof is an online adjunct professor for several universities across the United States. Her students participate from all parts of the world, including Afghanistan, Iraq, Qatar, Ghana, Germany, Japan, Puerto Rico, and other areas. She was a tenured full professor within The City University of New York; she is an international management organization analyst and mediator; among the publications she has authored is "The Executive Connection..." the first management study on press secretaries to elected mayors, and she has researched press secretaries to presidents of the United States from

the time of Roger Tubby to the week before James Brady and President Reagan were shot. She is also the author of "The Petology Series: Letters to Charlye," has had poetry published in several collections, as well as articles in professional journals and newspapers. Dr. Westerhof was a special negotiator to the U.S. Presidential Commission on Regulatory Affairs; the first female visiting professor at the U.S. Air War College; and in cooperation with the U.S. State Department set up public and business management programs in Ghana. She has spoken on U.S. presidential elections on BBC, London; was a political analyst for ABC News, and lectured at the CIA. Westerhof is a member of the Academy of International Business, has been CEO of a transportation-related corporation, as well as director of regulatory affairs for a multinational business. She is also a member of the American Society of Public Administration, the MidSouth Sociological Association, as well as other professional groups.

Academic Advisory Board

Correlation Guide

The *Annual Editions* series provides students with convenient, inexpensive access to current, carefully selected articles from the public press. **Annual Editions: Comparative Politics, 32/e** is an easy-to-use reader that presents articles on important topics such as *evaluating theories, political trends, institutional frameworks, administrative accountability and responsiveness, everyday politics,* and many more. For more information on *Annual Editions* and other *McGraw-Hill Create™* titles, visit www.mcgrawhillcreate.com.

This convenient guide matches the articles in **Annual Editions: Comparative Politics, 32/e** with **Comparative Politics: An Introduction, 1/e** by Klesner

Comparative Politics: An Introduction, 1/e	Annual Editions: Comparative Politics, 32/e
Chapter 1: Comparative Politics	Iran Press Report: Reactions to Developments in Lebanon, Egypt, and Syria Rumors of Central Command's Decline are Wishful Thinking U.S. Army Learns Lessons in N. Korea-like War Game We Shall Return What Caused the Economic Crisis? Will Tunisia Follow Egypt?
Chapter 2: Critical Thinking about Politics	The Coming Wave How India Stumbled: Can New Delhi Get Its Groove Back? Iran Press Report: Reactions to Developments in Lebanon, Egypt, and Syria Is Burma Democratizing? A New Growth Paradigm The Protesters and the Public Towards a Renewed Global Partnership for Development White House's Egypt Debate Heralds Shift Why Middle East Studies Missed the Arab Spring: The Myth of Authoritarian Stability Will Tunisia Follow Egypt?
Chapter 3: The State and Its Institutions	Africa's Turn: A Conversation with Macky Sall BJP Will Achieve Record Breaking Results in Lok Sabha Polls: Advani A Cautious Win in Egypt's Power Struggle The CIA's New Black Bag Is Digital David Cameron's Dangerous Game: The Folly of Flirting with an EU Exit Disabling the Constitution: Hungary's Illiberal Turn Foreign Talent and the Thriving Malaysian Economy How India Stumbled: Can New Delhi Get Its Groove Back? Intensive Care for the United Nations Is Burma Democratizing? Israel's Unity Government: A Bid to Represent the Majority Non-Telangana Ministers: MPs Oppose Division of Andhra Pradesh North Korea Rare Haven of Stability in Somalia Faces a Test Rumors of Central Command's Decline Are Wishful Thinking Srebrenica's Legacy: How the Lessons of the Balkans Animate Humanitarianism Today United Arab Emirates (UAE)—Government and Economy U.S. Army Learns Lessons in N. Korea-like War Game We Shall Return
Chapter 4: States and Nations	Africa's Turn: A Conversation with Macky Sall BJP Will Achieve Record Breaking Results in Lok Sabha Polls: Advani A Cautious Win in Egypt's Power Struggle Disabling the Constitution: Hungary's Illiberal Turn Exclusive: Eritrea Pays Warlord to Influence Somalia—U.N. Experts Non-Telangana Ministers: MPs Oppose Division of Andhra Pradesh North Korea Pakistan 2020: A Vision for Building a Better Future Rare Haven of Stability in Somalia Faces a Test The Technocrats and Tahrir Will Tunisia Follow Egypt?
Chapter 5: Democracy: What is it?	The Coming Wave Democracy in Cyberspace: What Information Technology Can and Cannot Do Is Burma Democratizing? Making Modernity Work: The Reconciliation of Capitalism and Democracy Twenty-Five Years, Fifteen Findings Will Tunisia Follow Egypt?

Comparative Politics: An Introduction, 1/e	Annual Editions: Comparative Politics, 32/e
Chapter 6: Democracy: How Does It Work?	How India Stumbled: Can New Delhi Get Its Groove Back? Is Burma Democratizing? Making Modernity Work: The Reconciliation of Capitalism and Democracy Twenty-Five Years, Fifteen Findings
Chapter 7: Democracy: What Does It Take?	The Coming Wave Democracy in Cyberspace: What Information Technology Can and Cannot Do How India Stumbled: Can New Delhi Get Its Groove Back? Is Burma Democratizing? Making Modernity Work: The Reconciliation of Capitalism and Democracy Twenty-Five Years, Fifteen Findings Will Tunisia Follow Egypt?
Chapter 8: Political Participation	BJP Will Achieve Record Breaking Results in Lok Sabha Polls: Advani The CIA's New Black Bag Is Digital Chile's Middle Class Flexes Its Muscles China's Cyberposse Exclusive: Eritrea Pays Warlord to Influence Somalia—U.N. Experts Few Good Choices for U.S. in Mideast Is Burma Democratizing? Making Modernity Work: The Reconciliation of Capitalism and Democracy The Protesters and the Public Srebrenica's Legacy: How the Lessons of the Balkans Animate Humanitarianism Today A Video Campaign and the Power of Simplicity White House's Egypt Debate Heralds Shift Why Middle East Studies Missed the Arab Spring: The Myth of Authoritarian Stability Will Tunisia Follow Egypt?
Chapter 9: Political Culture	Exclusive: Eritrea Pays Warlord to Influence Somalia—U.N. Experts The Famous Dutch (In)Tolerance Rare Haven of Stability in Somalia Faces a Test Srebrenica's Legacy: How the Lessons of the Balkans Animate Humanitarianism Today The Technocrats and Tahrir White House's Egypt Debate Heralds Shift Why Middle East Studies Missed the Arab Spring: The Myth of Authoritarian Stability Will Tunisia Follow Egypt?
Chapter 10: Ideology	Africa's Turn: A Conversation with Macky Sall David Cameron's Dangerous Game: The Folly of Flirting with an EU Exit A Cautious Win in Egypt's Power Struggle Defending an Open, Global, Secure and Resilient Internet Disabling the Constitution: Hungary's Illiberal Turn Exclusive: Eritrea Pays Warlord to Influence Somalia—U.N. Experts The Famous Dutch (In)Tolerance Iran Press Report: Reactions to Developments in Lebanon, Egypt, and Syria White House's Egypt Debate Heralds Shift
Chapter 11: Political Economy	Africa's Turn: A Conversation with Macky Sall The Coming Wave Economy Slows "Due to Rebalancing" Foreign Talent and the Thriving Malaysian Economy The Future of U.S.-Chinese Relations: Conflict Is a Choice, Not a Necessity How India Stumbled: Can New Delhi Get Its Groove Back? Making Modernity Work: The Reconciliation of Capitalism and Democracy A New Growth Paradigm The Protesters and the Public Recalibrating American Grand Strategy: Softening US Policies Toward Iran in Order to Contain China Singapore Poll Energizes Voters Taking the Arctic Route from China Technocrats and Tahrir Towards a Renewed Global Partnership for Development United Arab Emirates (UAE)-Government and Economy U.S., China Hopeful of BIT After Talks Reignited Wang, Yang Make the Rounds in DC What Caused the Economic Crisis?
Chapter 12: The Politics of Development	A New Growth Paradigm Pakistan 2020: A Vision for Building a Better Future Towards a Renewed Global Partnership for Development

Comparative Politics: An Introduction, 1/e	Annual Editions: Comparative Politics, 32/e
Chapter 13: The United Kingdom of Great Britain	David Cameron's Dangerous Game: The Folly of Flirting with an EU Exit
Chapter 14: Russia	The Protesters and the Public
Chapter 15: China	China's Cyberposse Economy Slows "Due to Rebalancing" The Future of U.S.-Chinese Relations: Conflict Is a Choice, Not a Necessity Recalibrating American Grand Strategy: Softening US Policies Toward Iran in Order to Contain China Taking the Arctic Route from China U.S., China Hopeful of BIT After Talks Reignited Wang, Yang Make the Rounds in DC
Chapter 18: South America	Chile's Middle Class Flexes Its Muscles
Chapter 19: Africa	Africa's Turn: A Conversation with Macky Sall Exclusive: Eritrea Pays Warlord to Influence Somalia—U.N. Experts Rare Haven of Stability in Somalia Faces a Test We Shall Return

Topic Guide

This topic guide suggests how the selections in this book relate to the subjects covered in your course. You may want to use the topics listed on these pages to search the Web more easily.

All the articles that relate to each topic are listed below the bold-faced term.

Asian politics and society

China's Cyberposse
The Coming Wave
Foreign Talent and the Thriving Malaysian Economy
The Future of U.S. – Chinese Relations: Conflict Is a Choice, Not a
  Necessity
How India Stumbled: Can New Delhi Get Its Groove Back?
Is Burma Democratizing?
North Korea
Recalibrating American Grand Strategy: Softening US Policies Toward
  Iran in Order to Contain China
Singapore Poll Energizes Voters
Taking the Arctic Route from China
U.S. Army Learns Lessons in N. Korea-like War Game
U.S., China Hopeful of BIT after Talks Reignited
Wang, Yang Make the Rounds in DC

Citizen participation and mobilization

BJP Will Achieve Record Breaking Results in Lok Sabha Polls: Advani
A Cautious Win in Egypt's Power Struggle
Chile's Middle Class Flexes Its Muscles
Democracy in Cyberspace: What Information Technology Can and
  Cannot Do
How India Stumbled: Can New Delhi Get Its Groove Back?
Is Burma Democratizing?
Israel's Unity Government: A Bid to Represent the Majority
Making Modernity Work: The Reconciliation of Capitalism and
  Democracy
The Protesters and the Public
Rare Haven of Stability in Somalia Faces a Test
Singapore Poll Energizes Voters
Srebrenica's Legacy: How the Lessons of the Balkans Animate
  Humanitarianism Today
Twenty-Five Years, Fifteen Findings
A Video Campaign and the Power of Simplicity
Why Middle East Studies Missed the Arab Spring: The Myth of
  Authoritarian Stability
Will Tunisia Follow Egypt?

The economy and economics

Africa's Turn: A Conversation with Macky Sall
The Coming Wave
Defending an Open, Global, Secure, and Resilient Internet
Disabling the Constitution: Hungary's Illiberal Turn
Economy Slows "Due to Rebalancing"
Foreign Talent and the Thriving Malaysian Economy
The Future of U.S. – Chinese Relations: Conflict Is a Choice, Not a
  Necessity
How India Stumbled: Can New Delhi Get Its Groove Back?
Making Modernity Work: The Reconciliation of Capitalism and
  Democracy
A New Growth Paradigm
Pakistan 2020: A Vision for Building a Better Future
The Protesters and the Public
Recalibrating American Grand Strategy: Softening US Policies Toward
  Iran in Order to Contain China
Singapore Poll Energizes Voters
Taking the Arctic Route from China
The Technocrats and Tahrir
Towards a Renewed Global Partnership for Development
U.S., China Hopeful of BIT after Talks Reignited
United Arab Emirates (UAE) – Government and Economy
Wang, Yang Make the Rounds in DC
What Caused the Economic Crisis?

Elections and regime types

Africa's Turn: A Conversation with Macky Sall
BJP Will Achieve Record Breaking Results in Lok Sabha Polls: Advani
A Cautious Win in Egypt's Power Struggle
Chile's Middle Class Flexes Its Muscles
The Coming Wave
David Cameron's Dangerous Game: The Folly of Flirting with an EU Exit
Disabling the Constitution: Hungary's Illiberal Turn
Exclusive: Eritrea Pays Warlord to Influence Somalia—U.N. Experts
The Famous Dutch (In)Tolerance
The Future of U.S. – Chinese Relations: Conflict Is a Choice, Not a
  Necessity
Iran Press Report: Reactions to Developments in Lebanon, Egypt, and
  Syria
Is Burma Democratizing?
Israel's Unity Government: A Bid to Represent the Majority
Making Modernity Work: The Reconciliation of Capitalism and
  Democracy
Non-Telangana Ministers, MPs Oppose Division of Andhra Pradesh
North Korea
The Protesters and the Public
Rare Haven of Stability in Somalia Faces a Test
Singapore Poll Energizes Voters
The Technocrats and Tahrir
Why Middle East Studies Missed the Arab Spring: The Myth of
  Authoritarian Stability
Will Tunisia Follow Egypt?

The executive or legislature in less democratic systems

A Cautious Win in Egypt's Power Struggle
Disabling the Constitution: Hungary's Illiberal Turn
Exclusive: Eritrea Pays Warlord to Influence Somalia—U.N. Experts
Iran Press Report: Reactions to Developments in Lebanon, Egypt, and
  Syria
Making Modernity Work: The Reconciliation of Capitalism and
  Democracy
North Korea
Rare Haven of Stability in Somalia Faces a Test
Why Middle East Studies Missed the Arab Spring: The Myth of
  Authoritarian Stability

The executive or legislature in parliamentary systems

David Cameron's Dangerous Game: The Folly of Flirting with an EU Exit
The Famous Dutch (In)Tolerance
How India Stumbled: Can New Delhi Get Its Groove Back?
Intensive Care for the United Nations
Is Burma Democratizing?
Israel's Unity Government: A Bid to Represent the Majority
Singapore Poll Energizes Voters

The executive or legislature in presidential systems

Africa's Turn: A Conversation with Macky Sall
A Cautious Win in Egypt's Power Struggle
Iran Press Report: Reactions to Developments in Lebanon, Egypt, and
  Syria
A New Growth Paradigm
Non-Telangana Ministers, MPs Oppose Division of Andhra Pradesh
North Korea
Pakistan 2020: A Vision for Building a Better Future

Unit 1

UNIT

Prepared by: Caroline Shaffer Westerhof,
California National University for Advanced Studies

Why Comparative Politics?

Why do we study foreign government institutions or the policies they make? Clearly, part of the answer is "interest" and to create understanding and develop awareness. That is, we study foreign government institutions, their policymaking processes, and the resultant policies. We need to comprehend what is similar or different from us, encapsulating our interests in foreign governments, institutions, and the policies that follow from such governments and institutions. It is important that we understand what happens in other countries, the ways they are different, and what motivates their changes.

It is imperative that we recognize issues, similarities, and dissimilarities in understanding comparative politics. Studying comparative politics helps us to become aware so that we may make projections regarding what will happen next to some of our closest allies or affect our largest trading partners. There is the strong humanitarian consideration: Before we are able to help, we need to gain knowledge and insights into foreign government institutions, their policymaking processes, and actual policies.

The security, political, and economic considerations capture the other parts of globalization: Globalization, which has brought with it many advantages from economic, social, and cultural exchange, has also left us more exposed to the frailties of foreign governments and policy failures. Whereas geography may previously pose a viable line of defense against weak or erratic governments, the increasing interconnectedness of countries through trade, migration, and the Internet—a process termed *globalization*—has rendered physical boundaries almost meaningless. As a result, we are no longer insulated from the ramifications of recalcitrant governments or citizens in foreign countries. Instead, issues ranging from the political unrest in the Middle East, civil war in Africa, and the economic crises across Europe are directly affecting our lives and livelihoods. These reverberations stress that we need to be cognitive to the activities, citizens, and actors in other countries.

The need to understand institutions and policy processes is all the more relevant given that we do not have successful regional or international institutions for mediating conflicts or addressing the humanitarian, welfare, or social problems that arise. History reminds us that many such regional or international agencies are far from functional. Further, with information disseminated at lightning speed, we are prone to inaccurate interpretations and incorrect conclusions without a basic political and social knowledge of any country. Even though we are witness to a country ravaged by civil strife, we must also be attentive to the fact that our offers of aid are often delivered with simplistic and unrealistic expectations. Such expectations may do more damage in the long run, particularly to political socioeconomic relations within and between countries.

Thus, consider, for instance, that the long history of aid extension to Africa has brought few successes, in part because the aid was fueled by the clamor to "do something." And, the poor success has spurred an "anti-aid" position that almost seems ideological. What does this tell us? More so than before, there is a need to for us to be equipped to participate as a global citizen: to gain knowledge and understanding of political institutions, processes, and systems in order to contribute meaningfully and empathetically. Also, the porous financial and geographical borders of globalization mean that we come face to face with the fallout of political and social instability more often and sooner than previous eras. And, these occur across industrialized democracies such as Norway and Britain, as well as less-industrialized countries of India, Afghanistan, and in the African continent. If we think we are insulated from the problems of failed political institutions and corruption, take a look at the reports of the felony and criminal charges that the United States Securities and Exchange Commission has filed, and think again. Should we consider—in light of the economic doldrums in the United States—that the experience in Britain may be more relevant to us than we would like to admit?

Clearly, there are humanitarian, economic, and social imperatives to learning about foreign government institutions and policy processes. This is relevant, not only from the perspective of an aid-giver; it is also important given that the porous borders of globalization may lead us to face the same political, social, or economic circumstances.

Now comes the challenge: How do we learn about foreign governments and policies? What do we need to take away from that learning? This is no small task: The UN recognizes 192 countries; this number does not include several that are not UN members.[1] The United States government recognizes 195 autonomous countries in the world.[2] The list easily expands beyond 250 if we include nations that are self-governing as well as those that are not. A nation is defined as "a group of people whose members share a common identity on the basis of distinguishing characteristics and claim to a territorial homeland."[3] Each of these nations or countries has long histories that may bear on the government's behaviors or the responses of their people and also influence what institutions and rules are considered and adopted. Clearly, learning about the particularities, of even one country, requires considerable time and effort, let alone the more than 100 formally recognized ones.

How do we accomplish this? From the political science perspective, it means we start with some fundamentals, such as:

What is comparative politics? What do we compare? How do we compare? Why do we compare? Who are the actors? How do we define the culture or multicultural aspects of the environment and its particular boundaries?

What is comparative politics? *Comparative Politics* refers to the study of governments and the potential of inter-relationships. That seems clear. Yet, popular dictionaries such as the Merriam-Webster's and Oxford Dictionary contain no less than five and as many as ten different ways of conceiving the word "government." They include[4]:

1. The exercise of authority over a state, district, or territory.
2. A system of ruling, controlling, or administering.
3. The executive branch of a government.
4. All the people and institutions that exercise control over the affairs of a nation or state.
5. The study of such systems, people, and institutions.

These definitions emphasize several concepts integral to comparative politics: authority, system, people and institutions, and state, district, or territory. In the broadest sense, comparative politics involves the systematic comparison of authority, systems, people, and institutions across states, districts, or other territories. Its focus is both formal and informal. Comparative politics focuses on the patterns of politics within a domestic territory, where political parties, interest groups, civil servants, the public, and the press interact under specified laws to influence who gets what, when, how, and why.

Comparative politics emphasizes careful empirical study as the way to gain knowledge about how people and governments behave and interact politically, given rules and institutions that are in place. It is important to note that other disciplines also study how people and governments behave; however, their goals or ends for such study are different.

We compare nation-states for several reasons: First, it provides a way to systematically consider how people and institutions across different countries, districts, or systems balance the competing goals of stability, change, security, freedom, growth, accountability, and responsiveness. Thus, for the political practitioner, analyst, or scholar, comparative politics is applied to describe, clarify, and, subsequently, understand change or stability. Second, we compare in order to enhance theory-building. Theory building is predicated on examination and evaluation, testing and retesting, in order to achieve, if possible, generalization and projections for the future, either negative or positive, or both. The comparative method in political science is one of the means toward this end of theory building.

Thus, comparative politics provides systematic generalizations regarding political behaviors, processes, and institutions to promote learning with greater efficiency. This understanding of why we compare in political science is important because it distinguishes political science from other disciplines. For example, the history discipline may also study governments; however, the focus of such study is directed at fact-finding and gathering to enhance interpretation and accuracy. Importantly, then, knowing a lot about a country or an area does not make one a comparative political scholar. It is the interrelationships that matter, and the baseline knowledge that is derived from particularities of observation, description, explanation, and through projection, possibly anticipated.

Our awareness of possible generalizations may be drawn regarding which countries democratize, how countries democratize, and why they democratize. At the most fundamental, what the people want from their governments in terms of accountability and representation is key. Thus, international political actors—including foreign governments and institutions such as the UN—will do well by paying attention to the domestic political conditions that contextualize how solutions are formulated and implemented. This is an ongoing process—no matter how far along a country appears in the political development spectrum (consider India)—the context of what people want drives their support of the government and the institutions. And, notwithstanding different countries and systems, there are fundamental behaviors, processes, and institutions needed to achieve the balance among the factors of stability, change, security, freedom, growth, accountability, and responsiveness. We seek the tasks of the identification of those behaviors, processes, and institutions in order to map out what is needed for the balance, and when possible, a global peace.

Note

1. The United Nations. un.org/News/Press/docs//2007/org1479.doc .htm

2. United States Department of State. www.state.gov/s/inr/rls/4250 .htm

3. Michael Sodaro. 2007. *Comparative Politics: A Global Introduction,* 3rd edition. New York: McGraw Hill.

4. *Oxford Dictionary.* oxforddictionaries.com/definition/government? region 5 us; *Merriam-Webster's Online Dictionary.* www.merriam-webster.com/dictionary/government

Article

Prepared by: Caroline Shaffer Westerhof,
California National University for Advanced Studies

David Cameron's Dangerous Game

The Folly of Flirting with an EU Exit

MATTHIAS MATTHIJS

Learning Outcomes

After reading this article, you will be able to:

- Explain the economic argument of why the United Kingdom should leave the EU.

- Explain the politics and policies of why many members of the Conservative Party in the United Kingdom have turned against Europe.

- Distinguish the politics of Franklin Roosevelt and Charles deGaulle relative to Prime Minister Winston Churchill's statement that if he had to pick between the two, he would always choose the leader of the United States.

Despite his innate caution and usually sound political instincts, British Prime Minister David Cameron is gambling with his country's future. In January, in a long-anticipated speech, he called for a wide-ranging renegotiation of the terms of the United Kingdom's membership in the European Union and promised to put the result up for a straight in-or-out popular referendum by the end of 2017 (assuming his party wins the next election, due in 2015). A British exit from the EU is now more likely than ever—and it would be disastrous not only for the United Kingdom but also for the rest of Europe and the United States.

If London does ultimately cut the rope, it will not be the result of rational political or economic calculations. British Euroskepticism boils down to a visceral dislike of Brussels—the host of a number of European institutions and the EU's de facto capital—on the part of an ill-informed conservative minority that clings to an antiquated notion of national sovereignty. These sentiments are on display every day in the right-wing tabloids, which play on voters' fears with vitriolic commentary and sensationalistic headlines, such as "Eu Wants to Merge UK With France" and "EU Will Grab Britain's Gas," both of which recently appeared in the *Daily Express*.

By caving in to the demands of the right wing of his party, Cameron appears to be falling into the same trap that his predecessors fell into. Both Margaret Thatcher and John Major, the previous two Conservative prime ministers, were eventually thrown out of office as their party tore itself apart over the issue of European integration during the late 1980s and mid-1990s. In 1995, these divisions among the Conservatives led a young Labour opposition leader named Tony Blair to ridicule Major on the floor of the House of Commons, scoffing, "I lead my party; he follows his." Even Cameron himself, back in 2006, less than a year after he took over the Conservative Party, wisely counseled his colleagues to "stop banging on about Europe" if they ever wanted to win elections again.

And yet, seven years later, Cameron faces a simmering rebellion on an issue that most Britons still do not care much about but that has once again turned toxic in his party. In a 2012 survey of the British electorate, only six percent of respondents described Europe as the most salient issue facing the country, compared with 67 percent who prioritized the economy, 35 percent who worried most about unemployment, and just over 20 percent whose main concerns were immigration and race relations.

With his January speech, Cameron had hoped to achieve four short-term objectives. First, he wanted to stop the growing threat on his party's right flank from the anti-EU and anti-immigration UK Independence Party, whose populist leader, Nigel Farage, positions himself as a champion of British common sense and defender of British sovereignty against Brussels' encroachment. Second, Cameron aimed to neutralize his own party's increasingly restless Euroskeptic backbenchers, many of whom also advocate a British exit from the EU. Third, he hoped to put the losing political issue of Europe to rest until the next parliament. Fourth, he tried to portray the country's economic woes as a result of the eurozone crisis rather than of his own government's biting austerity measures.

On all four fronts, however, it appears that Cameron miscalculated. The UK Independence Party wildly outperformed expectations in the local elections in May, earning close to a quarter of the overall vote. The Euroskeptics in the Conservative Party are still insisting on a referendum during the current parliament, underscoring once again that they cannot be appeased on the European question and do not trust the prime minister to deliver on it. Cameron's leadership is more tenuous than ever, especially after he pushed through a contentious bill in support of gay marriage, a stance that many party activists find hard to swallow. (The fact that one of Cameron's close advisers referred to these activists as "mad, swivel-eyed loons" has not helped.) And finally, a slew of recent scholarly studies, including one published by the International Monetary Fund, have blown a giant hole in the intellectual case for austerity, undercutting the government's economic strategy. But far more is at stake than one prime minister's political career. If the United Kingdom ends up abandoning Europe, it will feel the negative economic and political effects for decades to come.

A Marriage of Convenience

The United Kingdom's relationship with Europe has never been warm, much less passionate; it is more like a loveless arranged marriage. Based on cost-benefit analysis rather than lofty rhetoric about a common European destiny, the country's European affair has been fraught with abysmal timing and shattered hopes. When the country first knocked on Brussels' door in the 1960s, it found its applications unceremoniously rejected by France's Charles de Gaulle. In 1973, when Edward Heath, a Conservative prime minister, successfully steered the United Kingdom toward membership in the European Economic Community, the Western world was about to slip into its first deep postwar recession. The subsequent Labour government, facing opposition to European integration from its left-wing backbenchers, felt the need to put Heath's decision to a national referendum, which eventually passed in 1975 by a two-to-one margin.

During the 1980s, Thatcher told her European partners that the United Kingdom wanted "a very large amount of [its] own money back" and warned them that she had not successfully rolled back the frontiers of government at home only to see them reintroduced through the backdoor by Brussels. At the beginning of the next decade, against her better judgment, she let her country join Europe's Exchange Rate Mechanism, a precursor to the monetary union. Major, then chancellor of the exchequer, had convinced her that this was the best way to tame inflation, which had been creeping up again at the end of the 1980s. But joining the ERM meant dancing to the tune of Germany's monetary policy, and soaring German interest rates to fight inflation and finance German reunification meant that the Bank of England had to follow the Bundesbank's lead in hiking up interest rates. Doing so at the onset of another domestic recession meant political suicide, however, and the United Kingdom was forced to leave the ERM only a few years after it joined.

After succeeding Thatcher as prime minister, Major negotiated various areas in which the United Kingdom could opt out of the Maastricht Treaty, which created the EU, most notably keeping the United Kingdom out of the common currency while allowing it to retain full EU membership. Blair, who as prime minister passionately told the French National Assembly in a 1998 speech that be shared the European ideal, at one point sought to bring his country onto the euro, but he was blocked by his powerful chancellor of the exchequer, Gordon Brown.

In some ways, the United Kingdom's quandary today looks like it did 40 years ago, when the country first joined the European Economic Community. Then, as now, the British were in deep, mostly self-inflicted economic trouble. In the 1970s, however, the politics of the issue were flipped: the Conservatives saw integration with Europe as a liberalizing move, and the Heath government believed it was the only way to reverse the country's relative economic decline. Thatcher, for her part, campaigned strongly in favor of staying in the European Economic Community during the referendum of 1975, arguing that access to the large and growing continental market would fuel British growth. At the same time, a majority of Labour Party members, although not the leadership, resolutely opposed membership on the grounds that Brussels was too market-friendly.

Today, the British economy is again struggling to emerge from a slump, but this time, Europe is seen as the source of the malaise, not its cure. In an attempt to play down the negative effects of their austerity policies, both Cameron and his chancellor of the exchequer, George Osborne, have been blaming the European sovereign debt crisis for the British economy's lack of growth. They usually justify their draconian spending cuts by pointing to Greece's fiscal tragedy. And whereas Labour is now moderately in favor of staying in the EU, seeing the union as the guarantor of certain social rights in the United Kingdom, the majority of Conservatives have turned against Europe and want to see the repatriation of key powers back to the national government. According to the most recent opinion polls, more Britons are in favor of leaving the EU than are in favor of staying in it.

Cameron's stance on Europe constitutes a break with Conservative tradition. Although Thatcher was never enamored with Brussels, she was a driving force behind the effort to establish a European common market in the 1980s, which culminated in the signing of the Single European Act in 1986. She was always careful to nurture relationships with like-minded leaders on the continent and keen to avoid British isolation. Major had a tougher time navigating the European question, but in the end, he signed the Maastricht Treaty, albeit while opting out of the euro. But when Cameron decided in December 2011, during the height of the euro crisis, to completely stay out of a new fiscal pact, forcing the EU to move forward with an intergovernmental agreement without the United Kingdom, he radically changed that Conservative tradition. His demand for a renegotiation of his country's EU membership terms went one step further, and it has infuriated many European leaders, who fear it will reignite old debates that were settled through compromise a long time ago.

Better Together

The economic argument for why the United Kingdom should leave the EU goes something like this: The continent is preoccupied with fighting a full-fledged sovereign debt crisis, one that has fundamentally changed the dynamics of European integration. The crisis has made integration a much more inward-looking project, requiring all kinds of new regulations in the financial sector aimed at completing the monetary union with common banking supervision, joint deposit insurance, and closer fiscal cooperation. These new regulations will allegedly hurt the City of London (the United Kingdom's financial hub) and therefore the entire British economy. And since fixing the euro once and for all can be achieved only by granting more powers to European institutions, the role of the British parliament and government as the legitimate representatives of the country's citizens will be threatened. This would further widen the democratic deficit within the EU, a particularly sensitive issue for the United Kingdom.

But on close inspection, none of these concerns holds up. The idea that the United Kingdom would be better off outside the EU is misguided, since it is based on a finance-centric view of the British economy. This view holds that the United Kingdom's comparative advantage is in financial services, a sector that needs to be protected at all costs from burdensome regulations. According to this school of thought, Thatcher's liberalization and deregulation of the economy in the 1980s and Blair's consolidation of finance as the core sector of the British economy in the late 1990s were unmitigated successes.

Proponents of this view suffer from collective amnesia about what has happened to the British economy over the past five years. Although finance lifted many boats during good times (some much more than others), when the sector crashed in 2008, it led to a collapse in government revenue, as close to one-quarter of all the Treasury's income came from finance. Even as the government's coffers were emptying, London had to dole out large bailouts to the very banks that had caused the crisis. The Cameron government then chose to respond with big expenditure cuts, and the pain seems set to continue for at least another five years. And that is the optimistic scenario.

Surely, the Cameron government's alternative to the EU banking regulations designed to thwart future crashes is not to get rid of financial rules altogether. For better or worse, this is now a post–Lehman Brothers era, and some amount of regulation is politically inevitable. What is more, London would certainly not be able to maintain its status as the leading financial center in Europe if the British left the Common Market, since doing so would make capital flows from the continent to the United Kingdom more regulated and thus more restricted than they are now.

The moment the United Kingdom leaves the EU is also the moment it loses all influence on European economic policymaking. And London would still have to accept most of Brussels' regulations and standards if it wanted free access to a market of over 400 million well-off European consumers, who currently buy more than 50 percent of all British exports. By leaving, the United Kingdom would also miss out on the free movement of labor, forfeiting the ability to attract many of Europe's best brains and the ability to take advantage of an influx of low-wage workers from central Europe.

The fact that the United Kingdom today remains in the EU but out of the eurozone means that it can have its cake and eat it, too. An independent monetary policy has allowed the country to keep down the value of the pound, boosting British exports to Europe and the rest of the world. And thanks to its membership in the Common Market, the United Kingdom remains influential in setting its rules. It is difficult to imagine a better position.

A British exit from the EU would be equally disastrous for the United Kingdom's standing in the world. Speaking at West Point in 1962, former U.S. Secretary of State Dean Acheson observed that the United Kingdom had lost an empire and had yet to find a role. By the 1970s, that role had started to take shape: the British would help shepherd European integration and maintain a "special relationship" with the United States. The alliance between the United Kingdom and the United States saw its heyday during the 2003 invasion of Iraq, when U.S. Defense Secretary Donald Rumsfeld spoke of Europe as divided into an antagonistic "old Europe"—led by the United Kingdom's traditional rivals, France and Germany—and a more supportive "new Europe."

But at that time, Washington still feared a common European defense policy, seeing a unified continent as a potential competitor. A decade later, the Americans no longer hold that view. Because of Germany's renewed economic strength and quasi-hegemonic status within the eurozone, Washington now sees Berlin, not London, as its preferred partner in Europe. The interests of the United States and Europe are more closely aligned than they used to be, as both try to cope with an economic slump, rising powers, and common security threats. Although the Obama administration has made clear that it sees Asia as the strategic battleground of the future, it is also encouraging European countries to cooperate more closely on defense so that they can help the United States bear the burden of global security. It would be a strategic mistake for London to leave the EU just as Washington is starting to warm to it.

As austerity takes its toll on the British armed forces, the only way for the United Kingdom to play any role in global security is if it pools its resources with the rest of Europe. In a sign of things to come, Europe's two nuclear powers, the United Kingdom and France, have agreed to share their aircraft carriers. A truly common European defense policy, however, has remained elusive. As a French diplomat recently told me, "You cannot do anything without Britain, but you also cannot do anything with Britain."

Still, as the wars in Iraq and Libya demonstrated, EU membership has not stopped the United Kingdom from acting in its own interests. Those campaigns have shown that the EU member states less inclined to intervene militarily, such as Germany, will not prevent others from resorting to force. NATO countries have adopted the flexible strategy of acting in "coalitions of the willing"; there's no reason why a formal EU defense alliance could not do the same thing. And now is the right time for such a move, since London's strategic interests have never been more closely aligned with those of the rest of Europe.

The End of the Affair

On the eve of the Allied troops' landing in Normandy in June 1944, British Prime Minister Winston Churchill warned de Gaulle that "every time we have to decide between Europe and the open sea, it is always the open sea that we shall choose." Elaborating on his point, Churchill explained that if he ever had to make a choice between de Gaulle and Franklin Roosevelt, between Europe and the United States, he would always pick the latter.

Ironically, Churchill was one of the first European leaders to call for a "United States of Europe," not long after World War II. De Gaulle, however, would never forget Churchill's wartime rebuke, and it certainly was on his mind both times he vetoed the United Kingdom's application to join the European Economic Community. Today, almost 70 years after Churchill's comment, U.S. President Barack Obama is sending the opposite message to his British counterpart, in equally firm terms: if the United Kingdom wants to retain any influence on the open sea, it must choose Europe.

But Cameron might well have already set his country inexorably on the road to isolation and irrelevance. Even if some European leaders would be willing to make substantive concessions to the United Kingdom to help keep it in the club, they are unlikely to ever go far enough for Cameron to appease the Euroskeptics in his party, much less to convince those British voters who favor withdrawing from the EU. There is a real danger, then, that the United Kingdom will end its relationship with Europe—making the tragic mistake of trading genuine power for the mirage of national sovereignty.

Critical Thinking

1. Why are London's strategic interests more closely aligned with the rest of Europe than they have ever been?

2. What are the reasons that the British electorate is not too concerned with the EU at the present time?

3. Did Charles deGaulle's decision to twice veto the United Kingdom's application to join the European Economic Community after World War II affect the future of Great Britain?

Create Central

www.mhhe.com/createcentral

Internet References

Foreign Affairs
www.ForeignAffairs.com

Nigel Nelson on David Cameron
www.mirror.co.uk/news/uk-news/nigel-nelson-david-cameron-win-2149434

BBC News—UK and the EU: Better Off Out or In?
www.bbc.co.uk/news/uk-politics-20448450

U.K. Lawmakers Debate Leaving the European Union
www.washingtonpost.com/blogs/worldviews/wp/2013/05/13/u-k-lawmakers-debate-leaving-the-european-union/

UK Economy Grows Again
www.express.co.uk/news/uk/417369/UK-economy-grows-again-as-economist-says-a-real-tailwind-now-behind-the-recovery

MATTHIAS MATTHIJS is Assistant Professor of International Political Economy at Johns Hopkins University's School of Advanced International Studies.

Article

Prepared by: Caroline Shaffer Westerhof,
California National University for Advanced Studies

Defending an Open, Global, Secure and Resilient Internet

John D. Negroponte, Samuel J. Palmisano, and Adam Segal

Learning Outcomes

After reading this article, you will be able to:

- Explain the reality of Internet governance adjusting to changing developments through the emergence of new Internet powers in the developing world.

- Discuss the following question: If the laws of more than one state apply to the data of another, why should the higher standards be applied?

- Explain how global Internet traffic could result in 31 billion devices being connected to the Internet by 2020 and what will be involved to accomplish this.

Introduction: The Open and Global Internet Is under Threat

Since the idea of a worldwide network was introduced in the early 1980s, the Internet has grown into a massive global system that connects over a third of the world's population, roughly 2.5 billion people. The Internet facilitates communication, commerce, trade, culture, research, and social and family connections and is now an integral part of modern life. Another 2.5 billion individuals are expected to get online by the end of this decade, mainly in the developing world, and further billions of devices and machines will be used. This enlargement to the rest of the globe could bring enormous economic, social, and political benefits to the United States and the world. New technologies could reshape approaches to disaster relief, diplomacy, conflict prevention, education, science, and cultural production.

However, as more people are connected in cyberspace and more critical services such as telecommunications, power, and transportation are interconnected, societies are becoming more dependent and more vulnerable to disruption. Escalating attacks on countries, companies, and individuals, as well as pervasive criminal activity, threaten the security and safety of the Internet. The number of high-profile, ostensibly state-backed operations continues to rise, and future attacks will

become more sophisticated and disruptive. A global digital arms trade has now emerged that sells sophisticated malicious software to the highest bidders, including hacker tools and "zero-day exploits"—attacks that take advantage of previously unknown vulnerabilities.

U.S. government officials have increasingly warned of the danger of a massive, destructive attack, and the government and private sector are scrambling to prevent and prepare for future cyberattacks. *U.S. government warnings and efforts are important, but the United States should do more to prevent a potential catastrophic cyberattack. It also, in partnership with its friends and allies, must work to define the norms of cyberconflict.*

From its beginning, the Internet has been open and decentralized; its development and growth have been managed by a self-organizing, self-policing, and self-balancing collection of private and public actors. Today, as many countries seek increased security and control over the type of information and knowledge that flows across the Internet, that original vision is under attack. Some nation-states are seeking to fragment and divide the Internet and assert sovereignty over it; they are increasing their efforts to tightly regulate social, political, and economic activity and content in cyberspace and, in many cases, to suppress expression they view as threatening. At the December 2012 World Conference on International Telecommunications (WCIT), some countries moved to rewrite a 1988 treaty so that it sanctions government control of Internet technology and content. A truly global platform is being undermined by a collection of narrow national Internets.

For the past four decades, the United States was the predominant innovator, promoter, and shaper of cyberspace, but the window for U.S. leadership is now closing. In Asia, Latin America, and Africa, the number of networked users is rapidly increasing. Cyberspace is now becoming reflective of the world's Internet users. *The United States, with its friends and allies, needs to act quickly to encourage a global cyberspace that reflects shared values of free expression and free markets.*

Successfully meeting the challenges of the digital age requires a rethinking of domestic institutions and processes that were designed for the twentieth century. The rapid rate of technological change cannot help but outpace traditional legislative approaches and decision-making processes. The threats of the past were relatively slow developing and geographically rooted, so there was an appropriate distribution of authorities among defense, intelligence, law enforcement, and foreign policy agencies. Cyberattacks, however, can be launched from anywhere in the world, including from networks inside the United States, and their effects can be felt in minutes. Moreover, they do not always look like attacks. Many threats and actual compromises appear as little inconsistencies. Stolen data is not taken away, so the losses may never be noticed, but suddenly companies have new competitors or foreign actors have an uncanny insight into their enemies' activities.

In the United States, a lack of a coherent vision, the absence of appropriate authority to implement policy, and legislative gridlock are significant obstacles to global leadership. *The United States should act affirmatively to articulate norms of behavior, regulation, and partnership, or others will do so.* In addition, the effects of domestic decisions spread far beyond national borders and will affect not only users, companies, nongovernmental organizations (NGOs), and policymakers in other countries but also the health, stability, resilience, and integrity of the global Internet. *The bottom line is clear: digital foreign policy must begin with domestic policy.*

The opportunities for the United States in cyberspace are great, but a path needs to be found between a cyberspace that has no rules and one that permits governments to abuse their sovereignty. At the same time, policymakers have to realize that even the most successful digital policy will have limits to what it can accomplish. The United States' commitment to free speech, for example, is rooted in its history and culture, just as French and German attitudes are toward appropriate limits on online hate speech or the sale of Nazi paraphernalia. These differences are unlikely to completely disappear no matter how well policy is crafted.

To support security, innovation, growth, and the free flow of information, the Task Force recommends a U.S. digital policy based on four pillars:

- Alliances: The United States should help create a cyber alliance of like-minded actors—including governments, companies, NGOs, and the noncommercial sector—based on a common set of practices and principles.

- Trade: All future U.S. trade agreements should contain a goal of fostering the free flow of information and data across national borders while protecting intellectual property and developing an interoperable global regulatory framework for respecting the privacy rights of individuals.

- Governance: The United States should articulate and advocate a vision of Internet governance that includes emerging Internet powers and expands and strengthens the multi-stakeholder process.

- Security: U.S.-based industry should work more rapidly to develop a coherent industry-led approach to protect critical infrastructure from cyberattacks.

Defending the Open, Global Internet

Many of the benefits of cyberspace are self-reinforcing. Knowledge, information, and data cannot be shared across borders without some degree of security; an open and global Internet is likely to be more resilient than one that is fractured into multiple national intranets. Encouraging a healthy Internet ecosystem will preserve the Internet for future users. As a result, U.S. decision-makers do not have the luxury of pursuing Internet trade, freedom, and security policies in isolation.

In other instances, however, the demands for security, intellectual property protection, open access and innovation, privacy, and the free flow of information involve difficult trade-offs. Technologies that allow countries and companies to control and identify applications and content that pass through networks, for example, can increase security (and generate profit), but they can also cut against users' ability to develop new services and software. Technologies that ensure anonymity can be used by activists to oppose authoritarian regimes, but may also be abused by extremist groups. For example, in responding to the "Innocence of Muslims," the anti-Islam video made by a California resident and uploaded on YouTube, the State Department had to balance defending the U.S. tradition of free speech and condemning intolerance and hate speech, while acknowledging the legitimate fear of social media's power to quickly disseminate incendiary materials.

The year 2012 saw the battle over the Stop Online Piracy Act (SOPA) and Preventing Real Online Threats to Economic Creativity and Theft of Intellectual Property Act (PIPA). These two bills sought to make it harder for website operators—especially those outside the United States—to sell or distribute pirated copyrighted material or counterfeit goods. Though all sides in the debate agreed on the need to protect intellectual property from rogue foreign websites, technology companies, free speech activists, popular websites such as Wikipedia, and other critics argued that the provisions within the bills could result in the censorship of large quantities of noninfringing material, including political content, thereby severely limiting free expression and impairing future innovation. . . .

Cybersecurity cooperation and collaboration is being expanded among the Five Eyes (the Technical Cooperation Program composed of Australia, Canada, New Zealand, the United Kingdom, and the United States); the United States and Australia have declared that their mutual defense treaty applies to cyberattacks; and the United States, through integrated government agency participation or a "whole-of-government" approach, has begun to hold cyber bilateral meetings with India, Brazil, South Africa, South Korea, Japan, and Germany that include representatives from the Departments of Defense, State, Commerce, Justice, and Homeland Security. The United States is also working with its negotiating partners to make sure that the forthcoming Trans-Pacific Partnership (TPP) trade agreement codifies the free flow of information across national boundaries.

The United States has also had success in promoting the free flow of information and knowledge both by appealing to established national and international norms and by working in tandem with and sometimes ceding the lead to other countries.

For example, in 2011, the Netherlands organized a meeting of governments to stand up for free expression on the Internet. The eighteen governments that make up the Freedom Online Coalition are often able to conduct discussions without provoking the same level of suspicion and opposition that the United States alone has to overcome.

This traditional state-to-state diplomacy is necessary, but nowhere near sufficient for cyberspace. Righting domestic policy is important, but the United States cannot go it alone. *It is necessary for the United States to identify partners among governments, the business community, and civil society at home and abroad.* Sharing leadership in cyberspace is essential if the United States is to maintain and improve what it has helped to build.

Numerous civil actors such as the Global Network Initiative, Open-Net Initiative, Electronic Frontier Foundation, and the Center for Democracy and Technology advocate for openness and human rights on the Internet. Close coordination with Sweden and the Netherlands on efforts to promote the right to connect work in tandem with the U.S. State Department getting circumvention tools in the hands of individual users and running "tech camps" for NGOs around the world. Similarly, any effort to develop rules, institutions, and norms for cybersecurity should involve private companies, international law enforcement, and international legal experts. . . .

Despite fears that the Internet and globalization more generally would lead to greater cultural homogeneity, cyberspace has been a platform for linguistic, artistic, cultural, religious, and ethnic expression. Examples include the growth in minority languages through the use of the Internet to connect diaspora communities. The use of Catalan online has grown substantially over the past ten years, connecting eight million speakers, and Catalan content has increased since the introduction of the top-level domain (TLD) name—.cat—in 2006. A TLD is at the highest level of the hierarchical Domain Name System (DNS), the designation .com, .org, gov, and others that appears farthest to the right in an Internet address. Global Goods Partners, a nonprofit organization, is one of many websites that give artisans in developing countries a venue to sell traditional artwork and handicrafts to customers in developed countries. . . .

Opportunities

Global Internet traffic is expected to triple over the next five years, with rapid growth in Africa, Latin America, and the Middle East. The world's Internet population nearly doubled between 2007 and 2013, and is now estimated at 2.27 billion people. The Cisco Visual Networking Index forecasts that by 2016 there will be 18.9 billion network connections, or almost 2.5 connections for each person on earth, compared with 10.6 billion in 2011. New products and services will be born as more devices are interconnected. Chips and sensors, smaller and more powerful, can be embedded in more products, creating vast amounts of data and linking physical and digital systems. . . .

The economic impact of the Internet is global. No widely accepted methodologies or metrics for assessing the full effect of the Internet on national economies exist yet, but it is estimated that for every 10 percent increase in broadband penetration, global GDP increases by an average of 1.3 percent. In a 2011 McKinsey study of thirteen countries (the G8 plus Brazil, South Korea, India, China, and Sweden), the Internet economy accounted for 3.4 percent of GDP and 7 percent of growth in these countries over the past fifteen years. Measurement is even more difficult for developing economies, but early research suggests that increases in Internet penetration are associated with higher exports overall; increasing emerging-marked mobile broadband penetration to more than 50 percent would yield returns of $420 billion and up to fourteen. Over the course of the last four decades, the Internet has developed from an obscure government science experiment to one of the cornerstones of modern life. It has transformed commerce, created social and cultural networks wth global reach, and become a surprisingly powerful vehicle for political organization and protest alike. And it has achieved all of this despite—or perhaps because of—its decentralized character.

Critical Thinking

1. The Internet has developed from an obscure entity since the 1980s. How has it grown to become one of the cornerstones of modern life?

2. What are some of the social media tools that feed into hacking and defacing websites that are attacking economic and political competition?

3. Can an open and global Internet be prepared for a potential catastrophic cyberattack, and if so, how?

Create Central

www.mhhe.com/createcentral

Internet References

Council on Foreign Relations
 www.cfr.org

Norton Cybercrime Report, Symantec Corporation, 2012
 http://us.norton.com/cybercrimereport/promo

Leon E. Panetta, "Remarks by Secretary Panetta on Cybersecurity to the Business Executives for National Security, New York City," October 11, 2012
 www.defense.gov/transcripts/transcript.aspx?transcriptid=5136

NATO Cooperative Cyber Defence Centre of Excellence, "The Tallinn Manual"
 www.ccdcoe.org/249.html

Global Network Initiative
 www.globalnetworkinitiative.org

Segal et al., Adam. From *Defending an Open, Global, Secure and Resilient Internet*, no. 70, June 2013, excerpts pp. 3–6, 26–27, 8–11, ix. Copyright © 2013 by Council on Foreign Relations. Used with permission.

Article

Prepared by: Caroline Shaffer Westerhof,
California National University for Advanced Studies

Is Burma Democratizing?

Thomas Carothers

Learning Outcomes

After reading this article, you will be able to:

- Explain the impact of Burma's turning away from authoritarian rule.
- Explain the most difficult part of Burma's transition.
- Discuss the impact of the Arab Spring upon the developments in Burma.

The victory of Aung San Suu Kyi and several dozen of her National League for Democracy colleagues in Burma's April 1 legislative by-elections is a major event for the country.

In a Q&A, Thomas Carothers, who visited Burma in the run-up to the elections, assesses the significance of the vote and the prospects for a democratic transition in Burma. Drawing on his extensive experience with political transitions around the world, Carothers compares the situation in Burma to other transitions away from authoritarian rule, highlighting major challenges but also reasons for hope.

- Is Burma transitioning to democracy?
- What can we learn from other transitions away from authoritarian rule? How do they compare to Burma?
- Has the Arab Spring impacted the developments in Burma?
- What will be the most difficult part of Burma's transition?
- Is there reason to be hopeful about Burma's future?

Is Burma Transitioning to Democracy?

Although the elections involved fewer than 7 percent of the seats in the country's parliament, they were unquestionably a big step forward for a society that has experienced only manipulated or nullified elections for more than half a century.

Burma is experiencing a striking and largely unpredicted political opening, marked by the return to political life of Aung San Suu Kyi and the National League for Democracy, the release of many political prisoners, and the opening up of considerable space for political discussion and activity. President Thein Sein, although in power thanks to the military establishment and illegitimate elections in 2010, appears to have taken reform to heart. When I visited Burma last month, it was impossible not to be struck by the powerful sense among many Burmese that this is an enormous moment for the country, a political opportunity that many barely dared to hope for over the last twenty years.

Encouraging as they are, however, these developments represent only a doorway to a possible democratic transition. The country's power holders—a long-entrenched, antidemocratic military and the ruling Union Solidarity and Development Party (USDP)—have not yet given up any significant structural levers of power. Constitutional reform, essential to undoing the longstanding lock on power of the military and the USDP, is only just starting to be discussed seriously. The weight of the reformers in the government relative to those in the government and the military who oppose reforms is still highly uncertain.

While the government has initiated some encouraging economic reforms, notably the rationalization of currency exchange and reform of the banking system, it remains to be seen whether it can implement changes that would challenge the core prerogatives of the existing ruling establishment, an establishment whose economic approach defines the concept of crony capitalism.

So political opening? Yes. Economic reform? Likely. Democratic transition? Too early to tell.

What Can We Learn from Other Transitions Away from Authoritarian Rule? How Do They Compare to Burma?

Every political transition is of course unique, reflecting the almost unlimited variety of sociopolitical configurations and traditions around the world. At the same time, with over 100 attempted democratic transitions occurring during the past twenty-five years, certain patterns are identifiable and certain analogies, if approached cautiously, can be illuminating.

Burma's reform-from-above process—in which softliners in a military-based authoritarian power establishment worried about its legitimacy are attempting an unfolding set of iterative political and economic reforms—is reminiscent of at least some of the transitions away from military rule in South America in the 1970s and 1980s, though these varied greatly even compared to each other.

In Brazil, for example, a military establishment concerned about its waning popularity—which had been undercut by poor economic management and florid corruption—broke into softliner and hardliner camps. The softliners gradually reintroduced civilian rule, followed by credible electoral processes, and kept peace with the hardliners by allowing them to retain many of their economic prerogatives and avoid prosecution for their past wrongs.

Most of the South American transitions look fairly good in retrospect, but it is important to note how long and turgid they mostly were in practice. In Brazil again, more than ten years elapsed from the opening of political reform in 1974 until a civilian president took power through credible elections. And it was almost another ten years after that until the system really worked through many of the toxic legacies of previous authoritarianism.

In addition, most of the South American militaries had only been in power for a decade or two when they returned their countries to civilian rule and these countries had at least some significant past experience with civilian rule and democratic pluralism. The Burmese military has been running the country for fifty of the country's sixty-five years of independence, and there is no extended prior democratic experience to draw from.

Has the Arab Spring Impacted the Developments in Burma?

One does hear in the country that the Arab Spring rattled the Burmese generals and also fueled the softliners' determination to move ahead with reforms in an attempt to head off a potential explosion from below.

The top-down reform process in Burma, however, more closely resembles the political situation in many Arab countries in the decade leading up to the Arab Spring. In those years, various Arab governments carried out political and economic reforms—allowing opposition parties to gain representation in parliaments, permitting a certain space for independent civil society, and rationalizing some elements of economic life—in what analysts characterized as "defensive liberalization."

The steps taken by Arab governments were not democratizing reforms, rather they were carefully circumscribed efforts designed precisely to head off the possibility of true democratization by alleviating popular dissatisfaction with regimes. Some regimes, such as those in Morocco and Jordan, have managed to stay in place by persisting with such a strategy. Others, like in Egypt, faltered in the reforms, stagnating until they faced an eventual explosion.

What Will be the Most Difficult Part of Burma's transition?

Difficulties certainly abound—a deeply entrenched, anti-democratic military internally divided over its commitment to reform, devastating legacies of political repression, atrocious governance, economic deprivation, and a politically challenging region.

But what is especially daunting is that the country is confronting the profound challenge of moving away from fifty years of harsh, haphazard authoritarian rule while also grappling with the need to resolve the multiple aggravated ethnic conflicts that have festered for decades. Trying to work simultaneously through two interrelated processes of the distribution of power—democratization at the core of the political system and greater regional autonomy in sizeable parts of the country—will be extremely difficult. It is a bit like trying to drive across a narrow, badly paved bridge with steep drops on either side while at the same time struggling to stop a fight with a whole set of angry passengers inside the car.

But it's not impossible. If handled well, the two processes could be complementary. When Indonesia moved suddenly away from authoritarian rule in the late 1990s, many people worried that it would not be able to handle democratization while dealing with the push for greater autonomy in some of its provinces. Indonesia arguably faced greater internal problems at the time than Burma confronts today, as some of its internal territorial struggles were about secession whereas in Burma the demands from the ethnic areas are more limited. But Indonesia did make it through, and the end of the authoritarian regime actually facilitated a peaceful resolution with Timor-Leste.

Is There Reason to be Hopeful about Burma's Future?

Burma faces enormous challenges in undertaking democratization, but it is far from a lost cause. Few countries entering into a political opening do so with a vibrant, clearly pro-democratic opposition movement that has already proven its national appeal in prior elections, has a deeply respected leader of unquestionable national and international legitimacy, and has at least a certain amount of basic organizational capability.

Moreover, the reform wing in the power establishment contains some very credible figures, not the least of which is President Thein Sein himself. And although some countries in Burma's neighborhood are not likely to be friends of the democratization process, a wide range of important international actors, including the United States, Europe, and various Asian democracies, are ready to help.

Critical Thinking

1. How will Burma's transition away from authoritarian rule compare to other nation-state transitions?
2. Will there be stumbling blocks to Burma's transitioning to democracy?
3. How will the April 2012 election and victory for Aung Suu Kyi portend her potential run for the presidency of Burma?

Create Central

www.mhhe.com/createcentral

Internet References

Special Report—Myanmar: Pangs of Democratic Transition

www.ipcs.org/special-report/myanmar/myanmar-pangs-of-democratic-transition-130.html

Burma's Transition to Quasi-Military Rule: From Rulers to Guardians?

afs.sagepub.com/content/early2013/07/02/0095327X13492943.full.pdf

Burma's Transition to "Disciplined Democracy"

www.isn.ethz.ch/Digital-Library/Publications/Detail/?ots591=0c54e3b3-1e9c-be1e-2c24-a6a8c7060233&lng=en&id=134189

Spring in Myanmar

www.brookings.edu/research/opinions/2012/03/07-spring-myanmar-rieffel

THOMAS CAROTHERS is Vice President for Studies at the Carnegie Endowment for International Peace.

Article   Prepared by: Caroline Shaffer Westerhof,
                                   California National University for Advanced Studies

How India Stumbled: Can New Delhi Get Its Groove Back?

PRATAP BHANU MEHTA

Learning Outcomes

After reading this article, you will be able to:

- Explain how India's growth in two years went from "èmerging" to "slackening."

- Explain how India's political and business interests achieved access to nuclear technology despite stumbling blocks.

- Explain how access to basic services has made India a nation in political and economic disarray.

When the United Progressive Alliance, a group of center-left parties led by the Indian National Congress, came to power for a second term in 2009, it seemed that India could do no wrong. The economy had sailed through the worst of the global economic recession with gdp growing at a fast seven percent annually and accelerating (it reached 10.4 percent in 2010). Inflation was low, officials were finally starting to take India's social problems seriously, and politics in the world's largest democracy were contentious but robust. The rest of the world was even looking to the country as a serious global power. "India is not simply emerging," U.S. President Barack Obama told the Indian parliament in November 2010; "India has emerged."

Just two years later, however, India's growth is slackening, its national deficit is growing, and inflation is rising after having fallen between early 2010 and early 2012. Plans to build a more inclusive nation are in disarray. Income inequality has risen. According to the economists Laveesh Bhandari and Suryakant Yadav, the urban Gini coefficient (a measure of inequality, with zero indicating absolute equality and one indicating absolute inequality) went from 0.35 in 2005 to 0.65 today. And access to basic services, such as water, health care, and sanitation, remains woefully inadequate. Meanwhile, the country's democracy putters along, but in the absence of leadership, policymaking has ground to a halt. India seems to have gone from a near-sure thing to, as the financial analyst Ruchir Sharma put it in *Breakout Nations,* a 50-50 bet.

Yet the change in India's economic performance is not nearly as stark as the comparison between 2009 and 2012 suggests. The economy has been troubled all along; all the hype in 2009 disguised a number of real weaknesses. Despite some economic liberalization in the years before, a whole range of regulations still made India a stifling environment for most businesses. In addition, the Indian agricultural sector, which accounts for around 15 percent of the country's gdp and employs about 50 percent of its work force, was a constant cause for worry. Strictures such as tight labor regulations, the inconsistent application of environmental laws, and arbitrary land-acquisition practices made it difficult for producers to respond to any changes in demand. Swings in food prices, a heavy burden on India's poor and farmers, could have thrown the economy into disarray at any time.

That said, the current pessimism about India underestimates some real strengths. Even as a few indicators have soured since 2009, India's household savings rate has stayed above 30 percent (compared with under five percent in the United States). According to India's Central Statistical Office, the country's private consumption rate is around 60 percent (compared with China's 48 percent). These solid figures mean that India's economic ups and downs have neither overtaxed the public, forcing it to dip into its savings to make it through tough economic times, nor dampened its appetite for goods and services quite yet. Indian companies, too, are flush and can rapidly begin to invest in new labor, machinery, or production processes when they believe the timing is right. And for its part, the government still has plenty of room to make tax collection more efficient, so it can finance greater public spending without raising the burden on citizens. Beyond that, one must not discount the optimism among the country's poorest and most marginalized. Growth opened up new opportunities for them, and the correlation between caste and occupation continues to weaken. In addition, they have come to believe in the economic benefits of education and spend extraordinary amounts to send their children to good private schools.

In other words, just as in 2009, India is still fully capable of entering the ranks of world economic heavyweights. The problem, however, is that its politics are getting in the way.

Too Great Expectations

In a sense, melancholy about India's economic prospects is the result of miscalibrated expectations. When India's gdp growth surpassed ten percent in 2010, many in India projected that the economy would continue growing just as fast for years to come. And given the steady progress in the fight against poverty, they thought that India would soon be a world-class model for inclusive, high-growth democracy. That hope has dimmed, with the Indian economy's growth rate now projected to be as low as six percent annually. Of course, that is no small achievement by international standards, and expecting ten percent growth was wildly unrealistic to begin with. Still, there is no reason India cannot do better. And its failure to do so has cast a cloud over the country's future.

But the public did have some reasonable economic expectations, too, ones set by the government itself: when Manmohan Singh, now prime minster, served as finance minister in the early 1990s, he spearheaded a number of economic reforms that were supposed to create a new social contract for the country. Under his initiatives, the state would dismantle domestic controls on private enterprise, gradually integrate India into the world economy, rationalize the tax and taria structures, and provide transparent regulation. The resulting growth, he promised, would benefit everyone. It would expand the country's tax base and lead to a boost in government revenue. Those funds could be spent on health care, education, and improved infrastructure for the poor. Eventually, they, too, would become productive components in India's economic machine.

But India's social contract hasn't panned out as planned. In addition to slowing growth and rising interest rates and inflation, the country has seen the value of the rupee fall by around 20 percent since last summer. The economy can still pick up if the government makes wise policy choices. But New Delhi has yet to indicate how expansionary a monetary policy it is willing to pursue. It seems hesitant to consider the tradeoas: whether it would like to preside over an economy with six percent annual growth and four percent inflation or one with eight percent growth and eight percent inflation. Eight percent inflation might seem too high to be palatable, but it might be a lesser evil: just to absorb enough new workers into the labor force to keep unemployment levels steady, the Indian economy needs to expand by seven to eight percent each year. Until New Delhi sends a clear signal about its intentions, companies will be hard-pressed to make assumptions about the future and invest the cash they have on hand.

Singh's reforms also suggested that India would become more transparent in its economic policymaking. But one of the most disconcerting developments of the last two years has been the Finance Ministry's backtracking on that commitment. Two recent actions illustrate the trend. First, earlier this year, the government decided to sell shares of the state-owned Oil and Natural Gas Corporation, but there were no real buyers. So in March, it simply coaxed the state-owned Life Insurance Corporation of India into investing in ongc. The investment raised hackles in the financial community, and Moody's downgraded the Life Insurance Corporation to Baa3 from Baa2. Second, in May, New Delhi decided to retroactively tax the takeover by the British telecommunications company Vodafone of an Indian phone company; the move is still being disputed, but if it goes forward, it could generate between $2 billion and $4 billion. What this measure means for foreign investment has been hotly debated. Such investment does not always depend on transparency and regulatory clarity. China, for example, has been able to paper over its lack of either. But in India, which is not yet quite as economically dynamic as China, many fear that such arbitrary interventions will scare away foreign investment.

Moreover, the government's commitment to a kind of growth that could serve all Indians has been inconsistent. Rather than create a propitious environment for small businesses, which would boost entrepreneurship and add to India's economic dynamism and growth, New Delhi has gone out of its way to make life better for big businesses, granting them access to easy credit, dedicated power plants, and protection against currency fluctuations. That is a problem because India's big-business sectors, such as mining, land development, and infrastructure, are its most corrupt. The government's backing of them has started to erode the public's fragile consensus on capitalism, and the old association of capitalism with corruption has returned.

On the social side, the picture is mixed. India has indeed rolled out a number of entitlement and welfare schemes. The 2005 National Rural Employment Guarantee Act, which guaranteed 100 days of employment per year to at least one member of every rural household, has had the desired effect of raising wages in the countryside. (Although patterns vary across states, a majority of participants in the program are women.) And central government spending on the social sector, including health care and education, has risen from 13.4 percent of the total budget in 2007 to 18.5 percent today. But due to inefficiencies and corruption, much of that money never reaches the targeted beneficiaries. And it is too soon to assess whether the most hailed employment and educational schemes have built the skills people will need for longer-term participation in the economy. Furthermore, most of the initiatives reek of central planning, with New Delhi micromanaging the design of each program. States rightly complain that they are not given enough leeway to experiment with the programs in order to tailor them to the particular needs of their constituents.

Some have said that the Indian social contract has broken down entirely. They point to the continued Maoist insurgency in the country's east, farmer protests over government land grabs across India, and the disconcerting phenomenon of farmer suicides. But some historical perspective is in order. According to Devesh Kapur, director of the Center for the Advanced Study of India at the University of Pennsylvania, overall communal violence in India has "plummeted to a tenth of the 2002 level," and "in the last decade all forms of political violence have declined markedly, save one—Maoist-related violence." Most protesters today realize that they have something to lose if India's economy sours. And rather than a sign of economic stagnation, many of these uprisings signal that India's rise has created new expectations that New Delhi has yet to meet.

Delhi Deadlock

So why hasn't the government been able to fulfill the public's hopes? First, politics in India are deeply fragmented, which makes consensus hard to come by. For example, an important tax reform, the introduction of an integrated goods and services taria, has been delayed for three years. This national levy would replace various complicated state level taxation systems, and economists believe that it could boost growth and promote trade. Another example is the haggling over whether to to open up India's retail market to foreign megafirms, such as Walmart. For its part, the Singh administration has said that doing so would create more than three million jobs and could be implemented in a way that did not hurt small local stores. But after announcing a plan in late 2011 to open the sector, the government quickly backtracked because of protest among the opposition, within Singh's own party, and on the street.

Second, the authority of politicians has eroded considerably. To be sure, they have done an admirable job of keeping democracy going and improving political access among marginalized groups. But they have also been deeply inefficient and self-serving. The public has grown tired of their mismanagement of India's economy and welfare system. In addition, a series of scandals in 2010 and 2011—including the sale of telecommunications licenses to political allies, sweetheart deals for construction contracts, and the granting of real estate development rights allegedly in exchange for incredible sums of money—called the integrity of a whole range of institutions, from the courts to the army, into question.

The political leadership, instead of recognizing its failures and working to restore moral order, has evaded responsibility. The Indian National Congress' top brass, which includes Singh; Sonia Gandhi, the party's leader; and Rahul Gandhi, Sonia's son and political heir, seldom speak in parliament or give press conferences. When they do, they complain about India's governance problems without acknowledging that they, in fact, are the very center of government. For example, Sonia Gandhi, speaking in November 2010 at the tenth Indira Gandhi Conference, admitted that "graft and greed are on the rise" and lamented that India's "moral universe seems to be shrinking." Her tone indicated that she interpreted these developments as being someone else's problem. Indeed, the Congress' leaders use their offices as relay centers, simply forwarding concerns along rather than taking charge and addressing them. The political vacuum they have created has further eroded public confidence.

The government's favorite scapegoat for the dysfunction is coalition politics. "The difficult decisions we have to make," Singh told parliament in March, "are made even more difficult because we are a coalition government." That means, he continued, that "we have to formulate policy with the need to maintain consensus." There is some truth to what Singh said. The Congress party does not have the numbers to pass legislation on its own. And its alliance partners have routinely opposed important reforms, such as rationalizing energy prices by lifting subsidies for all but the country's poorest, implementing changes to the pension system, and creating a national counterterrorism

center. They argue that the moves would trample on states' rights. Of course, just as for the opposition parties, so it is for the Congress party's coalition partners: both gain power and public support if they can show that the Congress is not adept at governing.

Still, India has been governed by coalitions before, and they haven't always had trouble passing difficult legislation. In 2003, parliament, then in the hands of an alliance led by the Hindu nationalist Bharatiya Janata Party (bjp), passed the Fiscal Responsibility and Budget Management Act. The main goal of the legislation was to reduce India's budget deficit to three percent. Whether the bill had a positive outcome is debatable; some argue that it slowed growth in social-sector spending too much. But overall, the act signaled that the government was committed to prudent financial management and, more fundamentally, to governing. The Congress party, especially bad at managing the vagaries of Indian politics, has proved no such thing. And that is at the heart of the current malaise.

The Weakest Winner

The Congress party is something of a puzzle. It is India's dominant party, electorally competitive in more than 400 of the 545 seats in the directly elected lower house of parliament. It now holds 206 of them-more than any other party. It has ruled India for 53 out of the 64 years since independence, in 1947. Even so, it fails on a major score: state politics. In India, government often happens at the local level. Most voters never cross paths with central government officials, and thus they form judgments about political parties through their performance in the states.

Yet the Congress rarely fields strong state-level leaders. The party's leaders have historically been suspicious of politicians with independent bases of their own. So rather than letting local leaders emerge organically, the Congress party typically imposes them from afar. In the recent state elections in Uttarakhand, for example, the Congress party nominated Vijay Bahuguna as chief minister above the objections of local legislators. Bahuguna, a Gandhi loyalist, was previously chief minister of another state. There are exceptions to this pattern: for example, Y. S. Rajashekara Reddy, a politician whose populist bent got him elected as chief minister of Andhra Pradesh, one of India's largest states, in 2004. Reddy helped deliver the district to the Congress and skillfully managed local conflicts during his two terms. But when he died, in 2009, the Congress party was left with no local politician to promote.

Beyond such specific problems, the lack of local leadership means that the party is out of touch with grass-roots movements and demands. For example, it has continually misjudged the intensity of the demands by the population of Telangana, a region in Andhra Pradesh, for its own state, since it has not paid attention to local leader's voices. Worse, in April, the party even suspended eight parliamentarians from the region for disrupting the parliament's proceedings by agitating for a new state. Without strong ties to locals, the Congress party is also less able to explain its policy choices to an impatient public.

As a result of all these missteps, the Congress is increasingly thrown into complicated alliances with more regionally connected parties.

Democratizing the Congress party could help it overcome its problems-and India's. Most Indian political parties, the Congress included, have archaic decision-making structures that are controlled by small groups of elites. Their incentives are to service their existing power structures more than their constituents. There are no transparent processes by which decisions are made or party platforms are shaped, which means that there are no real checks on party leaders.

Rahul Gandhi, now the political face of the Congress, has talked up his intentions to democratize the party. He started the process by reforming the Indian Youth Congress, the Congress party's youth wing, of which he became chair in 2007. Since then, he has worked toward what he calls "internal democracy," opening up the group's membership to everyone and holding internal elections with impartial observers present. That is all well and good, but it has had a minimal impact on the rest of the party. For one thing, there has been little change at the top of the Congress party, where loyalty to the Gandhi family is rewarded more than competence.

The lack of democracy within the Congress party is all the more problematic given the little that is known of its soon-to-be leader's governing philosophy. Take, for example, a local's response to one of Rahul Gandhi's speeches in Bihar. As Gandhi pontificated on his pet theme, that there are two Indias, one shining and one increasingly leftbehind, a journalist asked a farmer in the audience for a reaction. The farmer replied, "For 50 years they have ruled, and now they say there are two Indias. If we give them five years more, they will come and tell us there are three Indias!" Gandhi and his party seem to assume that the two Indias in his story are unconnected. In fact, economic growth has given the state the resources it needs to address inequality. It is New Delhi's failure to use those resources to do so that has caused so much public distress. Gandhi and the Congress party cannot rescue India from its malaise by pointing out problems; they have to demonstrate actual achievement.

You Say You Want a Revolution?

To be fair to the Congress, India is undergoing a broad reformation of its political culture that any party would struggle to manage. Until recently, Indian politicians and bureaucrats all shared four basic management principles-vertical accountability, wide discretion, secrecy, and centralization-all of which made for a government that was representative but not responsive. Today, these principles are becoming obsolete.

In the past, vertical accountability meant that any official in the state was largely accountable to his or her superiors, not to citizens or other institutional actors. But now, government institutions such as the Supreme Court of India and the Office of the Comptroller and Auditor General are starting to exert more horizontal control, partly because there is a such a dearth of leadership at the center. The media, too, have become more powerful than they once were, as the number of television channels has expanded. Government functionaries are less and less able to act as if their superiors are the only people they must answer to.

No government can function without a range of discretionary powers. What matters is how governments justify the use of such powers to constituencies affected by their decisions. India's officials, preoccupied with keeping their superiors happy, have seldom seen fit to explain anything to the public. Take the recent scandal over the government's sale of millions of dollars' worth of cell-phone spectrum to politically connected companies. Indians were not only shocked by the magnitude of the deal; they were also outraged by the fact that the government never even tried to justify its decision not to auction the licenses. In the wake of that debacle, there is immense pressure on New Delhi to publicly record the reasons for its moves.

The Indian government has also historically used secrecy to hold on to power. In the past, the public could not easily access information of any kind: government files, statistics, explanations of procedures. Opacity made it hard for citizens to hold the state accountable and was the foundation of state power. That has changed dramatically. The current government's single greatest achievement in its first term was passing, in 2005, the Right to Information Act. This act gave citizens the right to request information from any public authority, which is required by law to reply within 30 days. The bill was the brainchild of Aruna Roy, a social activist, and had the full support of Sonia Gandhi, often against the wishes of other politicians in her party. Now, civil-society groups are able to challenge New Delhi and local governments on a whole range of issues, from corruption to the environmental impact of industrial policies. Many in government claim that New Delhi's paralysis is due to the fact that any new policy or reform is challenged at every turn and in every forum.

Finally, power in India is more decentralized than ever. In small steps, more functions are being transferred to local governments. For example, the program of the National Rural Employment Guarantee Act is administered by village councils, which can decide what projects to pursue and better ensure that workers actually show up to the job sites. But many procedures, including the yearly financial allocations of the central government's Planning Commission, which develops five-year economic plans for the country, do not take this new reality into account, causing conflict and tension along the way.

The evolution of India's traditional culture of governance has yet to work itself out. This is a process long in the making, and it will go on for some time. No one in the political class, not in the Congress or in the bjp, has quite figured out how to harness it. For its part, the Congress party will have to make drastic changes, first by putting a greater premium on performance and by purging a whole range of committee members and cabinet ministers. The party has a sufficiently centralized structure to be able to switch course swiftly, if it so decides. Second, it needs to restore authority to the office of the prime minister. Real power now lies in the hands of the Gandhi family. But on the books at least, Singh is the one tasked with the responsibility for governance. In other words, when something goes wrong, the wrong actor is held accountable. Singh is called ineffective while the real power brokers carry on.

The silver lining for the Congress is that the bjp is struggling with succession and organizational issues of its own. The bjp chapters in Karnataka and Rajasthan are in open revolt against the central leadership and may well defect. And recently, the party has not been able to articulate a coherent ideology. The next major face-off between the Congress party and the bjp will be the general elections in 2014, which is still a long way off. The side that understands that India is fundamentally changing and that old modes of governance no longer work will have the best chance of winning.

India's economic future depends on the country's politics, and that is both good and bad news. True, India's politics will often be mired in brinkmanship and inefficiency. But Indian politicians have a remarkable capacity for reinvention. They can rapidly change course when need be, and there is nothing like a crisis to concentrate their minds. It is difficult to imagine that the entrepreneurship India has unleashed, the growing strength of its civil society, and the sense of hope among India's poor for a better future will remain stymied for long. The anxiety among India's politicians is, in part, a recognition that something new is taking shape.

Critical Thinking

1. How can policymakers in India have the capability to anticipate risks and reduce them?

2. How did population from Europe become involved in India over the centuries, and what has this accomplished for India's growth?

3. How has "India stumbled" as the author discusses?

Create Central

www.mhhe.com/createcentral

Internet References

Pratap Bhanu Mehta CPRindia
www.cprindia.org

Pratap Bhanu Mehta—The Indian Express
www.indianexpress.com/columnist/pratapbhanumehta

Pratap Bhanu Mehta: When Business Bats Against Itself—Forbes India
http://forbesindia.com/article/independence-special-2013/pratap-bhanu-mehta-when-business-bats-against-itself/35875/1

"The Politics of Social Jusice in India" by Pratap Bhanu Mehta
www.youtube.com/watch?v=xBFSF7TwU8Q

Article

Prepared by: Caroline Shaffer Westerhof,
California National University for Advanced Studies

A Video Campaign and the Power of Simplicity

NOAM COHEN

Learning Outcomes

After reading this article, you will be able to:

- Understand the conflict and terror in Uganda.
- Understand the explosive power of social media and the film *Kony 2012* that has attracted some 50 million viewers.
- Understand "slacktivism"—a pejorative term for armchair activism.

Even as the Internet era has accelerated the news cycle, sometimes to mere minutes, there is still one idea that holds true: you need a lash before you can have a backlash.

Invisible Children, a charity based in San Diego, certainly had the lash, in the form of a 30-minute video about the Ugandan warlord Joseph Kony and his Lord's Resistance Army. The "Kony 2012" video, pitched to a 5-year-old's sense of right and wrong, was an attempt to bring attention—and justice—to the case of Mr. Kony, whose violent paramilitary group has long been accused of using children as soldiers.

"Kony 2012" went viral last week and, helped by Twitter messages and endorsements by celebrities like Oprah Winfrey and Mia Farrow, had exceeded 71 million views on YouTube by Sunday afternoon.

And that is when the backlash began.

The grounds for objection to the video are many. Some critics begin and end with its deep misrepresentation of the current state of play, including the fact that Mr. Kony has largely been defeated and is in hiding. Others chafe at the implicit "white man's burden" message of the video—that Western outsiders, and only Western outsiders, can remedy the situation.

Others object to the reduction of a complex situation to the story of a single "bad guy" whose capture would magically restore harmony to a conflict-scarred region, and surely some object to the casual invocation of Hitler (is it a coincidence that the day of action promoted in the video is April 20, Hitler's birthday?).

For some, the backlash becomes an opportunity to promote longstanding arguments. Evgeny Morozov, the author of "The Net Delusion: The Dark Side of Internet Freedom," objects that the video is another example of a kind of low-impact concern he calls slacktivism. The journal *Foreign Policy* immediately lectured on what should be obvious errors of context. And African bloggers—tired of the image of outsiders coming to the rescue, or worse, sending in troops—have asked to be left alone, to be respected for their own agency in their own land.

It can all evoke George Bernard Shaw's insight that "all professions are conspiracies against the laity." Yes, "Kony 2012" may be crude, simplistic and shallow, but can it really be counterproductive if it prompts young people to ask why a well-known warlord with 30 years of atrocities to his name has not been caught and prosecuted?

Similarly, online protests against conditions at the factories in China that produce Apple products were asking a simple question: Is this really the best the richest corporation in the world can do in treating its workers? The response of experts was equally dismissive: Clearly you have no idea how preferable a miserable factory job is to an even more miserable existence in rural China.

And in the case of Occupy Wall Street, the movement asked why the income gap was widening and whether the trend could be reversed. Many critics—Wall Street bankers and opinion page pundits—assailed the movement, asking what precise remedies it was advocating.

The criticisms miss the point. The Occupiers, like Apple's critics or the people behind "Kony 2012," are arguing for the right to keep it simple. I was struck by the power of that urge when I read a thoughtful, nuanced blog post by Ethan Zuckerman, an expert on social networking and Africa, that came down against the "Kony 2012" video.

Mr. Zuckerman relied in part on research done by Séverine Autesserre, a political scientist at Barnard College. Mr. Zuckerman wrote that "the focus on rape as a weapon of war, Autesserre argues, has caused some armed groups to engage in mass rape as a technique to gain attention and a seat at the negotiating table."

So we have gotten to the point that public outcry against the use of rape as a weapon in war can be viewed as helping spread the very thing it is trying to fight. You could understand why young people, who are connected globally in ways that were unthinkable even five years ago, might resist that kind of nuanced, professional reasoning.

Something changed with the Kony video. Watch the nearly 30-minute video, and you will note that so much of it is not about Mr. Kony, but about the viewer, especially the untapped power of the viewer.

The millions who watched the "Kony 2012" video—and donated or contacted a legislator—acting individually and however naïvely, might collectively force some big decisions. Already, some have credited efforts by Invisible Children before the video with spurring the United States government to send 100 advisers to help capture Mr. Kony.

We are entering an age when the shallow political power of the public—including those too young to vote—will increasingly help shape our policy debates. And yes, that is scary to professional foreign policy experts, much in the same way reference book authors with graduate degrees were rattled by the idea of an online encyclopedia created collectively by amateurs.

Navid Hassanpour, a researcher working at the Yale political science department whom I came to know from his work on the role of social media in the Arab Spring uprising, said he was currently studying questions raised by efforts like "Kony 2012." Undoubtedly, the effort is getting more people involved in world politics—spreading "information" about remote areas.

His initial thought, he said in an e-mail, is that by creating advocates for one side in an internal struggle in a foreign land, it could lead to more intervention by the United States and other Western powers.

"I can say that we might get ourselves involved in more and more of them as private entities like the I.C. campaign enter the picture," he wrote, referring to Invisible Children.

And that might be the biggest backlash of them all.

Critical Thinking

1. Why did the conditions in Uganda not develop a surge of awareness before the film's showing when previously President Obama had stated he had authorized deployment of American military advisers?
2. Why are some critics complaining about the film?
3. Identify the manipulations of propaganda and the truth as generated by social media.

Create Central

www.mhhe.com/createcentral

Internet References

Debating Matters
www.debatingmatters.com/topicguides/topicguides/social_media
Joseph Kony and the *New York Times* NYTimes eXmaniner
www.nytexaminer.com/2012/03/joseph-kony-and-the-new-york-times
Online Media NewsBusters
newsbusters.org/media-topics/online-media?page=82
Kony 2012: Inaudible Children Bully Bloggers
bullybloggers.wordpress.com/2012/03/12kony-2012-inaudible-children
Noam Cohen Reporter Archives Times Crest
www.timescrest.com/reporters/Noam-Cohen

NOAM COHEN is a reporter for the *New York Times*.

Article

Prepared by: Caroline Shaffer Westerhof,
California National University for Advanced Studies

Intensive Care for the United Nations

"A gap is steadily growing between the major challenges facing the planet and the ability of international decision-making processes to deal with them . . . ."

THOMAS G. WEISS

Learning Outcomes

After reading this article, you will be able to:

- Discover how the United Nations is either the focus or a central component in world politics.

- Discover the pros and cons of global critiques of the United Nations.

- Understand the legacy of the United Nations and its inherent difficulties.

In October 2010, the United Nations turned a venerable 65 years old. In the spirit of the Beatles song that once asked, "Will you still need me, will you still feed me, when I'm sixty-four?," now seems a good time to inquire whether the UN, a baby boomer from the post–World War II era, has aged well. Should the world body be retired—or should it be revitalized? What are the institution's prospects?

Most countries, and especially major powers like the United States, are loath to allow any overarching central authority to constrain their capacity for autonomous action. State sovereignty remains sacrosanct. Even so, the logic of globalization, interdependence, and technological advances—along with a growing number of trans-boundary crises—should increasingly raise doubts about the sanctity of sovereignty, even in Washington. It is not far-fetched to imagine that the community of nations in coming years will witness a gradual advance of intergovernmental agreements and powers, along the lines of what Europe has nurtured.

The former UN secretary-general Kofi Annan frequently speaks of "problems without passports." What he means is that many of the most intractable challenges facing humankind are transnational; they need no visas to cross borders. Such problems range from climate change, pandemics, and terrorism to unlawful migration, destabilizing financial flows, and the proliferation of weapons of mass destruction (WMD). Effectively addressing any of these threats requires policies and vigorous actions that are not unilateral, bilateral, or even multilateral—they must be global.

Yet the policy authority and the resources for tackling such problems remain vested in the 192 member states of the United Nations individually, rather than in the universal body collectively. The fundamental disjuncture between the growing number of global threats and the currently inadequate structures for international problem solving and decision making goes a long way toward explaining the world's fitful, tactical, and short-term local responses to challenges that require sustained, strategic, and longer-term global action.

For all of its shortcomings and weaknesses, the United Nations with its system of specialized agencies and programs is the closest approximation the global stage can offer to a central institutional presence. This is why the world organization urgently requires strengthening.

Indispensable but Sick

Shortly before his inauguration, US President Barack Obama announced not only that the United States was prepared to reengage with other countries (both friends and foes), but also that multilateralism in general and the UN in particular would be essential to American foreign policy under his administration. He declared straightforwardly that "the global challenges we face demand global institutions that work."

Many of Obama's first steps—which included paying America's back dues to the UN, funding programs for reproductive health, joining the Human Rights Council, moving ahead with nuclear arms reductions, and expressing support for the Comprehensive Test Ban Treaty—were steps in the right direction. But more vigorous and sustained efforts are needed.

The Group of 7 or 8, and even the Group of 20, which includes emerging powers, have their purposes. These groupings are not, however, "global institutions that work." Neither are the ad hoc "coalitions of the willing," such as were mustered for invasions of Iraq and Afghanistan, or the "league of democracies" that the policy analyst Robert Kagan favors. The world needs a universal body that can formulate global norms, make global law, and enforce global decisions. Anything less represents wishful thinking, a desire to escape the complexities of daunting global challenges.

As the Obama administration faces growing dissension regarding the morass in Afghanistan, it is worth pondering how best to fill holes in a global security order that has been an American obsession since the terrorist attacks of September 11, 2001. In this regard, Secretary of Defense Robert Gates's comments in December 2008—that "the United States cannot kill or capture its way to victory" and "is unlikely to repeat another Iraq or Afghanistan: that is, forced regime change followed by nation building under fire"—bear remembering. The sobering experiences of occupation in Iraq and Afghanistan have highlighted the limits of US military and diplomatic power, limits akin to Washington's equally obvious and mammoth inability to go solo in addressing the recent global financial and economic crises.

What other trans-boundary problems should be included on a sensible priority list for this or any other US administration? Most informed Americans would acknowledge that when it comes to spotting, warning of, and managing international health hazards—for example, the severe acute respiratory syndrome (SARS) outbreak in 2003, avian flu more recently, and AIDS perennially—the UN-based World Health Organization is indispensable and unrivaled. Also based within the UN system are capacities for monitoring international crime and the narcotics trade, policing nuclear power and human trafficking, and undertaking numerous other important global functions.

Washington's short list for UN involvement would presumably include post-conflict rebuilding in Afghanistan and Iraq, fighting terrorism (for instance, when it comes to sharing information and monitoring money laundering), pursuing environmental sustainability, providing humanitarian aid, addressing global poverty, rescheduling debt, and fostering trade. (Interestingly all of these items were on a laundry list presented by President George W. Bush in an address to the September 2005 World Summit on the occasion of the UN's 60th anniversary.) After attacks on shipping in the Gulf of Aden and elsewhere, we should add piracy to the list.

At the same time, the diagnosis of the world body is clear: The United Nations is paralyzed. But before we prescribe a course of treatment for the UN's ailments, we must first understand the underlying causes. Essentially there are four.

What Ails It

The first is the enduring concept of the international community as a system of sovereign states, a notion dating back to the 1648 Treaties of Westphalia. The basis for membership in the United Nations, of course, reflects the theoretical equality of states. But a gap is steadily growing between the major challenges facing the planet and the ability of international decision-making processes to deal with them; this is the result of sovereignty's continuing grip. This gap characterizes NATO, the Organization for Economic Cooperation and Development, and the European Union, as well as the UN—all bodies in which states make decisions based almost exclusively on narrowly defined national interests.

Indeed, for national decision makers and so-called realist scholars of international relations, vital national interests, narrowly defined, are apparently the *only* basis on which to make commitments, or avoid them. Paradoxically, the United Nations is the last and most formidable bastion of sacrosanct state sovereignty—even as technological advances, globalization, and the proliferation of trans-boundary problems render national borders less and less salient.

Paradoxically, the United Nations is the last and most formidable bastion of sacrosanct state sovereignty.

The myopically calculated interests of major powers, particularly the United States, thus create obstacles to action by the UN. But powerful states are not the only ones impeding collective, policy making. Smaller and poorer, newer and less powerful states are just as vehemently protective of their so-called sovereignty as the major powers are.

The second cause of the UN's problems stems from the burlesque that passes for diplomacy on Manhattan's First Avenue or Geneva's Avenue de la Paix. The main drama proceeds from an artificial divide between the aging acting troupes from the industrialized north and those from the developing countries of the global south.

The Nonaligned Movement and the Group of 77 developing countries—vehicles launched in the 1950s and 1960s as a way to create diplomatic space in security and economic negotiations for countries on the margins of international politics—once featured creative voices. Now they have become prisoners of their own rhetoric. These rigid and counterproductive groups, along with the toxic atmosphere and unnecessary divisions that they create, constitute almost insurmountable barriers to diplomatic initiatives. Serious conversation becomes virtually impossible and is replaced by meaningless posturing designed to score points back home.

Examples of marquee "stars" in this charade include Venezuelan President Hugo Chávez and the former US ambassador to the UN John Bolton. In the fall of 2006, in the limelight of the General Assembly's stage, Chávez gave a performance in which he referred to George W. Bush as the devil, said "it smells of sulfur," and complained that Bush "came here talking as if he were the owner of the world." Bolton responded by calling Chávez irrelevant and warned that Venezuela would be "disruptive" if elected to the UN Security Council. The former Canadian politician and senior UN official Stephen Lewis has written that "Men and women cannot live by rhetoric alone"—but clearly UN ambassadors and officials are exceptions.

The third cause of the UN's malady is a structural one, and it arises from the overlapping jurisdictions of various UN bodies, the lack of coordination among their activities, and the absence of centralized financing for the system as a whole. All this makes turf struggles more attractive than sensible cooperation. The UN's various moving parts work at cross purposes instead of in a more integrated, mutually reinforcing, and collaborative fashion. Agencies relentlessly pursue cutthroat fundraising to finance expanding mandates, pursue mission creep, and stake out territory.

The UN's organizational chart refers to a "system," but this term falsely implies coherence and cohesion. The body in reality has more in common with a feudal society than with a modern organization. At the UN, frequent use also is made of the word "family." This folksy term is actually preferable to "system" because, like many families, the UN is dysfunctional and divided. Former senior UN staff members Brian Urquhart and Erskine Childers correctly described the world organization when they wrote in 1994 that "The orchestra pays minimum heed to its conductor."

The UN's organizational chart refers to a "system," but this falsely implies coherence and cohesion.

Sir Robert Jackson—the Australian logistics genius who moved goods to Malta and the Middle East during World War II and subsequently over-saw a number of key UN humanitarian operations—observed in a 1969 evaluation of the UN development system that "the machine as a whole has become unmanageable in the strictest sense of the word. As a result, it is becoming slower and more unwieldy, like some prehistoric monster." The lumbering dinosaur is now four decades older but is certainly not better adapted.

The fourth cause of the UN's ailments is the overwhelming weight of the organization's bureaucracy, its low productivity, and the underwhelming leadership within international secretariats. The stereotype of the UN's administration as bloated is misleading in some ways because such a portrayal ignores the efforts of many talented and dedicated individuals. However, the world body's recruitment and promotion methods are certainly part of what ails it. The UN's successes usually have more to do with serendipity and individual personalities than with recruiting the best people for the right reasons or with institutional structures designed to foster collaboration.

Staff costs account for the lion's share of the UN's budget, and much of this money is poorly spent. This situation could quickly improve if the international civil service were regarded as a potential resource and its composition, productivity, and culture were changed. But the short run holds little hope of this, as Secretary-General Ban Ki-moon's lackluster leadership will last for at least another year, and perhaps even until the middle of this decade.

As it stands now, Rube Goldberg would be hard pressed to design something exceeding in futile complexity the UN's array of agencies, each focusing on a different substantive area, with relevant UN partners often located in different cities and maintaining separate budgets, governing boards, organizational cultures, and executive heads. Challenges such as climate change, pandemics, terrorism, and WMDs require multidisciplinary perspectives, inspired leadership, and firm central direction of cross-sector efforts. The UN rarely supplies any of these.

Rube Goldberg would be hard pressed to design something exceeding in futile complexity the UN's array of agencies.

Taking the Cure

Is it possible to heal the United Nations? Can palliatives, if not cures, be found? In fact, the four sources of the institution's illness themselves suggest ways to initiate surgery that, if not radical, would certainly be more than cosmetic.

The first remedy requires building on spotty yet significant progress made to date in recasting national interests in terms of good global citizenship and enhancing international responsibilities. This prescription for the Westphalian system's ailments consists of encouraging yet more recognition of the benefits of cooperating to provide global public goods and respecting international commitments. Democratic member states of the UN, whether large or small, should theoretically find this pill relatively easy to swallow; they have a long-term, rational, and vital interest, along with a moral responsibility, in promoting multilateral cooperation.

While this statement will undoubtedly have a Pollyannaish ring to American ears, a demonstrable therapeutic benefit can be derived from "good international citizenship" (an expression coined by Gareth Evans, the former Australian foreign minister and one-time president of the International Crisis Group). This notion under-pins the conviction that there is a relationship between the provision of basic rights and wider international security. Nothing illustrates the idea better than "the responsibility to protect," or "R2P," a doctrine that defines state sovereignty not as absolute but as contingent on a modicum of respect for human rights. R2P imposes the primary responsibility for human rights on governmental authorities, but it argues that if a state is unwilling or unable to honor its responsibility—or worse, if it is itself the perpetrator of mass atrocities—then the responsibility to protect the rights of individuals shifts upward to the international community of states.

This doctrine illustrates how to move in the direction of reframing state sovereignty, a break-through in values after centuries of passive, mindless acceptance of the proposition that state sovereignty is a license to kill. Both President Obama and Susan Rice, the current US ambassador to the United Nations, have clearly expressed the need for Washington to take the lead in addressing conscience-shocking situations around the world, instead of repeating mistakes such as President Bill Clinton's lamentable decision to stay out of Rwanda during the genocide there in 1994.

The Washington-based "Enough" project, which campaigns to prevent genocide in places like Darfur, the Democratic Republic of Congo, and Zimbabwe, has referred to Africa specialist Rice, Secretary of State Hillary Clinton, National Security Adviser General James Jones, and Samantha Power, the senior director for multilateral affairs at the National Security Council, as a "dream team." An essay that Obama published in *Foreign Affairs* while a presidential candidate attracted wide attention because he asserted the importance of "military force in circumstances beyond self-defense" and specifically listed the need to "confront mass atrocities."

To date there has been no indication of American diplomatic or military teeth behind that promising early rhetoric. One has to worry, for example, how Washington and the international community will respond if a January 2011 referendum in Sudan results in the breakup of Africa's largest state, producing in all likelihood mass atrocities and massive forced displacement.

Nonetheless, the history of international diplomacy and law shows us how states have gradually accepted limits on their conduct by ratifying treaties that have constrained their margins for maneuver. Additionally, the definition of sovereignty has been altered by the spread of ideas about human rights—by what Eleanor Roosevelt presciently predicted in 1948 would be "a curious grapevine." The challenge for the Obama administration, as well as for future administrations, will be to squarely face the reality that the domestic institutions on which the United States and every society depend to provide public goods do not exist at the global level—not for genocide prevention or for any other crucial international issue.

Not to put too fine a point on it, the international order has no power to tax, conscript, regulate, or quarantine. Are these not precisely the attributes required if global problems are to be effectively addressed through international decisions?

Less Posturing, Please

The second prescription for what ails the United Nations involves redressing the north-south quagmire. Fortunately, states have on occasion forged creative partnerships across the fictitious border that supposedly divides industrialized from developing countries. Examples of wide-ranging coalitions formed across continents and ideologies include those that have negotiated treaties to ban landmines and have agreed to establish the International Criminal Court.

Unfortunately, the United States has not joined those coalitions, and in fact during the Bush administration many divides became wider. In the future, Washington should build bridges on issues such as climate change, development finance, nonproliferation, reproductive rights, and terrorism, to name a few. The Obama administration at least has this advantage: Its actions are judged against the extremely poor cooperation record of its predecessor, an administration during which expectations in both the global south and the global north became very low. When it comes to key global challenges, Washington should seek to build within international institutions larger, more legitimate "coalitions of the willing" than the skimpy, illegitimate coalitions that were cob-bled together for Iraq and Afghanistan.

The United States also can build on the Global Compact, a UN effort to bring nonstate actors, including civil society and transnational corporations, into a more intense partnership with the UN. In any case, for the future health of the world organization and world politics, both north and south must engage in less posturing and role-playing.

The third course of treatment would be to pursue the possibility, however remote, of making the UN work more coherently (as advocated in "Delivering as One," a report initiated by Annan before his departure as UN secretary-general). Outside the body itself, the mere mention of reform that might improve coordination among UN agencies causes eyes to glaze over.

But as Mark Malloch Brown (the former administrator of the UN Development Program and *chef de cabinet* for Annan) has suggested, the UN is the only institution where reform is a more popular topic around water coolers than sex.

No reform effort to date has even modestly reduced the turf battles and unproductive competition for funds that characterize the so-called UN system. But could it? Yes—if donor nations would stop talking out of both sides of their mouths and actually insist on the centralization and consolidation that they often espouse in UN forums and before parliamentary bodies. This is not an impossible thing to imagine. Nor is it impossible to imagine adopting modest alternative means of financing for the world body—such as assessing infinitesimally low taxes on financial transfers or airline tickets. Washington, however, has routinely fought such measures in the past because they would give the world organization the autonomy that it requires.

The final element of therapy would be to reinvigorate the staff of the United Nations. Reviving the notion of an autonomous international civil service, as championed by the UN's second secretary-general, Dag Hammarskjöld, is urgently needed. (In fact, Hammarskjöld's ideal goes back to what a working group of the Carnegie Endowment for International Peace during World War II called the "great experiment" of the League of Nations.) Competence and integrity should outweigh nationality, gender considerations, and cronyism, which have become the principal criteria for recruitment, retention, and promotion.

Staff reform for the United Nations would involve recruiting people with integrity and talent. There are numerous ways in which more mobile, younger staff members could be attracted, at the same time that turnover and rotation from headquarters to the field are increased, fewer permanent contracts are offered, and the world organization's career development improves. Staff expenditures account for 90 percent of the organization's budget; near the top of any to-do list should be strengthening performance and productivity by improving output and efficiency.

Obama and the UN

The United States does not dominate the world the way it once did. China and India are rising, and multipolarity has returned in the form of the G-20. Moreover, the world is not desperately longing for Washington to make good on Ambassador Rice's commitment in her confirmation hearing "to refresh and renew America's leadership in the United Nations." But if the League of Nations represented a first generation of international institutions, and the UN system is the second generation, creating a third generation should move to the top of the US foreign policy agenda.

A next generation would have world-class and independent executive leadership with more centralization and better funding. As with the EU, community-wide calculations of interest on many issues would replace those based on narrowly conceived national interests. While not a world government by any stretch of the imagination, international institutions would incorporate elements of overarching authority and enhanced mechanisms for ensuring compliance—indeed, the World Trade Organization (WTO) already has some.

Instituting the four remedies described here would amount to the establishment of a third generation of international institutions. To be sure, there are few precedents for the deliberate destruction of existing international institutions and the establishment of new ones (other than the transfer of assets from the League of Nations to the UN and from the General Agreement on Tariffs and Trade to the WTO). Moreover, initial expectations surrounding the Obama administration were as impossibly high in the international arena as they were in the domestic one. Obama's honeymoon was short, and public appetite for foreign policy initiatives is limited. Nonetheless, the US administration has exercised modest leadership—in the Middle East, on nuclear nonproliferation, on climate change, and in the aftermath of the recent financial and economic crisis.

Will the United States sit on the sidelines; try to take charge unilaterally; or will it make the UN a central component of its strategic interests? It is also worth asking whether the UN—a heavily bureaucratic institution deeply troubled by its own failings—is ready for an energetic United States.

The global financial crisis and subsequent economic slowdown have made clear the risks, problems, and costs associated with a global economy that lacks adequate international institutions with democratic decision-making ability and the power to ensure compliance with collective decisions. No less towering a commentator than Henry Kissinger wrote this about the realities of a globalizing world and the limits of a self-regulating worldwide market: "The financial collapse exposed the mirage. It made evident the absence of global institutions to cushion the shock and to reverse the trend." Trillions of dollars, euros, and pounds have been used mainly to paper over the cracks that the crisis revealed. Business as usual remains the standard operating procedure, even in the wake of the Great Recession.

But can we perhaps learn from history? In a recent book about the origins of American multilateralism, Stewart Patrick, a senior fellow at the Council on Foreign Relations, made a persuasive case that "the fundamental questions facing the 1940s generation confront us again today. As then, the United States remains by far the most powerful country in the world, but its contemporary security, political, and economic challenges are rarely amenable to unilateral action."

Charles de Gaulle famously called the United Nations *le machin*, thereby dismissing international cooperation as frivolous in comparison with the real red meat of international affairs—national interests and realpolitik. But de Gaulle conveniently ignored the fact that the decision to create "the thing" was formalized not by the UN Charter signed in June 1945,

but rather by the "Declaration by the United Nations" adopted in Washington in January 1942. That is, the 26 countries that defeated fascism also viewed the establishment of a world organization as an essential extension of their wartime commitments. These were not pie-in-the-sky idealists. The UN system was viewed not as a liberal plaything but as a vital necessity for postwar order and prosperity.

Urquhart—one of the first individuals recruited by the United Nations, and undoubtedly the most respected commentator on the world organization—recalled the "remarkable generation of leaders and public servants" who led the United States during and after World War II. These pragmatic idealists, he observed, were "more concerned about the future of humanity than the outcome of the next election; and they understood that finding solutions to postwar problems was much more important than being popular with one or another part of the American electorate." Could this same farsighted political commitment rise again under the Obama administration—if not in the next two years, then at least by the end of a second term?

Critical Thinking

1. How is there a gap between the major challenges facing the planet and the abilities of international decision-making processes to deal with them?

2. Has the United Nations changed world politics since its founding?

3. How is the United Nations having an impact on global history?

Create Central

www.mhhe.com/createcentral

Internet References

Current History
http://currenthistory.com

United Nations Chronicle
www.un/org/webcast/pdfs/wc983.pdf

What's Wrong with the United Nations and How to Fix It
www.foreignaffairs.com/articles/64682/g-john-ikenberry/what%C3%A2%E2%82%AC%E2%84%A2s-wrong-with-the-united-nations-and-how-to-fix-it

Ralph Bunche Institute for International Studies
www.ralphbuncheinstitute.org/about

WorldViews: Foreign Intervention in Africa
worldviews.igc.org/awpguide/interven.html

THOMAS G. WEISS is Presidential Professor of Political Science at the City University of New York Graduate School, and Director of the Ralph Bunche Institute for International Studies.

From *Current History*, November 2010, pp. 322–330. Copyright © 2010 by Current History, Inc. Reprinted by permission.

Article

Prepared by: Caroline Shaffer Westerhof,
California National University for Advanced Studies

Srebrenica's Legacy: How the Lessons of the Balkans Animate Humanitarianism Today

ANNE C. RICHARD

Learning Outcomes

After reading this article, you will be able to:

- Discover what led to the Srebrenica massacre.
- Understand Annex VII in 1995 of the Dayton Peace Agreement.
- Discover how digitally networked technology (DNT) changes our lives and influences constructively or destructively the development of nation-states.

Open Borders in Bosnia

Some of those who managed to escape during the conflict and ethnic cleansing in Bosnia two decades ago fled to neighboring countries and others fled longer distances, even as some neighboring countries and several European nations restricted the number of Bosnian refugees allowed to enter.

One country that provided refuge to nearly 10,000 Bosnians in the 1990s was Turkey. This is the same Turkey that today has opened its doors to accommodate nearly a half-million refugees who have fled the brutal war and atrocities in Syria. Today, the Syria conflict has forced more than 1.7 million Syrians to escape into the neighboring countries of Turkey, Jordan, Lebanon, Egypt, and Iraq. The citizens and governments of those five countries have responded to the massive Syrian refugee influx, for the most part, with generosity and at tremendous financial expense. Open borders for refugees who need to flee are not only helping save the lives of Syrians. Open borders are helping save the lives of a quarter-million refugees from Darfur, Sudan who have fled to neighboring Chad; providing refuge to a million Somali refugees in the Greater Horn of Africa region; to Iraqi and Afghan refugees in Pakistan; to Burmese refugees in Thailand, and refugees elsewhere.

However, keeping national borders open is a challenge. Sometimes governments deny entry to refugees. In the Syria crisis refugees continue to cross borders even as resources and hospitality in neighboring countries begin to wear thin and options for restricting the flow of refugees are discussed. We cannot take these open borders for granted, especially as tensions mount in the countries neighboring Syria.

The Bureau that I lead at the Department of State works hard to encourage open borders around the world. We meet with governments to encourage them to fulfill their international obligations and commitments relating to refugees. The U.S. Government also realizes that one of the most effective ways to encourage governments to maintain open borders is by doing what we can to support humanitarian aid programs for refugees. We help refugee-hosting governments by sharing the costs. Last year, the State Department provided more than $1.8 billion to assist and protect more than 15 million refugees as well as vulnerable migrants and displaced people around the world. . . .

In Bosnia, the world witnessed what happens when aid deliveries are blocked and humanitarian access denied. Over months, convoys were unable to reach people in Gorazde, in Cerska, in Zepa, in Bihac, in Srebrenica, and elsewhere. Trucks loaded with relief supplies were directly targeted for attack, the drivers killed. Convoys with food, medicines, soap, and other basic supplies were forced to turn around only a few kilometers from their destinations. Relief convoys that did reach besieged villages managed to do so only after negotiating access at dozens of roadblocks. As you know, the international community mounted a humanitarian airlift to reach a number of towns that were cut off by road.

Let's shift to Syria today. Inside Syria, more than four million people are reported to be displaced; millions more need humanitarian relief. Many of those people are without adequate food or water, poor sanitation, and little or no medical care. Despite heroic efforts by international humanitarian agencies and local charities operating inside Syria, UN humanitarian officials report that emergency water and sanitation programs have reached only 40 percent of Syrians who need those programs. Emergency health programs are reaching fewer than 30 percent of those in need. Fewer than 15 percent have access to emergency shelter and other relief supplies.

Why is it so hard to get aid delivered to those who need it in Syria? Partly it is because of the extreme danger. A number of relief workers have lost their lives there in the line of duty. But it is also because the Assad regime, which has the responsibility to help its own displaced, has created barriers to the delivery of aid.

In April, a top UN humanitarian official accompanying an aid convoy reported that he had to negotiate his way through 54 checkpoints on the 300-kilometer road between Damascus and Aleppo. Some had been erected by the Asad regime, and others by opposition forces. Cumulatively, these roadblocks make travel across Syria by humanitarian workers an arduous and dangerous journey. Moreover, delivering aid inside Syria is incredibly challenging because of continuing violence and shifting battle lines. And in Damascus the Asad regime issues or denies visas to aid workers and keeps a list of approved non-governmental organizations—the number of which is shrinking.

Part of my job is to push to secure humanitarian access so that aid workers can reach and help those who are trapped. The U.S. Government condemns those who attack innocent civilians, calls out governments that are perpetrating crimes against their own citizens and calls on governments to allow aid to reach those in need. The United States has provided nearly $815 million in humanitarian aid since the start of the Syria crisis, more than any other country. Some of it helps refugees who have fled Syria and nearly half—nearly $385 million—has been allocated for relief programs inside the country. We know that international aid is reaching people in all 14 governorates in Syria. But we also know that access is limited within governorates, and aid is not reaching everyone who needs it.

Humanitarian Access and Protection Challenges in Other Places in The World

The challenge of maintaining humanitarian access to victims of conflict and providing them with some basic forms of protection does not exist only in Syria.

In Sudan's Darfur region, the government regularly impedes the flow of international relief to 1.4 million Darfurians living in bleak displacement camps. The Government of Sudan has made harassment of aid operations an art form. The government at times refuses to issue visas to international aid workers; at other times, Sudan officials revoke visas they have already issued. Medicines sit in warehouses until they expire. We are also worried about those in conflict areas of South Sudan, where access is being impeded, slowing delivery of relief supplies that are vital to the local population.

In remote areas of the Democratic Republic of the Congo, widespread insecurity, sporadic fighting, and often non-existent roads block regular humanitarian access to villages. A tragic hallmark of that conflict is that women and girls are targeted for violence and rape, just as was the case during the war in Bosnia. Disruptions to humanitarian deliveries were a problem for 20 years in Somalia and remain challenging; earlier this year we saw similar challenges operating in northern Mali, where insecurity prevented access to many. A few weeks ago I was in Colombia and met with people who were being displaced by threats and attacks even as peace negotiations are being held and the Colombian government takes laudatory actions to provide restitution to conflict victims.

Policies that Help Secure Humanitarian Access

Improving our access to help victims of conflict and prevent human rights abuses is far more than a logistical challenge; it is a political challenge first and foremost. The U.S. Government is committed to working with other States and organizations that share our concerns about this. We will continue diplomatic efforts to encourage governments—and when necessary to pressure them—to live up to their responsibilities to assist and protect vulnerable populations. Here are some of the methods we are using and steps we are taking to secure and maintain humanitarian access:

1. **Using Diplomatic and Legal Tools:** Sovereignty should not be used as a shield for genocide, ethnic cleansing, and other mass atrocities. We should use all the legal and normative frameworks at our disposal to push for international humanitarian access where needed, including human rights law, international humanitarian law, the UN Guiding Principles on Internal Displacement, and the concept of the Responsibility to Protect to which UN member states agreed in 2005. As Srebrenica demonstrated, as Syria demonstrates today, merely having laws and guidelines on the books will not be enough in many cases. But elsewhere there is evidence of an improving legal environment that may result in greater respect for these laws and guidelines. In Africa, where sustained humanitarian access has been a prevalent problem over the years, the U.S. Government is working to help governments implement the African Union's excellent treaty that protects the rights of persons who have become internally displaced due to conflict, instability, or natural disasters. In the United States, the administration of President Obama has launched an initiative to strengthen our government's ability to impose financial sanctions, export controls, and travel bans against those who support or perpetrate atrocities in other countries, and to prosecute individuals who participated in atrocities. We are also supporting local efforts to promote accountability and combat impunity.

2. **Strengthening Peacekeeping Operations:** Peacekeeping can play an important role in halting conflicts, supporting safe returns and opening up humanitarian access. One lesson of the Balkans, and of Srebrenica, is that peacekeepers need to be prepared for their environment and to protect civilians, and the military capacity and will to act must match mandates. We are working to make UN peacekeeping operations

more effective, better-trained, and properly equipped. Last year alone the United States provided training and equipment to support 16,000 peacekeepers in seven UN and regional peacekeeping operations. We have also focused on strengthening the protection of civilians in peacekeeping operations. Last year as Chair of the G8, the United States brought attention to badly needed tools—the development of doctrine, training, and mission planning on the protection of civilians for missions. In the Democratic Republic of Congo, the U.S. Government supported an innovative strategy that aims to combine peacekeeping and human rights analysis to make the entire peacekeeping effort more effective. Recently, a new peacekeeping mission in Mali was established which should increase access and support reconciliation to that divided country.

3. **Stronger Advocacy for International Humanitarian Operations:** As long as there is conflict, we will need international humanitarian relief organizations able to take on the incredibly difficult and dangerous work of helping people in need of relief. What we also know is that such work requires solid leadership. Those at the top of humanitarian agencies and operations must be strong leaders and advocates. They must negotiate with national and local authorities, talk to armed groups, and manage to get past roadblocks and checkpoints. That takes skill and patience, experience and planning. They must break down barriers to get relief supplies to vulnerable populations—and to tell the international community what is happening. That's why it's critical to find the best leaders for these positions, including those who lead UN agencies and serve as UN Resident Coordinators and UN Humanitarian Coordinators.

As an advocate on humanitarian issues, I know their work must be backed up with strong diplomatic support. My State Department colleagues and I are absolutely committed to raising our voices on urgent crises and engaging other governments, international organizations and citizens of foreign countries in what we call "humanitarian diplomacy". We know that open borders, humanitarian access, and the many other challenges facing humanitarian operations in the world today are mostly political problems for which political solutions are needed before the aid workers will be able to go home.

Preventing Displacement and Atrocities in the First Place

These issues I raise are part of our government's effort to reduce conflict and atrocities, through many means. In August 2011, President Obama put a spotlight on this goal, directing a dozen government departments and agencies to look at how to better prevent mass atrocities, declaring that "preventing mass atrocities and genocide is a core national security interest and a core moral responsibility of the United States." Certainly this initiative is aspirational, and one that looks to include atrocity

prevention in the daily business of our government. One result is a monthly meeting of a new group with members from across the government. It [is called the Atrocities Prevention Board and it] reviews key country situations and also ways to improve U.S. and international tools. In particular, this effort is aimed at better early warning and prevention. Prevention is the best way to reduce future atrocities—and humanitarian challenges.

As Deputy Assistant Secretary Reeker said in Sarajevo in May, ". . . we continue to extend a hand as friends and partners . . . the United States will continue to invest in future leaders and in developing a market based economy, the rule of law, and a strong democracy . . . , but local actors in Bosnia and Herzegovina, government officials, civil society, and ordinary citizens—all need to do their part for the county to move forward."

Conclusion

Ladies and gentleman, I want to end my remarks today by recalling a singular act that took place twenty years ago. At that time, Mina Jahic, a Bosniak, took into her home a young, seriously wounded Muslim man who, somehow, had managed to escape the execution squad. Mina took the risk that few of us would take. She sheltered the injured man, nursed him back to health, and helped him to escape a month later. Mina herself could have been executed for her actions. But she did the right thing, the moral thing, and inspired her neighbors to do likewise. In 2011 she was honored by the Secretary of State together with other heroic rescuers. Mina is here today and I can thank her myself: Mina, thank you.

Mina was not the only one in this country who opened her door to a victim in danger who needed a place of safety and I salute all of them. Nations of the world should do no less, by keeping their doors open—their borders open—to refugees who need to escape persecution and supporting deliveries of humanitarian relief to vulnerable people caught in the grip of conflict.

Critical Thinking

1. Can such devastation of mankind ever be stopped?
2. How does our education help us draw on the lessons of the early 20th century, given how the speed of thought impacts our lives today?
3. What is the legacy of the Bosnian war?

Create Central

www.mhhe.com/createcentral

Internet References

Articles about Srebrenica—*Los Angeles Times*
articles.latimes.com/keyword/srebrenica

Balkans Logistics News—*World News Report*
world.einnews.com/news/balkans-logistics

"Sergio" in Conversation/commemorating Balkans Legacies
   http://gongandme.wordpress.com/2011/01/08/sergio-in-conversation-
   commemorating-balkans-legacies

The Legacy Project: Bosnia/Serbia 2013
   thelegacyproject.com/bosit.html

Srebrenica's Legacy
   www.state.gov/j/prm/releases/remarks/2013/211793.htm

ANNE RICHARD is Assistant Secretary of State, Bureau of Population.

Richard, Anne C. From an address delivered in Sarajevo, Bosnia, July 10, 2013.

Unit 2

UNIT

Prepared by: Caroline Shaffer Westerhof, *California National University for Advanced Studies*

Studying Comparative Politics: Evaluating Theories, Learning from Cases, Generalizing Trends

This section builds upon the discussion of why we compare. In part, it describes how theory-building is achieved, that is, it describes the process of examination and evaluation, testing and retesting, verifying sources, and collecting credible evidence in order to achieve generalizability and predictive strength. Generalizations are essential for providing baseline knowledge from which particularities are observed, described, explained, and anticipated. To concretize what this means, this unit looks into one of the oldest theoretical debates in political science: democratic theory. We track how leading scholars ruminate about democratic theory before looking at how additional studies—on participation, mature democracies, transitioning regimes, and the relationship between capitalism and democracy—build on some of the theoretical foundations laid out.

Here, the tone is set for distinguishing between democracy as studied in political science and conventional usage. Democracy is a term most widely used among politicians; scholars actually "hesitate" to use it "because of the 'ambiguity' of the term." Nevertheless, given its popular use in both democratic and autocratic regimes, it is important to clarify what it is and what it is not. Importantly, democracy, clarified by scholars may be interpreted one way, and practitioners may consider other definitions. As the concept is researched, it is important, at the outset, to clarify its interpretations in terms of concepts, procedures, and principles.

There is a review of the study of democracy noting the process of theory-building. The essential parts of theory-building include of theories derived from systematic scholastic examination and evaluation through evidentiary support. Fifteen interesting conclusions or considerations from twenty-five years of democratic study are reviewed and included.

What is political science research? Such research is situated in the debate in the literature and based on evidentiary evaluation. In this regard Middle East studies demonstrate "how theory meets reality." Progress in Middle East studies notes that we need no longer explain Arab in cultural terms and to recognize that there is a belief within the Arab world to acknowledge the popularity of democracy as a concept. We do recognize the broad conflagration that is tearing apart this part of the world. It continues to be a bloody turmoil that is growing worse, day by day. The president of the United States is being faced with hard questions.

Discussion and argumentation, fact-finding, and evidentiary support are the essential elements to theory-building so that the patterns that are identified withstand scrutiny and evaluation. This is the "theoretically informed" comparative study. Indeed, it is because the theoretical fundamentals are in place that we observe particularities that evolve throughout our rationale of comparative politics. We note the promises and problems of citizen participation and mobilization across transitioning countries and mature democracies. Thus, whether in transitioning regimes or mature democracies, viable outlets for citizen participation are the key to maintaining political stability and enhancing development, although these do not always exist.

If we think that the debate is near exhaustion, consider this additional angle: Does capitalism drive democracy or does democracy lead to economic development? Is this a wrinkle to the theory? Or is it an elaboration of the theory, even as protestors appear to demand an end to capitalism or the existing democratic institutions, they are also encouraging alienated groups to return to the political fold by participating? That participation, in turn, leads to less dramatic or less revolutionary forms of change, such as petitions for policy or economic responses.

Must the United States rethink its strategy as it addresses the challenges of maintaining its primacy as a global power? Yet, as the world is becoming increasingly multi-polar, the world center of gravity has shifted to Asia. Although the United States may want to contain China, China is continuing to make history by developing a new shipping frontier.

Clearly, political scholars as well as practitioners will continue to assess how democratization occurs, what it takes to consolidate democracies, and what processes will enrich emergent and mature democracies. That is, theory building is likely to continue—as it well should—and policymakers will continue to evaluate the empirical applications of the theory. Importantly, the discussion, evaluation, and testing reveal to us the problems of letting our own biases dictate who gets to participate and how or when. In the process, we also learn a fundamental and important lesson about participation: If we provide for citizen participation, the expanded venues provide the release of any bottled up responses that may otherwise find relief through dangerous or extremist appeals. That is a generalization and baseline that will enhance political development in any country and region and may yet be a destructive force.

Article

Prepared by: Caroline Shaffer Westerhof,
California National University for Advanced Studies

Twenty-Five Years, Fifteen Findings

PHILIPPE C. SCHMITTER

Learning Outcomes

After reading this article, you will be able to:

- Discover the author's concept and actions describing how democratic transitions are or are not achieved as nations move away from authoritarian rule.

- Understand the concepts of democracy as viewed by several scholars.

- Explain why, despite the neoliberal enthusiasm for privatization and globalization, democratization continues to rely on the state.

When Guillermo O'Donnell and I were writing *Transitions from Authoritarian Rule: Tentative Conclusion about Uncertain Democracies* a quarter of a century ago, we had few cases and almost no literature upon which to draw.[1] Mostly we ransacked the monographs of colleagues who were taking part in the same Woodrow Wilson Center project as we were. We also reached back to the classics of political thought. I personally drew much inspiration from the work of Niccolò Machiavelli who, I discovered, had grappled some time ago with regime change in the opposite direction—that is, from "republican" to "princely" rule.

Neither of us imagined that the fledgling efforts we were then observing in Southern Europe and Latin America would soon be followed by more than fifty other regime transformations all around the world. These "divine surprises," especially the ones in Central and Eastern Europe and the former Soviet Union, brought not only much scientific opportunity and personal normative satisfaction, but also a major intellectual risk. To what extent could the assumptions, concepts, hypotheses, and "tentative conclusions" that we had derived from the early cases be stretched to fit a much larger and highly varied set of countries? The stretching that we were considering seemed even more problematic in light of how opposed our ideas were to most prevailing theories about "really existing democracies."[2]

We insisted, for example, on a clear distinction between liberalization and democratization. We refused to accept the notion that democracy requires some fixed set of economic or cultural prerequisites. We emphasized the key role of elite interaction and strategic choice during the transition and in most cases ascribed limited importance to mass mobilization from below. We pointed to the demobilizing effect of the electoral process and said that while civil society might have a significant role, it would be a short-lived one. We noted how most transitions began from within the previous autocratic regime, whose collapse or self-transformation by no means guaranteed the eventual success of democracy. Finally, and perhaps most subversively, we argued that it was possible (if not always probable) that one could bring about democracy *without* having any democrats on hand. In other words, the favorable cultural and normative traits or "civic culture" that comparative survey research had detected and found essential to all stable democracies was better conceived as a *product* of democracy rather than its producer.

As a comparativist, I welcomed the challenge of "stretching" our original work and applying it to such different cases. I found it gratifying to observe how often, how far away, and even how controversially these "cross-regional" comparisons were attempted, and I am convinced that they contributed to a fuller understanding of democratization. What I found much less gratifying was the tendency of critics and other readers to apply our book to topics that were manifestly not within its purview. It had been no accident that Guillermo and I had given the book a title stressing transitions *away from* authoritarianism rather than *to* democracy, yet many treated our tome as if it purported to contain a magic formula for success or even lessons in how to consolidate democracy.

Not only did we refuse to presume a *telos* that would lead to such a felicitous result, we were obsessed with the likelihood of regression to autocracy. Admittedly, we were concerned all along with the implications that different transitional situations might have for democracy's ability to emerge and persist, but we wrote nothing about what such an outcome might look like. Guillermo and I have since written a good deal on this topic, but nothing in our original joint effort allows one to assume that voluntaristic, structurally underdetermined action would continue to dominate the politics of new democracies once they passed through the highly uncertain transition period, or that strategic machinations among elites would continue to count for more than mass mobilization and popular participation.

Much has happened over the last two decades, including a burgeoning of democratization studies, from which I have learned much. The editors of the *Journal of Democracy* have asked me to share this retrospective wisdom with their readers:

1. Democratization has proven far easier to accomplish in the contemporary historical context than I had at first thought it would be. Back in the late 1970s, I estimated that in Latin America since 1900 roughly two of every three efforts to democratize had failed, with an obvious (and usually violent) relapse into autocracy ensuing within three to five years. I wince when I come across the accusation that, in choosing to compare South European and Latin American cases, Guillermo and I had been "cherry picking" the easy cases, with crippling implications for our tentative conclusions about supposedly harder cases elsewhere. Nothing could have been further from my mind, especially since I had been researching the highly tumultuous and uncertain transition that had been going on in Portugal since 1974. It is certainly not our fault that none of the countries in Southern Europe or Latin America has as yet suffered a manifest or sudden regression to autocracy, although several spent a long time in transition (Brazil), some have had close calls (Paraguay, Peru), and a few have developed symptoms of gradual deterioration (Bolivia, Ecuador, Nicaragua).

The lack of authoritarian regressions is all the more astonishing when one considers that many of the factors said to be vital (or at least helpful) to the consolidation of liberal democracy have been missing in many if not most of these cases. Rates of employment and economic growth have not always been higher under democracy as opposed to autocracy; social equality and income distribution have not always improved significantly; trust in rulers has often deteriorated; critical measures of "civic culture" have declined—and yet basic democratic institutions have remained in place.

It must be kept in mind, finally, that the distinction between "easy" and "hard" cases of transition can only apply to those cases in which, for whatever reasons, an actual transition to democracy is attempted, as signaled by the holding of free and fair "founding elections" complete with contending parties and an uncertain outcome. Cases in which some elite from the old autocracy keeps control of the process—typically allowing some degree of liberalization as a tactic to fend off democratization—do not count. This means that one must exclude all the Central Asian cases when considering transitions in the post-Soviet world, and that only Turkey and, more recently, Lebanon need be counted by "transitologists" who study the Middle East and North Africa.

2. Democratization may have been easier than I had anticipated, but it has also been less consequential. Considering the consequences of previous efforts at democratization, scholars and activists alike expected that such a transformation would bring about much more significant changes in power relations, property rights, policy entitlements, economic equality, and social status than those that have in fact occurred so far. This is not to claim that "nothing changed." In the realm of respect for human rights, more decent treatment of citizens by authorities,

and a sense of greater personal freedom, significant changes have occurred and citizens appreciate them (even if the changes are often rapidly "discounted"). But in terms of those factors that are most likely to influence the longer-term distribution of power and influence within the polity, recent democratizations have accomplished much less than did those in the past. In some cases—most of which are found in Central and Eastern Europe and the former USSR—those running the new democracies have close ties to (or may even be) the very people who ran the old autocracies. Try to imagine France or the young United States after their respective revolutions with officials from the time of monarchy peacefully back in power under the new modes and orders of the early republic!

Admittedly, with respect to the recent cases, the time frame for evaluating such consequences is foreshortened, and the typical mode of transition has hardly been revolutionary. In what Terry Karl and I have called "pacted" or "imposed" transitions, there is every reason to expect less consequential changes. Under such circumstances, major and irreversible shifts in the distribution of resources that can be converted into power and influence are more or less ruled out. Only after these transitional arrangements have ended, whether by mutual agreement or by one party pulling out, can one expect the sheer persistence of democracy to produce some of these changes through normal political competition. One could say that new democracies buy time to consolidate; only then do redistributive consequences begin to appear in response to competitive pressures.

3. Democratization has been easier than anticipated precisely because it has been less consequential than anticipated. During the uncertainty of the initial transitions, no one could have known this—I certainly did not. The Portuguese case suggested the contrary. Only later was I to learn how exceptional it had been, and how ephemeral had been its consequences. Spain and later several Latin American cases showed that the socially dominant and economically privileged had much less to fear from democratization than they might at first have thought. After things in Portugal settled down, and later after the USSR collapsed, it became clear that political freedoms and partisan competition under democratic conditions would not have to lead to either majority tyranny or minority radicalization. Rotation in power would not have to produce wild fluctuations in either policies or the distribution of benefits. My hunch is that the learning of these lessons sealed democracy's irreversibility in these countries. Those who had once backed autocracy began to realize that their interests would be better protected under democracy than they had been under authoritarianism—and without the added costs that the latter might bring in terms of violent repression, international opprobrium, and the like.

4. Really existing democracy has been disappointing to both its intended beneficiaries and to us academics. In countries that have democratized since 1974, disenchantment with both the practices and products of democracy is widespread. Analysts vie to find the most deprecating adjective to place in front of the word "democracy": defective, electoral, partial, pseudo, low-intensity, sham, ersatz, and, of course, delegative. This effort has contributed to the general impression—reflected in opinion polls—that most of the regime changes over the past 25 years have resulted in poor-quality regimes unworthy of the struggles and sacrifices that it cost to bring them about.

The first thing to note here is that such disenchantment is hardly restricted to new democracies. In the established ones as well, analogous "morbidity symptoms" are rife. Almost everywhere, voter turnout has declined, as have union membership, the prestige of politicians, the perceived importance of parliaments, the strength of party identification, the stability of electoral preferences, and the levels of trust in most public institutions. Conversely, there has been a rise in litigiousness, corruption charges (and convictions), and populist antiparty candidacies. While it would be an exaggeration to call this a full-scale "crisis" of democratic legitimacy, the striking ubiquity of these symptoms suggests (but does not prove) that there may be something more generically deficient in democracy's institutions and practices. Communism's collapse and democracy's spread have not brought about an "end of history" rooted in democracy's insuperability. Far from enjoying smooth sailing, today's really existing democracies face storms of criticism from many directions.

5. Really existing democracy may be especially disappointing where it has been recently attained, but the impact of this disaffection does not seem to threaten it. No matter how many citizens disapprove of their elected leaders and shun politics as unsavory, there is virtually no sign of mass desire for any form of government other than democracy, and few signs of growing support for avowedly undemocratic parties or politicians. Those agents who in the past frequently used force or fraud to bring about the breakdown of democracy are astonishingly absent. Economic and social crises that once would have been enough to trigger regime change now only shake up electoral politics or spur somewhat irregular depositions of elected officials and their replacement by others.

According to comparative survey research, satisfaction with present rulers and trust in existing institutions are both abysmal (with a certain amount of nostalgia for the autocratic "strong hand" not unknown either), but none of this does much if anything to make authoritarian regression more likely. Even in countries that have done fairly well in objective economic terms (Brazil, Chile, Hungary, and Poland), subjective assessments give democracy low performance grades without anyone expecting that this is going to mean autocracy's return. For a while in Latin America, the prospect of *autogolpes* ("self-coups" by means of which elected rulers extended their powers and perpetuated themselves in office by decree) seemed a plausible threat, but these gambits failed fairly quickly. My hunch is that this is a product of what I call the "second law of political dynamics"—namely, that no regime is ever displaced or replaced unless and until an alternative to it already exists. With no credible and appealing alternative form of rule in the offing, really existing democracy—however unbeloved—remains "the only game in town."

Moreover, it is at least debatable whether this should be considered a sign of democracy's intrinsic inferiority. Democratic theorists (but not theorists of democratization)

have tended to assume that democratic stability hinges on the flourishing of a "civic culture" replete with ample intergroup tolerance, trust in institutions, and readiness to compromise. What we seem to be observing in new democracies today is a political culture that is less "civic" than "cynical." I have a hunch and a hope about this. My hunch is that this may not be as corrosive or dangerous a situation as was once presumed. My hope is that if ruling elites can be tricked into playing the competitive-politics game (even in defective form) for fifteen or twenty years, then the next crisis will most likely be resolved by a shift to a different subtype of democracy rather than to a nondemocratic regime. Disenchantment with democracy, in other words, could lead not to autocracy, but to different and perhaps even better forms of democracy.

6. Democratization may have been different in "post-totalitarian" versus "post-authoritarian" settings, but not in the way that specialists predicted. Twenty years ago, it seemed reasonable to assume that democratizing the postcommunist states would be much harder than democratizing those states where some form of autocracy other than communism had held sway. The former states, after all, would need not merely political reform but also massive economic, social, and even cultural or mental transformations to undo decades of comprehensive and ideologically reinforced collectivism. This assumption was widespread, and it has been proven wrong. On the contrary, in Central and Eastern Europe and even in several of the more western republics of the former Soviet Union, the transition away from autocracy and the consolidation of democracy have proven to be easier—not to mention faster and more thorough—than they were in either Latin America or Southern Europe. Most of the horrors and dilemmas predicted for postcommunism have not happened. One could even argue that having to make so many changes at once was an advantage. It gave the new rulers an enlarged policy space in which they could negotiate with powerful holdover elites and reach compromises—not the least of which was an exchange of the claim to rule for the right to make money. Explosions of ethnic violence were mostly confined to what had once been Yugoslavia, where Soviet-style totalitarian rule and political culture had long been in decline. In the cases where nondemocratic regimes did install themselves immediately (the five Central Asian republics) or after a short competitive interlude (Belarus and Russia), transitions did not fail—rather, they were never even seriously attempted as ex-communists calling themselves nationalists and social democrats seized control, won noncompetitive elections, and used preexisting organizational advantages to keep themselves in power.

7. Pacts negotiated between old-regime elites and opposition groups do seem to have made a difference in the short to medium run, but their longer-term effect is more dubious. Along with transitions simply "imposed" by ruling elites, "pacted" transitions have since 1974 out-numbered the historically most common forms of democratic transition, which are revolution and reform. Hence it is worth pointing out a problem that pacted and imposed transitions share: Both have a tendency to "lock in" existing privileges and make redistributive reforms harder. What is particularly noxious for the future of democracy about such pacts is that they tempt elites to extend their agreements beyond the period of early uncertainty and reinforce a pattern of collusion between political parties that generates corruption and citizen disillusionment. Venezuela, long a classic case of pacted transition, illustrates these toxic dynamics.

8. Political parties matter, even if they usually play an insignificant role in bringing about the transition, but they have made less of a contribution to democratic stability than expected. No democratization process can afford to do without parties, especially once elections are convoked. For better or worse, parties seem to be indispensable in structuring competition for representation within territorially defined constituencies. For "founding elections" to have their effect, the full range of potential parties must be allowed to take part and to choose their candidates without exclusions. Depending on the rules adopted, later elections will see the number of parties shrink, but the effect of these initial contests (Guillermo and I called them "civic orgies") will persist. In earlier waves of democratization, revolutions from below tended to produce a single dominant party that governed for a substantial period and played a key role in crafting the new rules of the regime. More recently, pacted and imposed transitions have become much more common and produced different short-term outcomes. Pacts tends to spawn collusive two-party systems; an imposed transition usually leads to a far more fragmented party landscape—at least among those political forces that opposed the former autocracy. The unexpected outcome is that, when it comes to preventing authoritarian regression and consolidating democracy, both modes seem to work. This is so, puzzlingly, even though the new parties are often very weak, with few regular supporters, little fundraising ability, and scant public trust or esteem. New democracies in both Latin America and Eastern Europe have seen record-breaking levels of volatility from one election to another, as well as high rates of party birth and death. Citizens show strong political interest and fairly clear preferences, but have trouble translating these into stable partisan identifications. Since 1974, the winning parties in "founding elections" have only rarely been able to gain a second consecutive term. Turnover in power has become the rule. In other words, many a new democracy has "shocked the experts" by consolidating as a regime without having first consolidated its party system.

9. Civil society has figured prominently and favorably in the literature on democratic transition and consolidation, but it may be a mixed blessing. Its robust presence has been regarded as vital to the success of both processes. In "classic" reform transitions, the self-organization of excluded or marginalized groups and their threatening (but nonviolent) expressions of discontent spur ruling elites' concessions. Once transition occurs, the willingness of these organizations to play by the new rules supposedly ensures regime stability. Civil society did play a major role in the Philippines, South Korea, Peru, and Czechoslovakia, and later in the Georgian and Ukrainian "color revolutions," albeit more as a force for transition than for consolidation. Most cases of transition since 1974 have been close to the "pacted" or "imposed" sort, in which civil society's role is less clear. Civil society could not choose the nature or timing of change; at best, civil society played an indirect part by bringing old-regime softliners and moderate oppositionists to the table, or by convincing rulers that repression would cost too much. Once transitions began, civil society mobilized to push rulers beyond the comfort zone of mere liberalization and highly restrictive elections.

But civil society can also play an ambiguous or even malign role. In Yugoslavia, the mobilization of civil society (or societies) along mutually hostile ethnic lines helped to fuel protracted violence. Something similar occurred when the USSR began to break up and the Baltic and Caucasus regions witnessed various civil societies gearing up to assert nationalist claims, sometimes through force. There are certainly circumstances in which civil society mobilization can make it harder rather than easier to agree on new rules and stick by them.

10. Parliamentarism, decentralizaztion (federalism), and checks and balances (horizontal accountability) were thought to be magic ingredients of successful consolidation, but many countries have opted for different institutions and have done just as well. If I have learned one thing about institutions during the last 25 years, it is that there is no magic formula—nothing works everywhere. Latin American polities have not done so badly during this time with presidentialism,[3] and I see no evidence that either corruption or ethnic conflict is significantly greater in the region's more centralized states. Central and Eastern Europe have not done so badly with either parliamentarism or semi-presidentialism, and federalism ended with the disintegration of federal states in Czechoslovakia, Yugoslavia, and the USSR. The EU demanded more regional autonomy and horizontal-accountability from prospective members, but it is hard to tell just what difference this made apart from the more general (and definitely favorable) impact of EU membership itself. Where overweening presidentialism and centralism plus a lack of checks and balances have been associated with failures to democratize (Armenia, Belarus, Central Asia, and Russia), the problem has not been this or that institution so much as too many holdover ex-communist elites with too much power. These allegedly democracy-unfriendly institutions are symptoms, not causes. Thus it seems safest to conclude that the choice of institutions can make a difference (and is related to the mode of transition—or its absence), but that it does not make the same difference in all cases.

11. Of all the economic and cultural prerequisites or preconditions of democracy, the one that must command the most urgent attention is the need for prior agreement on national identity and borders. The notion that democratization is intrinsically dangerous because it will inflame ethnolinguistic tensions is widespread, and is sometimes cited as a reason why democratization should not be tried. It is certainly the case that democratic mechanisms cannot be used to discover who is a member of the *demos,* and only rarely will they be useful in determining contested borders. In our book, Guillermo and I did not pay attention to this. In the Southern Europe and Latin America of the 1970s, questions of borders and identities were (with few exceptions such as that of the Basques in Spain) not prominent. Later, to my surprise, ethnically based mobilizations became a major feature in the politics of several highly centralized Andean countries. These mobilizations have made politics more tumultuous, to be sure, but they have yet to threaten really existing democracy itself. It was in Central and Eastern Europe and the former USSR that "nationhood" issues became most salient. In all but the worst cases, however, ethnolinguistic disputes have neither stopped democracy from moving toward consolidation nor prevented borders from being agreed upon. Tensions persist, no doubt, but it appears that democracy can, if practiced long enough, prove a powerful force for producing a national *demos,* even if it is one that contains multiple identity groups with relative autonomy inside their respective internal borders.

12. *Despite the neoliberal enthusiasm for privatization and globalization, democratization continues to rely on a political unit with a capacity for exercising legitimate public coercion and implementing collective decisions within a distinct territory—that is, a state.* Although it is an exaggeration to claim that without a state there can be no democracy, citizens are likely to demand some reasonably coherent, resourceful, and permanent administrative apparatus to protect them and satisfy their demands. All regimes in the contemporary world—democratic or autocratic, legitimate or illegitimate—require some degree of "stateness" in order to survive (and autocratic or illegitimate ones require considerably more of it). What is especially problematic for new democracies in the short term is the likelihood that the transition will bring a steep perceived decline in stateness. Some newly enfranchised citizens will confuse regime change with freedom not to pay taxes or obey laws. And since crime and corruption are typically underreported in autocracies, things will seem worse than they are when democracy and its free flow of information arrive. Nearly all new democracies pass through such an uncomfortable period, and most recover (as a rule, crime and corruption are lower in consolidated democracies than in all types of autocracy). What then becomes key is not stateness itself, but its ideal nature and reach. These questions become the stuff of normal democratic political competition.

13. *Liberalization may still precede democratization in most cases, but is less and less a determinant of democratization's outcome.* Guillermo and I stressed the role of a revived civil society as the link between liberalization and subsequent democratization. Even in postcommunist cases, this sequence largely obtained. By the time of transition, most of the communist regimes had taken a step back from totalitarianism as communist parties found their grip slipping and citizens increasingly demanded and received a degree of respect for individual rights. Czechoslovakia, Romania, and certain ex-Soviet republics seem to have been exceptions, with transition experiences that differed accordingly. What has called the link between liberalization and democratization into question is the spectacle of Middle Eastern and North African autocrats who toy with liberalization, then switch it off with no ill effects. Why Arab-Islamic civil societies have proven so docile remains a bit of a mystery to me. It could be due either to the presence of suppressed religious or ethnic cleavages that liberalization makes dangerously threatening to incumbent rulers, or to the fragile and state-dependent nature of the region's middle classes.

14. *Democratization requires not just amateur citizens but also professional politicians.* There is a persistent myth that elected officials are just normal people who lend themselves temporarily to public service. Amateurs may lead the struggle against autocracy and occupy top posts early in a transition, but they will soon give way to political professionals. Politicians today need ample party and personal resources to win elections, require specialized knowledge in order to hold technocrats accountable, and must surround themselves with experts in polling and the like in order to stay in office. The rise of a professional political class may be unavoidable, but it is also one of the gravest sources of citizen disenchantment with really existing democracy. The social and cultural gap between citizens and those who claim to represent them is a serious problem, as is the politicians' growing dependence on funds raised from sources (such as higher taxes or shady private contributors) that arouse citizen resentment or suspicion.

15. *The international context has become an increasingly significant determinant of both the timing and the mode of transition, as well as its outcome.* Guillermo and I asserted the predominance of domestic factors as one of our "tentative conclusions." With regard to the cases from Southern Europe and Latin America that we were studying, I would stick by that claim. By contrast, those cases that occurred later in the Eastern bloc would have been unimaginable without a prior change in the hegemonic pretensions of the Soviet Union, and would not have gone as far and as fast as they did without the incentives offered by EU membership. Moreover, once the postcommunist transitions began (Poland was the first), a strong process of diffusion and imitation set in among them.

As a variable, the international context is notoriously difficult to pin down. It is almost by definition omnipresent, since complete political isolation is so hard to achieve in today's world. Yet the causal impact is often indirect, working in opaque and unintended ways through ostensibly national agents. It varies greatly according to the size, resource base, regional context, geostrategic location, and alliance structure of the country involved. Two of its aspects, however, we did not anticipate. The first is the formation of a vast number and variety of non- or quasi-governmental organizations devoted to promoting democracy and human rights across national borders; the second is the EU's assumption of a responsibility to assist nearby fledgling democracies materially and through incentives tied to the prospect of membership.

A whole new world "beneath and beyond the nation-state" opened up and literally enveloped transitional polities, first in Central and Eastern Europe and later in Asia and Africa. Private associations, movements, foundations, consultancies, and party internationals provided ideas, contacts, and minor financial support. National governments and regional or global organizations provided far more money and, in the EU's case, even a whole new form of external intervention—namely, "political conditionality." What made EU conditionality so compelling was the linking of possible membership in the "European club" to compliance with the *acquis communautaire* (which is EU-speak for the entire set of EU rules and decisions compiled since 1958) as well as to the assimilation of a newer set of political norms, the so-called Copenhagen Criteria, which had been devised explicitly to condition the behavior of candidate states. A toned-down version of conditionality now applies to all EU trade agreements made with the so-called ACP (Africa-Caribbean-Pacific) countries, and is supposed to guide the EU's "Neighbourhood" and "Mediterranean" policies regarding the areas to Europe's immediate east and south, respectively. Other regional organizations such as the Organization of American States, the (British) Commonwealth, and even the African Union have taken steps down a similar path by adopting formal agreements that commit their members to responding collectively in the event of "unconstitutional" regime changes.

Since really existing democracy is a perpetually unfinished product, democratization will always be on the research agenda of political scientists. And since nothing seems to work well everywhere, they will have plenty of explaining to do.

Notes

1. Guillermo O'Donnell and Philippe C. Schmitter, *Transitions from Authoritarian Rule: Tentative Conclusions about Uncertain Democracies* (Baltimore: John Hopkins University Press, 1986). This is the fourth volume of the collection *Transitions from Authoritarian Rule*, which was coedited by O'Donnell, Schmitter, and Laurence Whitehead.

2. A "really existing democracy" in my view must: a) call itself democratic; b) be recognized as such by other self-proclaimed democracies; and c) be classified as democratic by most political scientists applying standard procedural criteria.

3. The revival of "delegative democracy" or "hyperpresidentialism" in Latin America with the recent spate of regimes imitating that of Hugo Chávez in Venezuela does not seem (to me) to be the result of failed transitions, but rather a reaction to practices of consolidated democracies that were excessively collusive (Venezuela) or that were insensitive to the demands of excluded ethnic groups (Bolivia and Ecuador). Only in the case of Nicaragua can it be said to be the product of a protracted (and corrupted) transition.

Critical Thinking

1. Why, according to the author, is democracy not considered to have a single set of institutions?

2. Why, for some, is democracy an ambiguous concept?

3. Would the formula for democracy and its generic concepts be adequate to consider its definition as "a unique system for organizing relations between rulers and ruled"?

Create Central

www.mhhe.com/createcentral

Internet References

Project MUSE—What Democracy Is . . . and Is Not
http://muse.jhu.edu/journals/jod/summary/v002/2.3schmitter.html

Twenty-Five Years, Fifteen Findings—*Journal of Democracy*
www.journalofdemocracy.org/article/twenty-five-years-fifteen-findings

Alina Mungui-Pippidi, "The Other Transition"
www.sar.org.ro/amp/data/dox/academic/papers/The%20Other%20Transition%20(Summary%20and%20Cover).pdf

Editors' Introduction to the *Journal of Democracy's* Twentieth Anniversary Issue
www.journalofdemocracy.org/sites/default/files/Editors-Intro=21-1.pdf

PHILIPPE C. SCHMITTER has been professor emeritus at the European University Institute in Florence, Italy; also, Professor, Political Science and Director of the Center for European Studies at Stanford University.

From *Journal of Democracy*, vol. 21, no. 1, January 2010, pp. 17–28. Copyright © 2010 by National Endowment for Democracy and The Johns Hopkins University Press. Reprinted with permission of The Johns Hopkins University Press.

Prepared by: Caroline Shaffer Westerhof,
California National University for Advanced Studies

Article

Why Middle East Studies Missed the Arab Spring: The Myth of Authoritarian Stability

F. GREGORY GAUSE III

Learning Outcomes

After reading this article, you will be able to:

- Understand why Professor Gause states the United States should not encourage democracy in the Arab world.

- Understand the complexity among all forces and factions in the Middle East.

- Understand what is meant by the "Arab Spring."

The vast majority of academic specialists on the Arab world were as surprised as everyone else by the upheavals that toppled two Arab leaders last winter and that now threaten several others. It was clear that Arab regimes were deeply unpopular and faced serious demographic, economic, and political problems. Yet many academics focused on explaining what they saw as the most interesting and anomalous aspect of Arab politics: the persistence of undemocratic rulers.

Until this year, the Arab world boasted a long list of such leaders. Muammar al-Qaddafi took charge of Libya in 1969; the Assad family has ruled Syria since 1970; Ali Abdullah Saleh became president of North Yemen (later united with South Yemen) in 1978; Hosni Mubarak took charge of Egypt in 1981; and Zine el-Abidine Ben Ali ascended to Tunisia's presidency in 1987. The monarchies enjoyed even longer pedigrees, with the Hashemites running Jordan since its creation in 1920, the al-Saud family ruling a unified Saudi Arabia since 1932, and the Alaouite dynasty in Morocco first coming to power in the seventeenth century.

These regimes survived over a period of decades in which democratic waves rolled through East Asia, eastern Europe, Latin America, and sub-Saharan Africa. Even the Arab countries' neighbors in the Muslim Middle East (Iran and Turkey) experienced enormous political change in that period, with a revolution and three subsequent decades of political struggle in Iran and a quasi-Islamist party building a more open and democratic system in secular Turkey.

For many Middle East specialists, this remarkable record of regime stability in the face of numerous challenges demanded their attention and an explanation. I am one of those specialists. In the pages of *Foriegn Affairs* in 2005 ("Can Democracy Stop Terrorism?" September/ October 2005), I argued that the United States should not encourage democracy in the Arab world because Washington's authoritarian Arab allies represented stable bets for the future. On that count, I was spectacularly wrong. I also predicted that democratic Arab governments would prove much less likely to cooperate with U.S. foreign policy goals in the region. This remains an open question. Although most of my colleagues expressed more support for U.S. efforts to encourage Arab political reform, I was hardly alone in my skepticism about the prospect of full-fledged democratic change in the face of these seemingly unshakable authoritarian regimes.

Understanding what we missed and what we overestimated in our explanations of the stability of Arab authoritarianism—and understanding why we did so—is of more than just academic significance. Regional analysts must determine what changed in the forces that underpinned four decades of Arab regime stability and what new elements emerged to spark the current revolts. Doing so will allow U.S. policymakers to approach the Arab revolts more effectively by providing them insight into the factors that will drive postrevolutionary politics in the Arab world.

Arab States and Their Militaries

The first task is to establish what academia knew and did not know. To begin with, it is important to recognize that few, if any, political scientists working on the Middle East explained the peculiar stability of Arab regimes in cultural terms—a sign of progress over the scholarship of earlier eras. The literature on how Arab dictators endured did not include old saws about how Islam is inimical to democracy or how Arab culture remains too patriarchal and traditional to support democratic change. We recognized how popular the concept of democracy was in the Arab world and that when given real electoral choices, Arabs turned out to vote in large numbers. We also understood that Arabs did not passively accept authoritarian rule. From Algeria to Saudi Arabia, Arab autocrats were able to stay in power over the past 40 years only by brutally suppressing popular attempts to unseat them, whether motivated by political repression or food prices. Arab citizens certainly demonstrated the desire and ability to mobilize against their governments. But those governments, before 2011, were extremely successful in co-opting and containing them.

As a result, academics directed their attention toward explaining the mechanisms that Arab states had developed to weather popular dissent. Although different scholars focused on different aspects of this question, from domestic institutions to government strategies, most attributed the stability of Arab dictatorships to two common factors: the military-security complex and state control over the economy. In each of these areas, we in the academic community made assumptions that, as valid as they might have been in the past, turned out to be wrong in 2011.

Most scholars assumed that no daylight existed between the ruling regimes and their military and security services. That assumption was not unreasonable. Many Arab presidents served in uniform before they took office, including Ben Ali and Mubarak. In the wake of the Arab military coups of the 1950s and 1960s, Arab leaders created institutions to exercise political control over their armies and, in some cases, established rival military forces to balance the army's weight. Arab armies helped ruling regimes win their civil wars and put down uprisings. As a result, most Middle East experts came to assume that Arab armies and security services would never break with their rulers.

This assumption obviously proved incorrect. Scholars did not predict or appreciate the variable ways in which Arab armies would react to the massive, peaceful protests this year. This oversight occurred because, as a group, Middle East experts had largely lost interest in studying the role of the military in Arab politics. Although this topic once represented a central feature of U.S. scholarship on the Middle East—when the Arab military coups of the 1950s and 1960s occupied the academics of that era—the remarkable stability of the Arab regimes since then led us to assume that the issue was no longer important. Yet a preliminary review of the unfolding revolts suggests that two factors drive how Arab militaries react to public unrest: the social composition of both the regime and its military and the level of institutionalization and professionalism in the army itself.

The countries in which the military, as an institution, sided with the protesters, Egypt and Tunisia, are two of the most homogeneous societies in the Arab world. Both are overwhelmingly Sunni. (The Coptic Christian minority in Egypt plays an important social role there but has little political clout.) Both the Egyptian and the Tunisian armies are relatively professional, with neither serving as the personal instrument of the ruler. Army leaders in both nations realized that their institutions could play an important role under new regimes and thus were willing to risk ushering out the old guard.

In Arab countries featuring less institutionalized forces, where the security services are led by and serve as the personal instruments of the ruler and his family, those forces have split or dissolved in the face of popular protests. In both Libya and Yemen, units led by the rulers' families have supported the regimes, while other units have defected to the opposition, stayed on the sidelines, or just gone home.

In divided societies, where the regime represents an ethnic, sectarian, or regional minority and has built an officer corps dominated by that overrepresented minority, the armies have thus far backed their regimes. The Sunni-led security forces in Bahrain, a Shiite-majority country, stood their ground against demonstrators to preserve the Sunni monarchy. The Jordanian army remains loyal to the monarchy despite unrest among the country's Palestinian majority. Saudi Arabia's National Guard, heavily recruited from central and western Arabian tribes, is standing by the central Arabian al-Saud dynasty. In each country, the logic is simple: if the regime falls and the majority takes over, the army leadership will likely be replaced as well.

The Syrian army's reaction to the crisis facing the Assad regime will offer an important test of this hypothesis. Members of the Assad family command important army units, and Alawites and members of other minority groups staff a good portion of the officer corps in the Sunni-majority country. If minority solidarity with the regime endures, Assad is likely to retain power. Yet if disaffected officers begin to see the army as an instrument of the Assad family itself, they could bring down the regime. Either way, once the dust settles, Middle East scholars will need to reexamine their assumptions about the relationship between Arab states and their militaries—perhaps the key element in determining regime survival in a crisis.

The Reform Factor

State control over the economy in the Middle East was another pillar of regime stability identified by academics. Scholars posited that Arab states with oil reserves and revenues deployed this wealth to control the economy, building patronage networks, providing social services, and directing the development of dependent private sectors. Through these funds, Arab rulers connected the interests of important constituencies to their survival and placated the rest of their citizens with handouts in times of crisis. Indeed, since the current uprisings began, only Libya among the major oil exporters (Algeria, Iraq, Kuwait, Libya, Qatar, Saudi Arabia, and the United Arab Emirates) has faced a serious challenge. Buoyed by high oil prices, the other oil exporters have been able to head off potential opposition by distributing resources through increased state salaries, higher subsidies for consumer goods, new state jobs, and direct handouts to citizens. Qaddafi's example establishes that oil money must be allocated properly, rather than wasted on pet projects and harebrained schemes, for it to protect a regime. The recent Arab revolts, then, would seem to validate this part of the academic paradigm on regime stability.

Yet this year's revolts have called the economic foundations of the regime stability argument into question when it comes to non-oil-producing states. Although Arab petrostates have relied on their oil revenues to avoid economic reform, changes in the world economy and the liberalizing requirements of foreign aid donors have over the past two decades forced non-oil-producing states to modernize their economies. A number of Arab regimes, including in Egypt, Jordan, Morocco, and Tunisia, have privatized state enterprises, encouraged foreign investment, created incentives to kick-start the private sector, and cut subsidies and state expenditures that previously consumed government budgets. Such Washington consensus-style economic reforms exacerbated inequalities and made life more difficult for the poor, but they also opened up new opportunities for local entrepreneurs and allowed the upper classes to enjoy greater consumer choice through liberalized trade regimes. Some Middle East specialists thought that economic liberalization could establish new bases of support for Arab authoritarians and encourage the economic growth necessary to grapple with the challenges of growing populations (as economic reforms in Turkey have led to greater support for the ruling Justice and Development Party there). Meanwhile, Western governments pushed the idea that economic reform represented a step toward political reform.

But these economic reforms backfired on those governments that embraced them most fully: Cairo and Tunis. Although both Egypt and Tunisia had achieved decent economic growth rates and received praise from the International Monetary Fund as recently as 2010, politically driven privatizations did not enhance the stability of their regimes. Instead, they created a new class of superwealthy entrepreneurs, including members of the presidents' families in both countries, which became the targets of popular ire. And the academics' assumption that these beneficiaries of economic reform would support the authoritarian regimes proved chimerical. The state-bred tycoons either fled or were unable to stop events and landed in postrevolutionary prison. The upper-middle class did not demonstrate in favor of Ben Ali or Mubarak. In fact, some members became revolutionary leaders themselves.

It is supremely ironic that the face of the Egyptian revolt was Wael Ghonim, the Egyptian Google executive. He is exactly the kind of person who was poised to succeed in the Egypt of Mubarak—bilingual, educated at the American University of Cairo, and at home in the global business world. Yet he risked his future and life to organize the "We are all Khaled Said" Facebook page, in memory of a man beaten to death by Egyptian police, which helped mobilize Egyptians against the regime. For him and many others in similar economic circumstances, political freedom outweighed monetary opportunity.

Seeing what happened in Cairo and Tunis, other Arab leaders rushed to placate their citizens by raising state salaries, canceling planned subsidy cuts, and increasing the number of state jobs. In Saudi Arabia, for example, in February and March, King Abdullah announced new spending plans of more than $100 billion. The Saudis have the oil money to fulfill such pledges. In non-oil-producing states, such as Jordan, which halted its march down the road of economic reform once the trouble began, governments may not have the money to maintain the old social contract, whereby the state provided basic economic security in exchange for loyalty. Newly liberated Egypt and Tunisia are also confronting their inherited economic woes. Empowered electorates will demand a redistribution of wealth that the governments do not have and a renegotiation of the old social contract that the governments cannot fund.

Many Middle East scholars recognized that the neoliberal economic programs were causing political problems for Arab governments, but few foresaw their regime-shaking consequences. Academics overestimated both the ameliorating effect of the economic growth introduced by the reforms and the political clout of those who were benefiting from such policies. As a result, they underestimated the popular revulsion to the corruption and crony privatization that accompanied the reforms.

Oil wealth remains a fairly reliable tool for ensuring regime stability, at least when oil prices are high. Yet focused on how Arab regimes achieved stability through oil riches, Middle East scholars missed the destabilizing effects of poorly implemented liberal economic policies in the Arab world.

A New Kind of Pan-Arabism

Another factor missed by Middle East specialists had less to do with state policies and institutions than with cross-border Arab identity. It is not a coincidence that major political upheavals arose across the Arab world simultaneously. Arab activists and intellectuals carefully followed the protests of Iran's 2009 Green Movement, but no Arabs took to the streets in emulation of their Iranian neighbors. Yet in 2011, a month after a fruit vendor in Tunisia set himself on fire, the Arab world was engulfed in revolts. If any doubts remain that Arabs retain a sense of common political identity despite living in 20 different states, the events of this year should put them to rest.

Such strong pan-Arab sentiments should not have surprised the academic community. Much of the work on Arab politics in previous generations had focused on Arab nationalism and pan-Arabism, the ability of Arab leaders to mobilize political support across state borders based on the idea that all Arabs share a common political identity and fate. Yet many of us assumed that the cross-border appeal of Arab identity had waned in recent years, especially following the Arab defeat in the 1967 war with Israel. Egypt and Jordan had signed treaties with Israel, and the Palestinians and Syria had engaged in direct negotiations with Israel, breaking a cardinal taboo of pan-Arabism. U.S.-led wars against Iraq in 1990-91 and beginning in 2003 excited opposition in the Arab world but did not destabilize the governments that cooperated with the U.S. military plans—a sign of waning pan-Arabism as much as government immunity to popular sentiment. It seemed that Arab states had become strong enough (with some exceptions, such as Lebanon and post-Saddam Hussein Iraq) to fend off ideological pressures from across their borders. Most Middle East scholars believed that pan-Arabism had gone dormant.

They thus missed the communal wave of 2011. Although the events of this year demonstrate the continued importance of Arab identity, pan-Arabism has taken a very different form than it did a half century ago under the leadership of Egyptian

President Gamal Abdel Nasser. Then, Nasser, a charismatic leader with a powerful government, promoted popular ideas and drove events in other countries, using the new technology of his day, the transistor radio, to call on Arabs to oppose their own governments and follow him. Now, the very leaderless quality of the popular mobilizations in Egypt and Tunisia seems to have made them sources of inspiration across the Arab world.

In recent decades, Arab leaders, most notably Saddam during the Gulf War, have attempted to embrace Nasser's mantle and spark popular Arab movements. Even the Iranian leader Ayatollah Ruhollah Khomeini-a Persian, not an Arab-appealed to Islam to mobilize Arabs behind his banner. All these attempts failed. When the people of Tunisia and then Egypt overthrew their corrupt dictators, however, other Arabs found they could identify with them. The fact that these revolts succeeded gave hope (in some cases, such as in Bahrain, false hope) to other Arabs that they could do the same. The common enemy of the 2011 Arab revolts is not colonialism, U.S. power, or Israel, but Arabs' own rulers.

Academics will need to assess the restored importance of Arab identity to understand the future of Middle East politics. Unlike its predecessor, the new pan-Arabism does not appear to challenge the regional map. Arabs are not demonstrating to dissolve their states into one Arab entity; their agendas are almost exclusively domestic. But the Arab revolts have shown that what happens in one Arab state can affect others in unanticipated and powerful ways. As a result, scholars and policymakers can no longer approach countries on a case-by-case basis. The United States will have a hard time supporting democracy in one Arab country, such as Egypt, while standing by as other allies, such as Bahrain, crush peaceful democratic protests.

In addition, the new pan–Arabism will eventually bring the issue of Arab–Israeli peace back to the fore. Although none of the 2011 Arab revolts occurred in the name of the Palestinians, democratic Arab regimes will have to reflect popular opinion on Israel, which remains extremely low. Arab public opinion on the United States is influenced by Arabs' views on the Israeli-Palestinian conflict as much as by U.S. actions in other Arab countries. As a result, the United States will need to reactivate Israeli-Palestinian peace talks to anticipate the demands of Arab publics across the Middle East.

Back to the Drawing Board

Academic specialists on Arab politics, such as myself, have quite a bit of rethinking to do. That is both intellectually exciting and frightening. Explaining the stability of Arab authoritarians was an important analytic task, but it led some of us to underestimate the forces for change that were bubbling below, and at times above, the surface of Arab politics. It is impossible for social scientists to make precise predictions about the Arab world, and this should not be a goal. But academics must reexamine their assumptions on a number of issues, including the military's role in Arab politics, the effects of economic change on political stability, and the salience of a cross-border Arab identity, to get a sense of how Arab politics will now unfold.

As paradigms fall and theories are shredded by events on the ground, it is useful to recall that the Arab revolts resulted not from policy decisions taken in Washington or any other foreign capital but from indigenous economic, political, and social factors whose dynamics were extremely hard to forecast. In the wake of such unexpected upheavals, both academics and policymakers should approach the Arab world with humility about their ability to shape its future. That is best left to Arabs themselves.

Critical Thinking

1. Can democracy stop terrorism? Explain.
2. Does the Arab world of today represent stability or instability for the future? Explain.
3. Can it be explained why the young bloggers were the first who demonstrated against Hosni Mubarak? Explain.

Create Central

www.mhhe.com/createcentral

Internet References

Remember Cairo? Brookings Institution
 www.journalofdemocracy.org/sites/default/files/Editors-Intro=21-1.pdf
Authoritarianism
 pomeps.org/2012/09/authoritarianism
WPR Article Middle East: Authoritarian Democracy and Democratic Authoritarianism
 www.worldpoliticsreview.com/articles/3835/middle-east-authoritarian-democracy-and-democratic-authoritarianism

F. GREGORY GAUSE III is a leading Saudi Arabian expert, and Professor of Political Science, University of Vermont.

From *Foreign Affairs*, vol. 90, issue 4. July/August 2011, pp. 81–90. Copyright © 2011 by Council on Foreign Relations, Inc. Reprinted by permission of Foreign Affairs. www.ForeignAffairs.com

Article

Prepared by: Caroline Shaffer Westerhof,
California National University for Advanced Studies

Few Good Choices for the U.S. in Mideast

GERALD F. SEIB

Learning Outcomes

After reading this article, you will be able to:

- Understand the complexity of Sunnis facing off against Shiites.

- Understand why many secularists are filled with bigotry against Islamists, regardless of which part of the world they call home.

- Understand the political instability and tensions that plague the Middle East, the Arabian peninsula, and North Africa.

The Middle East has a tendency to eat up American presidencies, and suddenly that is a real danger facing President Barack Obama.

The region is much closer to a broad conflagration than most Americans realize, with Sunnis now facing off against Shiites, and secularists against Islamists across a wide swath of lands. The dream of fostering a new wave of democratic, multiethnic governments—embraced by two successive American administrations—may be withering before our eyes.

As a result, Mr. Obama is coming face-to-face with two hard questions: Does the U.S., with a shrunken checkbook and a weary military, have the power to steer events? And does the U.S., tired after a decade of war in Iraq and happy to be growing less dependent on Middle East oil, even care enough to try?

The problems start with the bloody turmoil in the streets of Egypt, the cornerstone of American influence in the region for 35 years. There, a new military strongman seems more intent on crushing the Muslim Brotherhood than heeding American counsel to find a way to include the Islamists in a new government.

Meantime, Syria has become a proxy war for the entire region, pitting Shiites against Sunnis and drawing in combatants from all over. The nasty Alawite/Shiite axis of Syrian President Bashar al-Assad, Iran and Hezbollah has fought back to even with Sunni opposition forces, armed by Persian Gulf states and, soon, the U.S.

This now is essentially a sectarian war, and it's starting to spread next door to Lebanon. Sunnis there resent the fact that Hezbollah's Shiite fighters have been using Lebanon as a springboard to enter the fight on behalf of Mr. Assad. Car bombs and street fights between Sunni and Shiite groups are popping up; Lebanon is in danger of sliding back into its familiar rut of sectarian war.

Iraq now also seems infected. While most Americans have largely checked out of Iraqi news, a new wave of Sunni-Shiite violence is building. On Monday alone, 18 bombs exploded, killing at least 58 people. Whatever stability a decade of American military presence left behind seems newly imperiled.

Nearby, Jordan is becoming home to a giant, destabilizing refugee population of Syrians fleeing the fighting in their homeland. An estimated 650,000 refugees have entered Jordan; one refugee camp now is Jordan's fourth-largest city. It is an economic and demographic crisis of the first order for Jordan's king, one of America's most reasonable and reliable allies.

Oh, and Libya, home to a vast stockpile of weapons that seem to be finding their way around the region, is drifting into lawlessness; a thousand inmates were sprung in a giant jail break over the weekend.

In the middle of all this sits Israel. It now is surrounded by trouble and the march of Islamist forces in every direction—in Egypt to the west, Jordan to the east, Syria to the northeast and Lebanon to the north. It's no wonder that Israel agreed, after extensive prodding from Secretary of State John Kerry, to open new peace talks with the Palestinians in Washington this week. Amid this mess, it needs to buy a little stability on the home front if it can.

The impulse is to think the U.S. should do something—anything—to contain the risks.

But what? The U.S. once had great leverage over the Egyptian government because it provided the biggest chunk of aid. No longer. Saudi Arabia now writes much bigger checks, and it is urging the military leader there, Gen. Abdel Fattah Al Sisi, to hang tough against the Muslim Brotherhood. Each of the rival sides in Cairo's streets seems to think Washington is supporting the other, limiting American influence with both.

The U.S. military once might have waded into the mess in Syria, but the president is wary and the Pentagon tends to view engagement in Syria right now as a losing proposition. More broadly, the notion that Mr. Obama's relative popularity in, and overtures of friendship toward, the Islamic world could temper behaviors has faded in a period when hard power is what seems to matter.

The counter temptation is for the U.S. to simply step away, tending to the economy at home and pivoting toward Asia abroad. The problem is that history teaches that the Middle East doesn't like being ignored. Through soaring energy prices, or the scourge of terrorism, or some other calamity, it has a habit of insinuating itself onto the American agenda.

That leaves the U.S. the unsatisfying option of working with allies on a series of half-steps to move the region back from the brink so transformation can start anew: With the Saudis to convince Gen. Sisi in Egypt to contain his security forces; with the Europeans to help Jordan to contain the refugee crisis; with Arab allies to exert enough pressure to expel Syrian President Assad before Syria fractures permanently.

Not a satisfying list, but perhaps the only one available.

Critical Thinking

1. Can the Middle East ever achieve stability?
2. Is such tension in the Middle East generated by deep-seated hatred, or is it a manifestation of bigotry in the 21st century?

3. Is such tension and bombings a result of power politics, regardless of the actors?

Create Central

www.mhhe.com/createcentral

Internet References

In Mideast, Obama Finds He Has Limited Leverage—WSJ.com
http://online.wsj.com/article/SB10001424127887324170004578635810011536562.html

Islam: Sunnis and Shiites—About.com Middle East Issues
http://middleeast.about.com/od/religionsectarianism/a/me070907sunnis.htm

The Shia/Sunni Conflict in the Middle East Wars—Syria into Focus
http://worldpoliticsuncovered.wordpress.com/2013/09/28/the-shiasunni-conflict-in-the-middle-east-wars-syria-into-focus/

Video—Fueled by Anger, Iraqi Sunnis Make Push for Power
http://live.wsj.com/video/fueled-by-anger-iraqi-sunnis-make-push-for-power/9266CF4D-8744-4342-A4CE-0D96ACCFEBBB.html#!9266CF4D-8744-4342-A4CE-0D96ACCFEBBB

The Solution to America's Collapsing Confidence—WSJ.com
http://online.wsj.com/article/SB10001424127887323993804578613782547946130.html

GERALD SEIB is assistant managing editor, executive Washington editor of *The Wall Street Journal,* and a writer for WSJ. He is also a regulator commentator on Washington news for Fox Business.

Article

Prepared by: Caroline Shaffer Westerhof,
California National University for Advanced Studies

Making Modernity Work:
The Reconciliation
of Capitalism and Democracy

GIDEON ROSE

Learning Outcomes

After reading this article, you will be able to:

- Examine the concept, as some write, "We are living… through an ideological crisis."

- Understand why the author maintains that we are not living in "ideological upheaval but stability."

- Examine the theory that there are just as many examples of "democracies failing as there are of capitalism failing…"

We are living, so we are told, through an ideological crisis. The United States is trapped in political deadlock and dysfunction, Europe is broke and breaking, authoritarian China is on the rise. Protesters take to the streets across the advanced industrial democracies; the high and mighty meet in Davos to search for "new models" as sober commentators ponder who and what will shape the future.

In historical perspective, however, the true narrative of the era is actually the reverse-not ideological upheaval but stability. Today's troubles are real enough, but they relate more to policies than to principles. The major battles about how to structure modern politics and economics were fought in the first half of the last century, and they ended with the emergence of the most successful system the world has ever seen.

Nine decades ago, the political scientist Harold Laski noted that with "the mass of men" having come to political power, the challenge of modern democratic government was providing enough "solid benefit" to ordinary citizens "to make its preservation a matter of urgency to themselves." A generation and a half later, with the creation of the postwar order of mutually supporting liberal democracies with mixed economies, that challenge was being met, and as a result, more people in more places have lived longer, richer, freer lives than ever before. In ideological terms, at least, all the rest is commentary.

The Birth of the Modern

In the premodern era, political, economic, and social life was governed by a dense web of interlocking relationships inherited from the past and sanctified by religion. Limited personal freedom and material benefits existed alongside a mostly unquestioned social solidarity. Traditional local orders began to erode with the rise of capitalism in the eighteenth and nineteenth centuries, as the increasing prevalence and dominance of market relationships broke down existing hierarchies. The shift produced economic and social dynamism, an increase in material benefits and personal freedoms, and a decrease in communal feeling. As this process continued, the first modern political ideology, classical liberalism, emerged to celebrate and justify it.

Liberalism stressed the importance of the rule of law, limited government, and free commercial transactions. It highlighted the manifold rewards of moving to a world dominated by markets rather than traditional communities, a shift the economic historian Karl Polanyi would call "the great transformation." But along with the gains came losses as well—of a sense of place, of social and psychological stability, of traditional bulwarks against life's vicissitudes.

Left to itself, capitalism produced longterm aggregate benefits along with great volatility and inequality. This combination resulted in what Polanyi called a "double movement," a progressive expansion of both market society and reactions against it. By the late nineteenth and early twentieth centuries, therefore, liberalism was being challenged by reactionary nationalism and cosmopolitan socialism, with both the right and the left promising, in their own ways, relief from the turmoil and angst of modern life.

The catastrophic destruction of the Great War and the economic nightmare of the Great Depression brought the contradictions of modernity to a head, seemingly revealing the bankruptcy of the liberal order and the need for some other, better path. As democratic republics dithered and stumbled during the 1920s and 1930s, fascist and communist regimes seized control of their own destinies and appeared to offer compelling alternative models of modern political, economic, and social organization.

Over time, however, the problems with all these approaches became clear. Having discarded liberalism's insistence on personal and political freedom, both fascism and communism quickly descended into organized barbarism. The vision of the future they offered, as George Orwell noted, was "a boot stamping on a human face-forever." Yet classical liberalism also proved unpalatable, since it contained no rationale for activist government and thus had no answer to an economic crisis that left vast swaths of society destitute and despairing.

Fascism flamed out in a second, even more destructive world war. Communism lost its appeal as its tyrannical nature revealed itself, then ultimately collapsed under its own weight as its nonmarket economic system could not generate sustained growth. And liberalism's central principle of laissez faire was abandoned in the depths of the Depression.

What eventually emerged victorious from the wreckage was a hybrid system that combined political liberalism with a mixed economy. As the political scientist Sheri Berman has observed, "The postwar order represented something historically unusual: capitalism remained, but it was capitalism of a very different type from that which had existed before the war—one tempered and limited by the power of the democratic state and often made subservient to the goals of social stability and solidarity, rather than the other way around." Berman calls the mixture "social democracy." Other scholars use other terms: Jan-Werner Müller prefers "Christian Democracy," John Ruggie suggests "embedded liberalism," Karl Dietrich Bracher talks of "democratic liberalism." Francis Fukuyama wrote of "the end of History"; Daniel Bell and Seymour Martin Lipset saw it as "the end of ideology." All refer to essentially the same thing. As Bell put it in 1960:

Few serious minds believe any longer that one can set down "blueprints" and through "social engineering" bring about a new utopia of social harmony. At the same time, the older "counter-beliefs" have lost their intellectual force as well. Few "classic" liberals insist that the State should play no role in the economy, and few serious conservatives, at least in England and on the Continent, believe that the Welfare State is "the road to serfdom." In the Western world, therefore, there is today a rough consensus among intellectuals on political issues: the acceptance of a Welfare State; the desirability of decentralized power; a system of mixed economy and of political pluralism.

Reflecting the hangover of the interwar ideological binge, the system stressed not transcendence but compromise. It offered neither salvation nor utopia, only a framework within which citizens could pursue their personal betterment. It has never been as satisfying as the religions, sacred or secular, it replaced. And it remains a work in progress, requiring tinkering and modification as conditions and attitudes change. Yet its success has been manifest—and reflecting that, its basic framework has remained remarkably intact.

The Once and Future Order

The central question of modernity has been how to reconcile capitalism and mass democracy, and since the postwar order came up with a good answer, it has managed to weather all subsequent challenges. The upheavals of the late 1960s seemed poised to disrupt it. But despite what activists at the time thought, they had little to offer in terms of politics or economics, and so their lasting impact was on social life instead. This had the ironic effect of stabilizing the system rather than overturning it, helping it live up to its full potential by bringing previously subordinated or disenfranchised groups inside the castle walls. The neoliberal revolutionaries of the 1980s also had little luck, never managing to turn the clock back all that far.

All potential alternatives in the developing world, meanwhile, have proved to be either dead ends or temporary detours from the beaten path. The much-ballyhooed "rise of the rest" has involved not the discrediting of the postwar order of Western political economy but its reinforcement: the countries that have risen have done so by embracing global capitalism while keeping some of its destabilizing attributes in check, and have liberalized their polities and societies along the way (and will founder unless they continue to do so).

Although the structure still stands, however, it has seen better days. Poor management of public spending and fiscal policy has resulted in unsustainable levels of debt across the advanced industrial world, even as mature economies have found it difficult to generate dynamic growth and full employment in an ever more globalized environment. Lax regulation and oversight allowed reckless and predatory financial practices to drive leading economies to the brink of collapse. Economic inequality has increased as social mobility has declined. And a loss of broad-based social solidarity on both sides of the Atlantic has eroded public support for the active remedies needed to address these and other problems.

Renovating the structure will be a slow and difficult project, the cost and duration of which remain unclear, as do the contractors involved. Still, at root, this is not an ideological issue. The question is not what to do but how to do it—how, under twenty-first-century conditions, to rise to the challenge Laski described, making the modern political economy provide enough solid benefit to the mass of men that they see its continuation as a matter of urgency to themselves.

Critical Thinking

1. Is democracy too slow to respond to crises and too short to plan for the long term?

2. What is this so-called "political paralysis" that makes the governing challenges so complicated?

3. Do you agree with Gideon Rose that the post-war reconciliation of capitalism and liberal democracy had adapted to challenges in the past, and would so again?

Create Central

www.mhhe.com/createcentral

Internet References

The Reconciliation of Capitalism and Democracy
www.ihavenet.com/World-The-Reconciliation-of-Capitalism-and-Democracy-Foreign-Affairs.html

Capitalism and Democracy—On Point with Tom Ashbrook
http://onpoint.wbur.org/2012/01/17/capitalism-and-democracy

International Politics and Society—FES
www.fes.de/ipg/ONLINE2_2001/LESELISTEE.htm

GIDEON ROSE is editor of *Foreign Affairs,* and is a former National Security Council official.

Article

Prepared by: Caroline Shaffer Westerhof,
California National University for Advanced Studies

Taking the Arctic Route from China

COSTAS PARIS

Learning Outcomes

After reading this article, you will be able to:

- Discover the trading and global benefits for China in navigating the Northern Sea Route.

- Discover why the first container-transporting vessel to sail to Europe from China through the Arctic will increase the financial bottom line.

- Discover the difficulties inherent in traveling the Northern Sea Route.

China's Yong Sheng is an unremarkable ship that is about to make history. It is the first container-transporting vessel to sail to Europe from China through the Arctic rather than taking the usual southerly route through the Suez Canal, shaving two weeks off the regular travel time in the process.

The 19,000-ton Yong Sheng, operated by China's state-controlled Cosco Group, left the port of Dalian Aug. 8 and is scheduled to reach Rotterdam, in the Netherlands, via the Bering Strait Sept. 11. The travel time of about 35 days compares with the average of 48 days it would normally take to journey through the Suez Canal and Mediterranean Sea.

Chinese state media have described the roughly 3,400-mile Northern Sea Route, or NSR, as the "most economical solution" for China-Europe shipping. Cosco has said that Asian goods could be transported through the northern passage in significant volumes.

The NSR, at roughly 8,100 nautical miles, is about 2,400 nautical miles shorter than the Suez Canal for ships traveling the benchmark Shanghai-to-Rotterdam journey, according to the NSR Information Office.

"The Arctic route can cut 12 to 15 days from traditional routes, so the maritime industry calls it the Golden Waterway," Cosco said when the Yong Sheng's voyage was announced earlier this year.

The Yong Sheng's Arctic journey is possible because of warmer weather, which has kept the passage relatively free of ice for longer than in recent decades.

The Russian-run NSR Administration has so far issued 393 permits this summer to use the waters above Siberia, compared with 46 last year and a mere four in 2010. The travel window usually opens in July and closes in late November when the ice concentration becomes prohibitive for sailing.

"Our best months are September and October, where there is barely any ice across the whole route," said Sergey Balmasov, head of the NSR Information Office.

"We expect a substantial increase in permit applications if temperatures continue to rise in coming years," he added. "But climate change could work both ways, so if temperatures come down the route will become impenetrable without ice-breaking escort ships."

Mr. Balmasov said even ships without ice-breaking capabilities received permits as the weather became warmer. "This cuts the cost of operators as the seaway is free of ice and the voyage time significantly lower," he said.

Arctic ice covered 860,000 square miles last year, off 53% from 1.8 million square miles in 1979, according to the National Snow and Ice Data Center of the U.S.

The rate of change has astounded the scientific community, said Mark Serreze, director of the Colorado-based center, which is funded through grants from groups including the National Aeronautics and Space Administration, the National Science Foundation and the National Oceanic and Atmospheric Administration.

"It's warming very quickly in the Arctic and I would not be surprised if we see summers with no ice at all over the next 20 years. That's why shipping companies are so excited over the prospects of the route," Mr. Serreze said.

"Over the past 50 years temperatures in the Arctic have gone up by around four degrees Celsius, which is a dramatic increase," he added. "This is much higher than the global average of around one degree." A change of four degrees Celsius is equivalent to a change of 7.2 degrees in Fahrenheit.

The benchmark Asia-to-Europe shipping route accounts for 15% of total trade. Ships from China sail across the Bering Strait, through the East Siberian Sea and Vilkitsky Strait and then on to European ports.

China has made no secret of its interest in the new Arctic passage. In May Beijing obtained "permanent observer" status at the Arctic Council, which consists of eight countries with territory in the region.

Shipowners recognize the potential of the route, but say it will take years to determine whether it will become commercially viable.

"We are looking into it but there are still many unknowns," said a Greek shipowner whose vessels are chartered by a number of Chinese companies that trade with Europe. "The travel window is short and if ice forms unexpectedly your client will be left waiting and your cost will skyrocket to find an ice-breaker. But if climate change continues to raise temperatures, the route will certainly become very busy."

Lars Jensen, chief executive of Copenhagen-based SeaIntel Maritime Analysis, says owners are increasingly investing in bigger ships to cut transport costs but these larger vessels aren't suited to sail in the Arctic. Those ships burn on average 25% less fuel per container than older and smaller vessels using less-efficient engines. "Even though an Arctic route is shorter, the fuel consumption per container on a much smaller vessel might simply not be attractive," he said.

Lloyd's List, a shipping-industry data provider, estimates that in 2021 about 15 million metric tons of cargo will be transported using the Arctic route. That will remain a small fraction of the volumes carried on the Suez Canal. More than 17,000 vessels carrying more than 900 million tons of cargo plied the canal route last year.

Critical Thinking

1. What is the thesis behind the concept that shipping lanes through the Arctic Ocean won't put the Suez and Panama canals out of business?

2. How does global warming affect the Northern Sea Route?

3. How does China's use of the Northern Sea Route (NSR) affect its global trading?

Create Central

www.mhhe.com/createcentral

Internet References

The Northern Sea Route versus the Suez Canal
www.husdal.com/2011/05/22/the-final-frontier-the-northern-sea-route

Ship Travels Arctic from China to Europe — WSJ.com
http://online.wsj.com/news/articles/SB100014241278873234238045790229823646814 64

Chinese Shipping Firm opens Northern Sea Route
http://ajw.asahi.com/article/economy/business/AJ201308130047

China's Voice of Discovery to Cover the Less Frozen North
www.japantimes.co.jp/news/2013/08/23/world/chinas-voyage-of-discovery-to-cross-the-less-frozen-north-2/

The Arctic Institute — Center for Circumpolar Security Studies
www.thearcticinstitute.org/

Costas Paris is senior correspondent for Dow Jones Newswires.

Article   Prepared by: Caroline Shaffer Westerhof,
California National University for Advanced Studies

Recalibrating American Grand Strategy: Softening US Policies Toward Iran in Order to Contain China

Samir Tata

Learning Outcomes

After reading this article, you will be able to:

- Examine the premise that if U.S. policies toward Iran are softened, China can be contained.

- Examine the political and policy difficulties inherent in implementing strategy.

- Examine Clausewitz's philosophy on the influence of war and strategy.

Over the next decade, the United States will have to rethink its grand strategy as it addresses the challenge of maintaining its primacy as a global power in an increasingly multipolar world whose center of gravity has shifted to Asia. The task will be all the more daunting because significant fiscal and economic constraints imposed by a federal government debt that has mushroomed to nearly $16 trillion or about 100 percent of GDP, and a continuing economic slowdown that has been the deepest and longest since the Great Depression will force difficult tradeoffs as the United States seeks to realign and streamline vital national interests with limited resources.[1] The overarching national security objective of the United States must be crystal clear: to counterbalance and contain a rising China determined to be the dominant economic, political, and military power in Asia.

While China's rise will not be a straight line, its trajectory to great power status is obvious.[2] A twenty-first century version of a Greater East Asia Co-Prosperity Sphere with China at the epicenter is emerging.[3] China is the biggest economy in Asia, having surpassed Japan in 2010.[4] China is the largest trading partner of Japan, South Korea, Taiwan, Australia, India, and the ten countries of the Association of Southeast Asian Nations (ASEAN). Unquestionably, China is the economic engine of Asia, displacing both Japan and the United States. According to US government projections, China is expected to be the world's

largest economy by 2019 in terms of purchasing power parity (which adjusts for cost of living) with a forecasted gross domestic product (GDP) of $17.2 trillion compared to an expected US GDP of $17 trillion.[5]

From a strategic perspective, the "Achilles heel" of China is its overwhelming dependence on Persian Gulf energy imports to fuel its rapidly growing economy. The sea lines of communication (SLOCs) over which these vital oil and gas imports are transported by tanker—from the Strait of Hormuz in the Persian Gulf to the Arabian Sea and Indian Ocean, continuing on to the Bay of Bengal and through the Malacca Straits into the South China Sea—is China's jugular vein. Virtually all Persian Gulf energy exports destined for China (as well as for Japan, South Korea, and Taiwan) flow through this route. Two important alternatives to the Malacca Straits are the Sunda and Lambok Straits in Indonesia linking the eastern Indian Ocean to the Java Sea which continues to the South China Sea. Another key energy route flows from Saudi ports on the Red Sea (principally the port of Yanbu) to the Bab el Mandab in the Gulf of Aden proceeding on to the Arabian Sea and the Indian Ocean and continuing to the Malacca Straits, or the Sunda and Lambok Straits. The five critical choke points—Hormuz, Bab el Mandab, Malacca, Sunda and Lambok—and the SLOCs linking them are controlled by the US Navy.

China's economic and military security is inextricably intertwined with its energy security. Since 2000, China has been a net importer of oil and gas, primarily from the Persian Gulf. China became the world's largest energy consumer in 2009, with 96.9 quadrillion British thermal units (BTU) of annual energy consumption compared to 94.8 quadrillion BTU for the United States.[6] By 2011, China surpassed the United States as the largest importer of Persian Gulf oil, importing 2.5 million barrels per day (bbls/d) from the region (representing about 26 percent of total Chinese oil consumption of 9.8 million bbls/d), overtaking the United States which imported 1.8 million bbls/d from the Persian Gulf (representing about 10 percent of total US oil consumption of 18.8 million bbls/d).[7] In fact, over half of US oil imports come from three countries in the Americas: Canada, Venezuela, and Mexico, with Canada being the single most important foreign supplier.[8]

The US Energy Information Administration (EIA) projects that by 2030 oil imports, mainly from the Persian Gulf, will represent 75 percent of total Chinese oil consumption. By contrast, US oil imports are expected to decline sharply and account for only 35 percent of total US oil consumption by 2030.[9] Clearly, Persian Gulf oil imports will be far more crucial to China than to the United States. Accordingly, for China, ensuring access to Persian Gulf oil and gas will loom large as a vital national interest. By contrast, for the United States, a key strategic priority will be denial of access to Persian Gulf energy resources to its adversaries.

China, of course, which has domestic oil reserves of about 20 billion barrels and domestic gas reserves of 107 trillion cubic feet (Tcf), is seeking oil and gas resources which it can effectively control in its own backyard.[10] In the East China Sea, low-end estimated oil reserves are 60 billion barrels, and in the South China Sea, low-end estimated oil reserves are 11 billion barrels.[11] Not surprisingly, the potential energy resources of these areas have generated intense rival claims involving China, Japan, South Korea, Vietnam, and the Philippines. However, the East and South China Seas have yet to be explored systematically, and their oil and gas resources are a long way from being developed and produced. By comparison, the proved oil reserves of Saudi Arabia alone amount to 263 billion barrels, and the combined proved oil reserves of Iran and Iraq are about 252 billion barrels.[12] Thus, from the Chinese viewpoint, the strategic importance of access to Persian Gulf oil and gas resources is not significantly changed even with Chinese control over access to oil and gas resources in the East and South China Seas.

If the United States is to counterbalance China successfully, it must be able to threaten China's energy security. Ideally, the United States should be in a position in which it can persuade the Persian Gulf oil producers, if necessary, to turn off the tap and decline to supply China with oil and gas. Furthermore, the United States must be able to put in place anti-access, area denial strategies (a) in the eastern Indian Ocean and Bay of Bengal to blockade the Malacca, Sunda and Lambok Straits; and (b) in the western Indian Ocean and the Arabian Sea to blockade the arc between the Bab el Mandab to the Strait of Hormuz. Indonesia, India, and Iran will be critical to the success of a recalibrated American grand strategy to contain China.

Notes

1. For total public debt outstanding, see US Department of the Treasury, Daily Treasury Statement, August 31, 2012, Table III-C, https://fms.treas.gov/fmsweb/viewDTSFiles?dir=a&f name=12083100.pdf For total GDP see Bureau of Economic Analysis (BEA), National Income and Product Accounts, August 29, 2012, http://www.bea.gov.

2. China is likely to face a pension and social security bomb by 2050. The combined impact of a low fertility rate (1.56) and skewed male to female ratio at birth (1.18 to 1) means that

"Unlike the rest of the developed world, China will grow old before it gets rich." See "Demography: China's Achilles heel," The Economist, April 21, 2012, http://www.economist.com and "China's population: The most surprising demographic crisis," The Economist, May 5, 2011, http://www.economist.com.

3. Japan's original version of the Greater East-Asian Co-Prosperity Sphere was enunciated in August 1940 to serve as the rationale for the Japanese Empire being carved out by Japanese militarists. See Warren I. Cohen, East Asia at the Center: Four Thousand Years of Engagement with the World (New York: Columbia University Press, 2000), 352.

4. BBC News, "China overtakes Japan as world's second biggest economy," 14 February 2011, http://www.bbc.co.uk.

5. US Energy Information Administration (EIA), "World gross domestic product (GDP) by region expressed in purchasing power parity, Reference case," International Energy Outlook 2011, http://www.eia.gov.

6. US Energy Information Administration, Table A1 "World total primary energy consumption by region, Reference case," in International Energy Outlook 2011, http://www.eia.gov.

7. For total Chinese oil consumption and imports, see US Energy Information Administration (EIA), China: Country Analysis Brief, September 4, 2012, http://www.eia.gov; for total US oil consumption and imports see EIA, "Energy in Brief: How dependent are we on foreign oil?" July 13, 2012, http://www.eia.gov; and EIA, "Petroleum and Other Liquids: US Net Imports by Country," August 30, 2012, http://www.eia.gov.

8. Ibid. In particular see "Energy in Brief: How dependent are we on foreign oil?"

9. Ibid. For further details regarding the forecasted dramatic drop in US oil imports, see figure 114 "US net imports of petroleum and other liquids fall in the Reference case" in EIA, Annual Energy Outlook 2012," June 25, 2012, http://www.eia.gov.

10. US Energy Information Administration, China: Country Analysis Brief, September 4, 2012, http://www.eia.gov.

11. EIA, East China Sea: Analysis Brief, September 12, 2012, http://www.eia.gov; South China Sea: Analysis Brief, February 7, 2013, http://www.eia.gov.

12. "2011 World Proved Reserves," http://www.eia.gov.

Critical Thinking

1. Can the U.S. contain a rising China that is determined to become the economic, political, and military power in Asia?

2. Can the U.S. rethink its strategy in order to maintain its primacy as a global power?

3. Will the U.S. be successful in pursuing a policy of containment toward China?

Create Central

www.mhhe.com/createcentral

Internet References

Carl Von Clausewitz on War; Sun Tzu, The Art of War and Strategy

www.sonshi.com/clausewitz.html

Demography: China's Achille's Heel
www.economist.com/node/21553056

Samir Tata—Journal of International Affairs
jia.sipa.columbia.edu/authors-listing/author/samir-tata

NATO: Time to Refocus and Streamline /ISN
www.isn.ethz.ch/Digital-Library/Articles/Detail/?id=167376

Parameters—Strategic Studies Institute–U.S. Army
www.strategicstudiesinstitute.army.mil/pubs/parameters

Samir Tata is a foreign policy analyst. He served as an analyst with the National Geospatial-Intelligence Agency, researcher with Middle East Institute, Atlantic Council, & National Defense University. He has a B.A. in Foreign Affairs & History from the University of Virginia, and an M.A. in International Affairs from George Washington University.

Tata, Samir. From *Parameters,* Winter/Spring 2013, pp. 47-49. Copyright © Samir Tata. Published by U.S. Army War College. Reprinted by permission of the author.

Unit 3

UNIT

Prepared by: Caroline Shaffer Westerhof,
California National University for Advanced Studies

Participating in Politics: Acting within and out of Institutional Frameworks

This section builds upon diverse elements of political theory. It discusses payments to warlords in an area that bars journalists and is under United Nations sanctions. In contrast to this article, there is discussion of stability in the same region, but it is not considered a nation-state. Somaliland is not recognized as a country because of its breakaway status following the disintegration of Somalia in 1991. Somaliland seeks to be an example of free and fair elections based on inclusive citizenship to buttress political stability.

This brings us to the most widely used form of organizing citizen preferences and most common expression of citizen participation: voting. Voting is a requirement for citizenship in many countries; it is both an entitlement and a privilege. Given the significance of the vote outcome, who are the citizens that regularly exercise their voting privileges? Many studies note that the young tend to abstain from voting, with participation growing with age and peaking around those in their forties and fifties.

Why is it important to ensure that voting is the preferred choice of citizen participation? Consider this: If citizens are not voting, how do they express their policy preferences? Even in the United States, a common outlet of expression includes protesting, even bedding down in tents and the like in certain neighborhoods. A majority of protestors in Russia have more income, are better educated, and are likely to get their news from the Internet than the general public, and some are protesting in groups, risking jail. Street protests are taking place not only in a government that has been defined by top-down political control, but even in the United States where we speak of grassroots democracy.

If voters are not voting, their disenfranchisement may lead to the pursuit of extralegal means to access the political system or make demands on the government. With the increasing interconnectedness through cellphones, texting, and the Internet, the geographical and physical impediments to such extralegal means of participation means that they likely had negligible effect. Social networking and electronic access provide venues and the setting for raising awareness.

Importantly, social movements mobilized through these nontraditional contexts have grown in the face of possible government clampdown, in part because their large numbers provide anonymity and some insulation against adverse government repression and because such activism has led to a redefinition of civic associations and how they mobilize to improve political conditions and civil rights. Such use is seen in China, where technology is being used to mobilize netizens not only against the government but against other citizens. Such activity demonstrates that use of the Internet may lead to citizen vigilantism and campaigns of "harassment, mass intimidation, and public revenge."

It is to be noted that, while mass protests and demonstrations are useful, sole reliance on such mass demonstrations does not generally achieve the desired objectives. Is success based, if there is such, on regular or even institutionalized funding and organization to raise awareness, support, and defuse challenges to their agenda? Citizen participation and involvement are important, although they may be dangerous in a controlled political regime. Citizen participation is fundamental to political development and social stability; but such venues must not generate a negative political arena. There has to be purpose, organization, and funding. Actors in the system have to listen, understand, and provide the impetus for the new changes that will happen or there will be continued destruction as we are witnessing today.

Such is being questioned in Egypt, where the present rulers have $12 billion to spend. The reality of many theorists and practioners is that "No government erected on the ruins of Mohamed Morsi's regime will be deemed to be legitimate."

And yet within the Expat Focus, there are successful and fast growing economies. What makes the United Arab Emirates and Malaysian economy successful? The UAE has an open economy, and the government has increased spending on job creation and infrastructure. Malaysia has a flexible form of governance and welcomes foreign talent. Such, for both nations, encourages further growth, continued progress, and long-term challenges. The reality demonstrates that nation-states working with their citizens in an open society, and not against them, will encourage positive economic growth and political stability.

Article

Prepared by: Caroline Shaffer Westerhof,
California National University for Advanced Studies

Exclusive: Eritrea Pays Warlord to Influence Somalia—U.N. Experts

LOUIS CHARBONNEAU

Learning Outcomes

After reading this article, you will be able to:

- Examine the reality of Eritrea paying warlords to influence Somalia.

- Examine why mining companies are the biggest source of funding for some of the worst regions in the world.

- Examine why money for hire is a great inducement for regional terrorism.

Eritrea is undermining stability in conflict-ravaged Somalia by paying political agents and a warlord linked to Islamist militants to influence the Mogadishu government, U.N. sanctions experts said in a confidential report.

The Eritrean government has long denied playing any negative role in Somalia, saying it has no links to Islamist al Shabaab militants fighting to overthrow the Somali government. It says the U.N. sanctions imposed on it in 2009 for supporting al Shabaab were based on lies and has called for the sanctions to be lifted.

The latest annual report by the U.N. Monitoring Group on Somalia and Eritrea to the Security Council's Somalia/Eritrea sanctions committee casts fresh doubt on Asmara's denials, undermining its case for lifting the sanctions against it.

"The Monitoring Group has received numerous reports about the warming of relations between Asmara and Mogadishu, and has obtained evidence of Asmara's control of political agents close to the Somali presidency and some of the individual spoilers," the group said in the report, seen by Reuters.

One such operative, the monitors said, is "Eritrean agent of influence Abdi Nur Siad 'Abdi Wal,' . . . who is reported to have a close relationship with a senior al Shabaab commander."

The monitors describe Abdi Wal as a "warlord."

"Abdi Wal is now a close ally of former ARS-Asmara (a Somali Islamist network in Eritrea) leader Zakaria Mohamed Haji Abdi, for whom he provides security in Mogadishu," the monitors said. "He is known to command the allegiance of about 100 fighters in Mogadishu and is involved in contract killings."

The monitors said in their report that they have "obtained direct testimonies and concrete evidence of Eritrean support to Abdi Wal and Mohamed Wali Sheikh Ahmed Nuur." The Monitoring Group has reported on Ahmed Nuur in the past, describing him as a "political coordinator for al Shabaab" and a recipient of funds from Eritrea.

"A source on the Eritrean payroll in direct contact with Abdi Wal has confirmed that Abdi Wal has admitted in closed-door meetings that he is acting as an agent for the Eritrean government," the group said in its latest report.

Eritrea's U.N. mission did not respond to a request for comment.

Russian and Italian Complaints

The latest report said that Ahmed Nuur, also known as Ugas Mohamed Wali Sheikh, has repeatedly held meetings in Khartoum with Mohamed Mantai, Eritrea's ambassador to Sudan and, since December, Iran.

"During these meetings, options for Eritrean financial support to Ahmed Nuur were discussed," the report said.

"Mantai, a former military intelligence officer, has a history of operating in Somalia and was expelled from Kenya in 2009 after he returned from Somalia following meetings with al Shabaab agents," the monitors said.

In addition to their nearly 500-page report on Somalia and Eritrea, the Monitoring Group produced a separate report of around 80 pages focusing solely on Eritrea.

Council diplomats said the longer Somalia/Eritrea report will be made public soon, but the shorter Eritrea report will not be published because of Russian objections.

According to a letter the Russian delegation sent to Ambassador Kim Sook, chairman of the Somalia/Eritrea sanctions committee, Russia "objects to the publication of the (Eritrea) report due to the biased and groundless conclusions and recommendations contained in it."

Italian Ambassador Cesare Maria Ragaglini also wrote to Kim complaining about the report because of "misleading information and undocumented implications of violations of the arms embargo." Reuters has obtained both letters.

According to diplomats familiar with the U.N. monitors' shorter Eritrea report, an Italian helicopter exported to Eritrea for mining survey purposes was seen at a military facility there, raising the possibility of a sanctions breach.

The monitors said Italian authorities failed to provide additional information as requested, the diplomats added.

Ragaglini dismissed that allegation, saying "we did provide the information they requested (e.g. on financial flows), but there is no evidence whatsoever of military assistance from Italy to sustain the undocumented claims of the experts."

China, diplomats say, is annoyed about references in the Eritrea report to Chinese machine tools procured for a large government depot in Eritrea that houses tanks, missiles and dual-use civilian trucks. But the envoys said there was no suggestion the Chinese government was violating U.N. sanctions.

Critical Thinking

1. Has there been a case for lifting United Nations sanctions against the Eritrea region? Explain.
2. Is the United Nations montoring group capable of handling the Eritrea/Somalia terrorist activities? Explain.
3. Is the Security Council the proper body of the United Nations to handle such conflict? Explain.

Create Central

www.mhhe.com/createcentral

Internet References

Eritrea Pays Warlord to Influence Somalia—*The New York Times*
www.reuters.com/article/2013/07/17/us-somalia-eritrea-un-idUSBRE96G06U20130717

Monitoring Group Report on Somalia
http://davidshinn.blogspot.com/2013/07/un-monitoring-group-report-on-somalia.html

Russia, Italy and China Scoff at U.N. Monitoring Report on Eritrea
www.tesfanews.net/russia-italy-and-china-object-u-n-eritrea-monitoring-report/

Eritrea Extorts UK Refugees to Fund Somalia's al-Shabaab Islamist Fighters
www.ibtimes.co.uk/articles/495268/20130729/eritrea-shabaab-somalia-diaspora-tax-horn-islam.htm

Saudi Ban Lifting Boosts Somaliland Cattle Trade
www.allkismayo.com/?p57019

LOUIS CHARBONNEAU is Reuters United Nations Bureau Chief.

Article   Prepared by: Caroline Shaffer Westerhof,
                                        California National University for Advanced Studies

Rare Haven of Stability in Somalia Faces a Test

Jeffrey Gettleman

Learning Outcomes

After reading this article, you will be able to:

- Examine how, although the city of Mogadishu has been devastated, it is now going through a transition.

- Examine how the Somalia militants mix business and terror.

Burao, Somalia—The rallies usually start early in the morning, before the sunshine hurts.

By 8 A.M. on a recent day, thousands of people were packed into Burao's sandy town square, with little boys climbing high into the trees to get a peek at the politicians.

"We're going to end corruption!" one of the politicians boomed, holding several microphones at once. "We're going to bring dignity back to the people!"

The boys cheered wildly. Wispy militiamen punched bony fists in the air. The politicians' messages were hardly original. But in this corner of Africa, a free and open political rally—led, no less, by opposition leaders who could actually win—is an anomaly apparently worthy of celebration.

The crowd that day helped tell a strange truth: that one of the most democratic countries in the Horn of Africa is not really a country at all. It is Somaliland, the northwestern corner of Somalia, which, since the disintegration of the Somali state in 1991, has been on a quixotic mission for recognition as its own separate nation.

While so much of Somalia is plagued by relentless violence, this little-known slice of the Somali puzzle is peaceful and organized enough to hold national elections this week, with more than one million registered voters. The campaigns are passionate but fair, say the few Western observers here. The roads are full of battered old Toyotas blasting out slogans from staticky megaphones lashed to the roofs.

Somalilanders have pulled off peaceful national elections three times. The last presidential election in 2003 was decided by a wafer-thin margin, around 80 votes at the time of counting, yet there was no violence. Each successful election feeds the hope here that one day the world will reward Somaliland with recognition for carving a functioning, democratic space out of one of the most chaotic countries in the world.

But this presidential election, scheduled for Saturday, will be one of the biggest tests yet for Somaliland's budding democracy.

The government seems unpopular, partly because Somaliland is still desperately poor, a place where even in the biggest towns, like Burao or the capital, Hargeisa, countless people dwell in bubble-shaped huts made out of cardboard scraps and flattened oil drums. Most independent observers predict the leading opposition party, Kulmiye, which means something akin to "the one who brings people together," will get the most votes.

But that does not mean the opposition will necessarily win.

In many cases in Africa—Ethiopia in 2005, Kenya in 2007, Zimbabwe in 2008—right when the opposition appeared poised to win elections, the government seemed to fiddle with the results, forcibly holding on to power and sometimes provoking widespread unrest in the process.

"There's probably not going to be many problems with the voting itself, but the day after," said Roble Mohamed, the former editor in chief of one of Somaliland's top websites. "That is the question."

Many people here worry that if Somaliland's governing party, UDUB, tries to hold on to power illegitimately, the well-armed populace (this is still part of Somalia, after all) will rise up and Somaliland's nearly two decades of peace could disappear in a cloud of gun smoke.

"I know this happens in Africa, but it won't happen in Somaliland," promised Said Adani Moge, a spokesman for Somaliland's government. "If we lose, we'll give up power. The most important thing is peace."

Easily said, infrequently done. Peaceful transfers of power are a rarity in this neighborhood. In April, Sudan held its first national elections in more than 20 years (the last change of power was a coup), but the voting was widely considered superficial because of widespread intimidation beforehand and the withdrawal of several leading opposition parties from the presidential race.

Last month's vote in Ethiopia, in which the governing party and its allies won more than 99 percent of the parliamentary seats, was also tainted by what human rights groups called a campaign of government repression, including the manipulation of American food aid to starve out the opposition.

Then there is little Eritrea, along the Red Sea, which has not held a presidential election since the early 1990s, when it won independence. And Djibouti, home to a large American military base, where the president recently pushed to have the Constitution changed so he could run again.

South-central Somalia, where a very weak transitional government is struggling to fend off radical Islamist insurgents, is so dangerous that residents must risk insurgents' wrath even to watch the World Cup, never mind holding a vote.

So in this volatile region, Somaliland has become a demonstration of the possible, sustaining a one-person one-vote democracy in a poor, conflict-torn place that gets very little help. While the government in south-central Somalia, which barely controls any territory, receives millions of dollars in direct support from the United Nations and the United States, the Somaliland government "doesn't get a penny," Mr. Said said.

Because Somaliland is not recognized as an independent country, it is very difficult for the government here to secure international loans, even though it has become a regional model for conflict resolution and democratic-institution building—buzzwords among Western donors.

In many respects, Somaliland is already its own country, with its own currency, its own army and navy, its own borders and its own national identity, as evidenced by the countless Somaliland T-shirts and flags everywhere you look. Part of this stems from its distinct colonial history, having been ruled, relatively indirectly, by the British, while the rest of Somalia was colonized by the Italians, who set up a European administration.

Italian colonization supplanted local elders, which might have been one reason that much of Somalia plunged into clan-driven chaos after 1991, while Somaliland succeeded in reconciling its clans.

Clan is not the prevailing issue in this election. The three presidential candidates (Somaliland's election code says only three political parties can compete, and they take turns campaigning from day to day) are from different clans or subclans. Yet, many voters do not seem to care.

In the middle of miles and miles of thorn bush stand two huts about 100 feet apart, one with a green and yellow Kulmiye flag flapping from a stick flagpole, the other with a solid green UDUB flag.

Haboon Roble, a shy 20-year-old, explained that she liked UDUB: "They're good. They hold up the house."

But about 100 feet away, her uncle, Abdi Rahman Roble, shook his head. "This government hasn't done anything for farmers," he complained. "We can't even get plastic sheets to catch the rain."

He said he was voting for Kulmiye. "But I don't tell anyone how to vote," Mr. Abdi Rahman said. "That's their choice."

And like the other adults in the family, he proudly showed off his new plastic voter card, which he usually keeps hidden in a special place in his hut, along with other valuables.

Critical Thinking

1. How has Somalia sustained financial support?
2. Can Somalia, with its famine, drought, and powerful warlords involved in its political instability, ever become a peaceful and stable government?
3. Can "qat," a mild stimulant, known to increase aggressiveness for warlords and pirates, ever become a controlled substance?
4. Why was and has the decision been made by the United States to suspend all aid?

Create Central

www.mhhe.com/createcentral

Internet References

Somali Militants Mixing Business and Terror
www.nytimes.com/2013/10/01/world/africa/officials-struggle-with-tangled-web-of-financing-for-somali-militants.html?pagewanted=all&_r=0

Rare Haven of Stability in Somalia Faces a Test
www.nytimes.com/2010/06/26/world/africa/26somaliland.html

Lawrence Solomon: Capitalist haven | Somalilandpress.com . . .
http://somalilandpress.com/lawrence-solomon-capitalist-haven-29183

Somaliland—20 years of success?
www.samorg.net/nyheter/somaliland

EAPI
www.eastafricapi.com

JEFFREY GETTLEMAN is the East Africa bureau chief for *The New York Times*.

Article   Prepared by: Caroline Shaffer Westerhof,
                                       California National University for Advanced Studies

China's Cyberposse

TOM DOWNEY

Learning Outcomes

After reading this article, you will be able to:

- Explain the concept of "netizens."

- Explain human-flesh search engines.

- Understand contemporary China's fault lines.

The short video made its way around China's Web in early 2006, passed on through file sharing and recommended in chat rooms. It opens with a middle-aged Asian woman dressed in a leopard-print blouse, knee-length black skirt, stockings and silver stilettos standing next to a riverbank. She smiles, holding a small brown and white kitten in her hands. She gently places the cat on the tiled pavement and proceeds to stomp it to death with the sharp point of her high heel.

"This is not a human," wrote BrokenGlasses, a user on Mop, a Chinese online forum. "I have no interest in spreading this video nor can I remain silent. I just hope justice can be done." That first post elicited thousands of responses. "Find her and kick her to death like she did to the kitten," one user wrote. Then the inquiries started to become more practical: "Is there a front-facing photo so we can see her more clearly?" The human-flesh search had begun.

Human-flesh search engines—*renrou sousuo yinqing*—have become a Chinese phenomenon: they are a form of online vigilante justice in which Internet users hunt down and punish people who have attracted their wrath. The goal is to get the targets of a search fired from their jobs, shamed in front of their neighbors, run out of town. It's crowd-sourced detective work, pursued online—with offline results.

There is no portal specially designed for human-flesh searching; the practice takes place in Chinese Internet forums like Mop, where the term most likely originated. Searches are powered by users called *wang min*, Internet citizens, or Netizens. The word "Netizen" exists in English, but you hear its equivalent used much more frequently in China, perhaps because the public space of the Internet is one of the few places where people can in fact act like citizens. A Netizen called Beacon Bridge No Return found the first clue in the kitten-killer case.

"There was credit information before the crush scene reading 'www.crushworld.net,' " that user wrote. Netizens traced the e-mail address associated with the site to a server in Hangzhou, a couple of hours from Shanghai. A follow-up post asked about the video's location: "Are users from Hangzhou familiar with this place?" Locals reported that nothing in their city resembled the backdrop in the video. But Netizens kept sifting through the clues, confident they could track down one person in a nation of more than a billion. They were right.

The traditional media picked up the story, and people all across China saw the kitten killer's photo on television and in newspapers. "I know this woman," wrote I'm Not Desert Angel four days after the search began. "She's not in Hangzhou. She lives in the small town I live in here in northeastern China. God, she's a nurse! That's all I can say."

Only six days after the first Mop post about the video, the kitten killer's home was revealed as the town of Luobei in Heilongjiang Province, in the far northeast, and her name—Wang Jiao—was made public, as were her phone number and her employer. Wang Jiao and the cameraman who filmed her were dismissed from what the Chinese call iron rice bowls, government jobs that usually last to retirement and pay a pension until death.

"Wang Jiao was affected a lot," a Luobei resident known online as Longjiangbaby told me by e-mail. "She left town and went somewhere else. Li Yuejun, the cameraman, used to be core staff of the local press. He left Luobei, too." The kitten-killer case didn't just provide revenge; it helped turn the human-flesh search engine into a national phenomenon.

At the Beijing headquarters of Mop, Ben Du, the site's head of interactive communities, told me that the Chinese term for human-flesh search engine has been around since 2001, when it was used to describe a search that was human-powered rather than computer-driven. Mop had a forum called human-flesh search engine, where users could pose questions about entertainment trivia that other users would answer: a type of crowd-sourcing. The kitten-killer case and subsequent hunts changed all that. Some Netizens, including Du, argue that the term continues to mean a cooperative, crowd-sourced investigation. "It's just Netizens helping each other and sharing information," he told me. But the Chinese public's primary understanding of the term is no longer so benign. The popular meaning is now not just a search *by* humans but also a search *for* humans, initially performed online but intended to cause real-world consequences. Searches have been directed against all kinds of people, including cheating spouses, corrupt government officials, amateur pornography makers, Chinese citizens who are perceived as unpatriotic, journalists who urge a moderate stance on Tibet and rich people who try to game the Chinese system. Human-flesh searches highlight what people are willing to fight for: the political issues, polarizing events and contested moral standards that are the fault lines of contemporary China.

Versions of the human-flesh search have taken place in other countries. In the United States in 2006, one online search singled out a woman who found a cellphone in a New York City taxi and started to use it as her own, rebuffing requests from the phone's rightful owner to return it. In South Korea in 2005, Internet users identified and shamed a young woman who was caught on video refusing to clean up after her dog on a Seoul subway car. But China is the only place in the world with a nearly universal recognition (among Internet users) of the concept. I met a film director in China who was about to release a feature film based on a human-flesh-search story and a mystery writer who had just published a novel titled "Human-Flesh Search."

The prevailing narrative in the West about the Chinese Internet is the story of censorship—Google's threatened withdrawal from China being only the latest episode. But the reality is that in China, as in the United States, most Internet users are far more interested in finding jobs, dates and porn than in engaging in political discourse. "For our generation, the post-'80s generation, I don't feel like censorship is a critical issue on the Internet," Jin Liwen, a Chinese technology analyst who lives in America, told me. While there are some specific, highly sensitive areas where the Chinese government tries to control all information—most important, any political activity that could challenge the authority of the Communist Party—the Western media's focus on censorship can lead to the misconception that the Chinese government utterly dominates online life. The vast majority of what people do on the Internet in China, including most human-flesh-search activity, is ignored by censors and unfettered by government regulation. There are many aspects of life on and off the Internet that the government is unwilling, unable or maybe just uninterested in trying to control.

The focus on censorship also obscures the fact that the Web is not just about free speech. As some human-flesh searches show, an uncontrolled Internet can be menacing as well as liberating.

On a windy night in late December 2007, a man was headed back to work when he saw someone passed out in the small garden near the entryway to his Beijing office building. The man, who would allow only his last name, Wei, to be published, called over to the security guard for help. A woman standing next to the guard started weeping. Wei was confused.

Wei and the guard entered the yard, but the woman, Jiang Hong, was afraid to follow. As they approached the person, Wei told me, he realized it was the body of someone who fell from the building. Then he understood why Jiang wouldn't come any closer: the body was that of her sister, Jiang Yan, who jumped from her apartment's 24th-floor balcony while Hong was in the bathroom. Two days earlier, Yan, who was 31, had tried to commit suicide with sleeping pills—she was separated from her husband, Wang Fei, who was dating another woman—but her sister and her husband had rushed her to the hospital. Now she had succeeded, hitting the ground so hard that her impact left a shallow crater still evident when I visited the site with Wei a year and a half later.

Hong soon discovered that her sister kept a private diary online in the two months leading up to her death and wanted it to be made public after she killed herself. When Hong called her sister's friends to tell them that Yan had died, she also told them that they could find out why by looking at her blog, now unlocked for public viewing. The online diary, "Migratory Bird Going North," was more than just a reflection on her adulterous husband and a record of her despair; it was Yan's countdown to suicide, prompted by the discovery that her husband was cheating on her. The first entry reads: "Two months from now is the day I leave . . . for a place no one knows me, that is new to me. There I won't need phone, computer or Internet. No one can find me."

A person who read Yan's blog decided to repost it, 46 short entries in all, on a popular Chinese online bulletin board called Tianya. Hong posted a reply, expressing sadness over her sister's death and detailing the ways she thought Yan had helped her husband: supporting him through school, paying for his designer clothes and helping him land a good job. Now, she wrote, Wang wouldn't even sign his wife's death certificate until he could come to an agreement with her family about how much he needed to pay them in damages.

Yan's diaries, coupled with her sister's account of Wang's behavior, attracted many angry Tianya users and shot to the top of the list of the most popular threads on the board. One early comment by an anonymous user, referring to Wang and his mistress, reads, "We should take revenge on that couple and drown them in our sputa." Calls for justice, for vengeance and for a human-flesh search began to spread, not only against Wang but also against his girlfriend. "Those in Beijing, please share with others the scandal of these two," a Netizen wrote. "Make it impossible for them to stay in this city."

The search crossed over to other Web sites, then to the mainstream media—so far a crucial multiplier in every major human-flesh search—and Wang Fei became one of China's most infamous and reviled husbands. Most of Wang's private information was revealed: cellphone number, student ID, work contacts, even his brother's license-plate number. One site posted an interactive map charting the locations of everything from Wang's house to his mistress's family's laundry business. "Pay attention when you walk on the street," wrote Hypocritical Human. "If you ever meet these two, tear their skin off."

Wang is still in hiding and was unwilling to meet me, but his lawyer, Zhang Yanfeng, told me not long ago: "The human-flesh search has unimaginable power. First it was a lot of phone calls every day. Then people painted red characters on his parents' front door, which said things like, 'You caused your wife's suicide, so you should pay.'"

Wang and his mistress, Dong Fang, both worked for the multinational advertising agency Saatchi & Saatchi. Soon after Netizens revealed this, Saatchi & Saatchi issued a statement reporting that Wang Fei and Dong Fang had voluntarily resigned. Wang's lawyer says Saatchi pushed the couple out. "All the media have the wrong report," he says. "[Wang Fei] never quit. He told me that the company fired him." (Representatives for Saatchi & Saatchi Beijing refused to comment.) Netizens were happy with this outcome but remained vigilant. One Mop user wrote, "To all employers: Never offer Wang Fei or Dong Fang jobs, otherwise Moppers will human-flesh-search you."

What was peculiar about the human-flesh search against Wang was that it involved almost no searching. His name was revealed in the earliest online-forum posts, and his private information was disclosed shortly after. This wasn't cooperative detective work; it was public harassment, mass intimidation and populist revenge. Wang actually sought redress in Chinese court and was rewarded very minor damages from an Internet-service provider and a Netizen who Wang claimed had besmirched his reputation. Recently passed tort-law reform may encourage more such lawsuits, but damages awarded thus far in China have been so minor that it's hard to imagine lawsuits having much impact on the human-flesh search.

For a westerner, what is most striking is how different Chinese Internet culture is from our own. News sites and individual blogs aren't nearly as influential in China, and social networking hasn't really taken off. What remain most vital are the largely anonymous online forums, where human-flesh searches begin. These forums have evolved into public spaces that are much more participatory, dynamic, populist and perhaps even democratic than anything on the English-language Internet. In the 1980s in the United States, before widespread use of the Internet, B.B.S. stood for bulletin-board system, a collection of posts and replies accessed by dial-up or hard-wired users. Though B.B.S.'s of this original form were popular in China in the early '90s, before the Web arrived, Chinese now use "B.B.S." to describe any kind of online forum. Chinese go to B.B.S.'s to find broad-based communities and exchange information about everything from politics to romance.

Jin Liwen, the technology analyst, came of age in China just as Internet access was becoming available and wrote her thesis at M.I.T. on Chinese B.B.S.'s. "In the United States, traditional media are still playing the key role in setting the agenda for the public," Jin told me. "But in China, you will see that a lot of hot topics, hot news or events actually originate from online discussions." One factor driving B.B.S. traffic is the dearth of good information in the mainstream media. Print publications and television networks are under state control and cannot cover many controversial issues. B.B.S.'s are where the juicy stories break, spreading through the mainstream media if they get big enough.

"Chinese users just use these online forums for everything," Jin says. "They look for solutions, they want to have discussions with others and they go there for entertainment. It's a very sticky platform." Jin cited a 2007 survey conducted by iResearch showing that nearly 45 percent of Chinese B.B.S. users spend between three and eight hours a day on them and that more than 15 percent spend more than eight hours. While less than a third of China's population is on the Web, this B.B.S. activity is not as peripheral to Chinese society as it may seem. Internet users tend to be from larger, richer cities and provinces or from the elite, educated class of more remote regions and thus wield influence far greater than their numbers suggest.

I found the intensity of the Wang Fei search difficult to understand. Wang Fei and Jiang Yan were separated and heading toward divorce, and what he did cannot be uncommon. How had the structure of the B.B.S. allowed mass opinion to be so effectively rallied against this one man? I tracked down Wang Lixue, a woman who goes by the online handle Chali and moderates a subforum on Baidu.com (China's largest search engine, with its own B.B.S.) that is devoted entirely to discussions about Jiang Yan. Chali was careful to distance herself from the human-flesh search that found Wang Fei and Dong Fang. "That kind of thing won't solve any problems," she told me. "It's not good for either side." But she didn't exactly apologize. "Everyone was so angry, so irrational," Chali says. "It was a sensitive period. So I understand the people who did the human-flesh search. If a person doesn't do anything wrong, they won't be human-flesh-searched."

Chali was moved by the powerful feeling that Wang shouldn't be allowed to escape censure for his role in his wife's suicide. "I want to know what is going to happen if I get married and have a similar experience," Chali says. "I want to know if the law or something could protect me and give me some kind of security." It struck me as an unusual wish—that the law could guard her from heartbreak. Chali wasn't only angry about Jiang Yan's suicide; she also wanted to improve things for herself and others. "The goal is to commemorate Jiang Yan and to have an objective discussion about adultery, to talk about what you want in your marriage, to find new opinions and have a better life," Chali says. Her forum was the opposite of the vengeful populism found on some B.B.S.'s. The frenzy of the occasional human-flesh search attracts many Netizens to B.B.S.'s, but the bigger day-to-day draw, as in Chali's case, is the desire for a community in which people can work out the problems they face in a country where life is changing more quickly than anyone could ever have imagined.

The plum garden Seafood Restaurant stands on a six-lane road that cuts through Shenzhen, a fishing village turned factory boomtown. It has a subterranean dining room with hundreds of orange-covered seats, an open kitchen to one side and a warren of small private rooms to the other. Late on a Friday night in October 2008, a security camera captured a scene that was soon replayed all over the Chinese Internet and sparked a human-flesh search against a government official.

In the video clip, an older man crosses the background with a little girl. Later the girl runs back through the frame and returns with her father, mother and brother. The subtitles tell us that the old man had tried to force the girl into the men's room, presumably to molest her, and that her father is trying to find the man who did that. Then the girl's father appears in front of the camera, arguing with that man.

There is no sound on the video, so you have to rely on the Chinese subtitles, which seem to have been posted with the video. According to those subtitles, the older man tells the father of the girl: "I did it, so what? How much money do you want? Name your price." He gestures violently and continues: "Do you know who I am? I am from the Ministry of Transportation in Beijing. I have the same level as the mayor of your city. So what if I grabbed the neck of a small child? If you dare challenge me, just wait and see how I will deal with you." He moves to leave but is blocked by restaurant employees and the girl's father. The group exits frame left.

The video was first posted on a Web site called Netease, whose slogan is "The Internet can gather power from the people." The eighth Netizen comment reads: "Have you seen how proud he was? He's a dead man now." Later someone chimed in, "Another official riding roughshod over the people!" The human-flesh search began. Users quickly matched a public photo of a local party official to the older man in the video and identified him as Lin Jiaxiang from the Shenzhen Maritime Administration. "Kill him," wrote a user named Xunleixing. "Otherwise China will be destroyed by people of this kind."

While Netizens saw this as a struggle between an arrogant official and a victimized family of common people, the staff members at Plum Garden, when I spoke to them, had a different take. First, they weren't sure that Lin had been trying to molest the girl. Perhaps, they thought, he was just drunk. The floor director, Zhang Cai Yao, told me, "Maybe the government official just patted the girl on the head and tried to say, 'Thank you, you're a nice girl.'" Zhang saw the struggle between Lin and the family as a kind of conflict she witnessed all too often. "It was a fight between rich people and officials," she says. "The official said something irritating to her parents, who are very rich."

Police said they did not have sufficient evidence to prosecute Lin, but that didn't stop the government from firing him. It was the same kind of summary dismissal as in the kitten-killer case—Lin drew attention to himself, and so it was time to go. The government had the technology and the power to make a story like this one disappear, yet it didn't stand up to the Netizens. That is perhaps because this search took aim at a provincial-level official; there have been no publicized human-flesh searches against central-government officials in Beijing or their offspring, even though many of them are considered corrupt.

Rebecca MacKinnon, a visiting fellow at Princeton University's Center for Information Technology Policy, argues that China's central government may actually be happy about searches that focus on localized corruption. "The idea that you manage the local bureaucracy by sicking the masses on them is actually not a democratic tradition but a Maoist tradition," she told me. During the Cultural Revolution, Mao encouraged citizens to rise up against local officials who were bourgeois or corrupt, and human-flesh searches have been tagged by some as Red Guard 2.0. It's easy to denounce the tyranny of the online masses when you live in a country that has strong rule of law and institutions that address public corruption, but in China the human-flesh search engine is one of the only ways that ordinary citizens can try to go after corrupt local officials. Cases like the Lin Jiaxiang search, as imperfect as their outcomes may be, are examples of the human-flesh search as a potential mechanism for checking government excess.

The human-flesh search engine can also serve as a safety valve in a society with ever mounting pressures on the government. "You can't stop the anger, can't make everyone shut up, can't stop the Internet, so you try and channel it as best you can. You try and manage it, kind of like a waterworks hydroelectric project," MacKinnon explained. "It's a great way to divert the *qi*, the anger, to places where it's the least damaging to the central government's legitimacy."

The Chinese government has proved particularly adept at harnessing, managing and, when necessary, containing the nationalist passions of its citizens, especially those people the Chinese call *fen qing*, or angry youth. Instead of wondering, in the run-up to the 2008 Beijing Olympics, why the world was so upset about China's handling of Tibet, popular sentiment in China was channeled against dissenting individuals, painted as traitors. One young Chinese woman, Grace Wang, became the target of a human-flesh search after she tried to mediate between pro-Tibet and pro-China protesters at Duke University, where she is an undergraduate. Wang told me that her mother's home in China was vandalized by human-flesh searchers. Wang's mother was not harmed—popular uprisings are usually kept under tight control by the government when they threaten to erupt into real violence—but Wang told me she is afraid to return to China. Certain national events, like the Tibet activism before the 2008 Olympics or the large-scale loss of life from the Sichuan earthquake, often produce a flurry of human-flesh searches. Recent searches seem to be more political—taking aim at things like government corruption or a supposedly unpatriotic citizenry—and less focused on the kind of private transgressions that inspired earlier searches.

After the earthquake, in May 2008, users on the B.B.S. of Douban, a Web site devoted to books, movies and music, discussed the government's response to the earthquake. A woman who went by the handle Diebao argued that the government was using the earthquake to rally nationalist sentiment, and that, she wrote, was an exploitation of the tragedy. Netizens challenged Diebao's arguments, saying that it was only right for China to speak in one voice after such a catastrophe. These were heady days, and the people who disagreed with Diebao weren't content to leave it at that. In Guangzhou, the capital of Guangdong, Feng Junhua, a 25-year-old man who on the Internet goes by the handle Hval, was getting worried. Feng spent a lot of time on Douban, and, he told me later, he saw where the disagreement with Diebao was going—the righteous massing against the dissenter. He e-mailed Diebao, who lived in Sichuan Province, to warn her of the danger and urge her to stop fighting with the other Netizens. "I found out that the other people were going to threaten her with the human-flesh search engine," he told me. "She wrote back to me, saying she wanted to talk them out of it."

The group started to dig through everything Diebao had written on the Internet, desperate to find more reasons to attack her. They found what they were looking for, a stream-of-consciousness blog entry Diebao posted right after the earthquake hit: "I felt really excited when the earthquake hit. I know this experience might happen once in a lifetime. When I watched the news at my aunt's place, I found out that it caused five people to die. I feel so good, but that's not enough. I think more people should die." Diebao wrote this right after the earthquake struck her city, possibly while she was still in shock and before she knew the extent of the damage.

The group tried to use this post to initiate a human-flesh search against Diebao. At first it didn't succeed—no one responded to the calls for a search. (There are hundreds, maybe thousands of attempts each week for all kinds of human-flesh searches, the vast majority of which do not amount to much.) Finally they figured out a way to make their post "sparkle," as they say in Chinese, titling it, "She Said the Quake Was Not Strong Enough" and writing, of Diebao: "We cannot bear that an adult in such hard times didn't feel ashamed for not being able to help but instead was saying nonsense, with little respect for other people's lives. She should not be called a human. We think we have to give her a lesson. We hereby call for a human-flesh search on her!"

This time it took hold. A user named Little Dumpling joined the pile-on, writing: "Earthquake, someone is calling you. Please move your epicenter right below [Diebao's] computer desk." Juana0906 asked: "How could she be so coldblooded? Her statement did greater harm to the victims than the earthquake." Then from Expecting Bull Market, the obligatory refrain in almost every human-flesh search, "Is she a human?"

Feng, the user who tried to warn Diebao of the impending search, became angry that so many people were going after Diebao. "I cannot stand seeing the strong beating the weak," he told me. "I thought I should protect the right of free speech. She can say anything she wants. I think that she just didn't think before she spoke." But the searchers managed to rally users against Diebao. "Her school read a lot of aggressive comments on the Internet and got pressure from Netizens asking them to kick out this girl," Feng told me. Shortly after the human-flesh search began, Diebao was expelled from her university. "The school announced that it was for her own safety, to protect her," Feng says.

Feng decided to get revenge on the human-flesh searchers. He and a few other users started a human-flesh search of their own, patiently matching back the anonymous ID's of the people who organized against Diebao to similar-sounding names on school bulletin boards, auction sites and help-wanted ads. Eventually he assembled a list of the real identities of Diebao's persecutors. "When we got the information, we had to think about what we should do with it," Feng says. "Should we use it to attack the group?"

Feng stopped and thought about what he was about to do. "When we tried to fight evil, we found ourselves becoming evil," he says. He abandoned the human-flesh search and destroyed all the information he had uncovered.

Critical Thinking

1. Explain "iron rice bowls"?

2. How is the human-flesh search engine activated in other countries besides China?

3. How did the human-flesh search engine derive its momentum?

Create Central

www.mhhe.com/createcentral

Internet References

What Is a 'Human Flesh Search,' and How Is It Changing China?
www.theatlantic.com/international/archive/2012/10/what-is-a-human-flesh-search-and-how-is-it-changing-china/263258/

Online Vigilante Justice in China: China's Cyberposse
www.economist.com/blogs/banyan/2010/03/online_vigilante_justice_china

The Dawn of the Cyber Posse
www.zdnet.com/the-dawn-of-the-cyber-posse-1339338618/

Behind the Curtain | An Insider's Guide to US-China Relations
http://levinehank.wordpress.com/

Cyber Security: The New Arms Race for a New Front Line
www.csmonitor.com/USA/Military/2013/0915/Cyber-security-The-new-arms-race-for-a-new-front-line

Tom Downey is a freelance documentary producer, writer for *The New York Times* and global, major publications, including a dominant author on major issues of the twentieth and twenty-first centuries.

Article

Prepared by: Caroline Shaffer Westerhof,
California National University for Advanced Studies

The Protesters and the Public

Putinism Under Siege

Denis Volkov

Learning Outcomes

After reading this article, you will be able to:

- Explain how citizens' demands in Russia were handled by a government that has been defined by top-down political control.

- Define the handling of Putin's slogan and its importance in 2011: "Stability and Order."

- Explain the social mobilization movement in Russia.

The mass protests that shook Russia in December 2011 and March 2012 (with more in May) caught both domestic and international observers by surprise. Yet there were warning signs, including internal conflict in Russia's political system and growing civic activism.

Since the global economic crisis began to hit Russia in 2008, Russians have had a growing sense of uncertainty about the future, coupled with a feeling that the country is moving in the wrong direction. Indicators of public optimism have declined, as has approval for Vladimir Putin, Dmitri Medvedev, and their ruling United Russia party.[1]

This mood of uncertainty and vulnerability has touched all socioeconomic groups, including those living in comparatively prosperous regions such as Moscow. Russians universally lament the arbitrariness of government and its security agencies, the inability to protect one's rights, and the impossibility of directly impacting the broader state of affairs in the country. For Russia's "privileged minority," the confluence of material privilege with political impotence and defenselessness is highly irritating.

Isolated protests have occurred in recent years, and independent civic initiatives including protest committees, labor unions, and ecological organizations have appeared, but the participants form only a tiny percentage of the total population. Inevitably, these groups have run into the corrupt practices of Russia's government elite and business interests, and have become politicized in the process. This increased public activism has naturally led to conflict, which is compounded by the inability of citizens to address Russia's systemic corruption through legislative or judicial means.

Open conflict has increasingly become a regular feature of Russia's political system. The system of top-down control favored by Putin's regime is designed to block rather than ease systemic change. Authorities tend to ignore problems until citizens' frustrations spill over into (not necessarily peaceful) protest, at which point officials adopt some mixture of repression plus halfhearted measures to redress grievances, hoping that unrest will subside and the public mood will improve. Thus protest is a given, even if saying exactly where, when, and how the next one will break out is difficult in a partly closed society such as Russia's, where civic problems and social stresses are not openly discussed.

In December 2011, civic mobilization took place in two phases: first, in the form of a protest vote during the December State Duma elections, and second, during the post-election street protests in Moscow and in Russia's larger regional capitals. The number of participants far exceeded past opposition protests, bringing hundreds of thousands of Russians out into the street for the first time in several years.

Although any number of factors fed the protest vote during the State Duma elections, prominent irritants included the September 2011 maneuver by which Medvedev ceded the United Russia presidential nomination to Putin, as well as the fraud and abuses of power which characterized that party's conduct of the parliamentary campaign. All this happened, moreover, against a backdrop of anxiety and uncertainty caused by the global economic crisis.

The fraud hardly came as a surprise. Civic groups in major urban areas made known their dissatisfaction with both the campaign environment and the election results. Their complaints reached the general public and shaped public discussion in the weeks following the election. For those who united around the election-monitoring organizations GOLOS and Citizen Observer, and who followed Russia's independent press—which gathered information from thousands of activists on election day—the arbitrary repression that the government carried out was unacceptable. Herein lies the primary difference between Russia's civil society and the "patient majority." Civil society will publicly and repeatedly defend itself and its positions, thus defining the civic nature of the

2011 and 2012 protests. Going forward, the difficulties in reconciling the interests of these disparate groups may intensify. Studying the causes of instability in developing countries for a book first published in 1968, Samuel P. Huntington noted that during the modernization process "all groups, old as well as new, traditional as well as modern, become increasingly aware of themselves as groups and of their interests and claims in relation to other groups."[2]

The Demographics of Protest

The Levada Center's public-opinion polls allow us to examine the protests at their peak.[3] Those who witnessed the initial December 2011 protests in Moscow noted the preponderance of youth in attendance, as well as their mobility and aptitude for using online social networks to aid in organization and recruiting. Quickly, however, the demographics of the protests began to broaden, incorporating people of all ages. By February 2012, participants in the 18-to-24 age bracket were accounting for just a fifth of all participants, roughly the same number as those aged 55 and older. Most protesters were middle-aged. Thus, what began as a youth protest did not stay that way.

A majority of those participating in the protests identified themselves as "democrats" or "liberals" (between 60 and 70 percent). Practically all participants expressed dissatisfaction with Putin. The principal motivations of those participating included "dissatisfaction with the current situation in Russia" (73 percent), "indignation over electoral fraud" (73 percent), "dissatisfaction that key decisions were being made by politicians without citizen input" (52 percent), and disillusionment with President Medvedev's promises of modernization (42 percent). Few expressed solidarity with opposition parties (15 percent) or individual protest organizers (13 percent).

Protest participants differed from the general population in more than just their political sympathies. They were atypical of Russians in general, and even of Moscow residents. About 80 percent had at least some post-secondary education; only 30 percent of all Russians can claim that much schooling. Almost two-thirds were male, while Russia's general population is mostly female. As key sources of information, protesters cited the Internet (70 percent), radio (about 45 percent), friends and acquaintances (about 30 percent), television (17 to 18 percent), and newspapers (15 to 18 percent). By contrast, 81 percent of Russians in general receive the bulk of their news from television, while just 13 percent read news online. Finally, around 70 percent of protesters reported themselves as relatively well off while only half of all Muscovites and a quarter of all Russians did so.

The Levada Center's polls captured the key differences between the political demands of the protesters and those of the Russian public in general. For example, 97 percent of protesters called for the removal of Vladimir Churov, the head of Russia's Central Election Commission, while just 39 percent of Russians felt similarly. Almost 85 percent of protesters called for the release of political prisoners; only 35 percent of Russians shared a similar sentiment. Ninety-five percent of protesters called for new parliamentary elections; only 29 percent of Russians agreed. Eighty-nine percent of protesters liked the slogan "Not one vote for Vladimir Putin!"; only 24 percent of Russians agreed.

The gap between Russia's privileged, protest-friendly minority and its patient majority was clearly evident during and after the elections. The bulk of Russia's people live in relative poverty away from major cities, get much of their income from the state in the form of pensions, and rely on state-run television for news. Among this portion of the populace, there is widespread passivity and a Soviet-holdover tendency to regard repressive government as normal. Most of the changes that these Russians have lived through have only made things worse for them. In surveys, the public says it mainly believes that people come to pro-Putin rallies in order to oppose "dangerous ongoing changes in the nation."

The majority, fearing change, meant to vote for the devil it knew. Given this intention, and given a political scene deliberately stripped of alternatives by official bans on certain parties, by state control of the major television channels, and by systematic regime efforts to discredit opponents, it is small wonder that the voting's outcome seemed predetermined.

Yet it must be said that the active minority has been sadly inactive when it comes to bridging the gap between itself and the passive majority. The opposition parties that appeared in the 1990s ignored average Russians and consisted of members of the ranks of the old Soviet elite. Nor did the Russian public, having few political skills and beset by a sea of changes, demand involvement.

To the extent that various social groups in Russia are gradually beginning to identify their own political interests and to attempt to protect them when possible, existing parties may become impediments to the development of grassroots political change as long as they remain elite networks that exclude these new civic initiatives.

Today, more than half of Russians think that a political opposition is needed. Moreover, approximately 25 to 30 percent affirm that they would not mind seeing opposition figures such as Grigory Yavlinsky, Vladimir Ryzhkov, Garry Kasparov, Mikhail Kasyanov, and Eduard Limonov in parliament. Despite this support, Russians have consistently refused to vote for opposition politicians or their parties. In the eyes of Russian voters, liberal parties and their leaders who took part in the organization of the 2011 and 2012 protests do not represent a sufficiently broad cross-section of Russian society. Thus in mid-2011, just 5 percent of Russians believed that the liberal-democratic party Yabloko represented the interests of the whole population. By comparison, polling data for United Russia shows that roughly 20 percent of the general population feels that this party of the Putin regime represents the collective interest. In the eyes of a huge 74 percent majority, moreover, United Russia is the only real political power in the country—no other party comes close. The Levada Center's polling data tend to reinforce the common criticism of the opposition parties as groups that "just talk and do nothing."

It is noteworthy that the general public, in surveys, more than adequately identified the protesters' motives. Many agreed that the protesters were motivated by their discontent with the current political system (37 percent), their indignation with electoral fraud (25 percent), and the ruling party's refusal to consider their opinions (22 percent). Meanwhile, the active minority, or what some observers call Russia's "liberal society," does not seem to have reciprocated. Its members still show little or no sign that they understand the motives of the majority that fears change. Until the protest movement learns to take the majority's concerns seriously and to address them with concrete stands on real issues, it will remain in minority status and find its aspirations harder to achieve than they might otherwise be.

The Putin regime, meanwhile, faces grave troubles of its own. In order to match the protests, it has spurred countermobilizations and staged mass demonstrations by its own supporters. But since the regime, as Lev Gudkov has pointed out, leans so heavily on the suppression of independent political activities of any kind,[4] *any* mobilization is risky for it and threatens to undermine its grip on power. By drawing Russians into politics, the regime may be writing its own death warrant.

The rise of protest and the emancipation of social groups currently being witnessed in Russia are byproducts of the absence of any real mechanisms for aggregating public preferences: This absence leaves a vacuum into which public outrage flows. Yet outrage alone may not be enough to force constructive change toward more systematically inclusive (that is, more democratic) forms of decision making. In Russia, the links between wealth and government are such that the short-term preservation of wealth and power always trumps the need for systemic adaptation. We could be witnessing a case of what Shmuel Eisenstadt called "modernization breakdown."

Civic Choices

The Levada Center's polling shows that civic organizations working on concrete social issues are far more popular than opposition political parties or abstract political movements. Assisting children, protecting the greater Moscow area's Khimki Forest from highway development, and even battling with Kremlin officials over the flashing blue lights that they use to drive recklessly and with impunity around the capital all attract higher support than opposition parties or movements backing more abstract causes.

Václav Havel called such bottom-up civic activities "parallel structures," and noted how they address "the vital needs of specific people."[5] Spontaneously arising around specific problems, these structures tend to be open, self-governing, and inclined to raise their own funds. For a time, they are able to exist "alongside" the political system or at least on its edges. Politicization always beckons, however, and in Russia can take place quickly. This may not be a bad thing, since civic leaders who become active in politics may be key to the reform

and humanization (in Havel's sense) of Russian politics. Those representing the interests of specific groups must seek to draw the broadest possible public support, with a focus on finding new partners.

To its credit, the Russian opposition was able to quickly tie the problem of electoral fraud to the current structure of the Russian political system, and speedily organized large protest rallies in response. Yet more needs to be done. The interests of different social groups need to be articulated and aggregated.

The protests of 2011 and 2012 have shown that significant numbers of Russian citizens are not content to be indifferent. Perhaps the mass protests finally forced many Russians to think about their country's political system and the possibility of taking part in politics. Many Muscovites, including some under the age of 25, decided to participate in the Moscow municipal elections, and they helped to elect independent candidates to slightly more than a fourth of the seats in Moscow's municipal assemblies. Among these newly elected deputies are a number of well-known civic activists, who are already attempting to unite independent deputies and coordinate their efforts.

Thanks to the protests, new civic activists have become prominent beyond Moscow. The upcoming mayoral elections in Russia's larger cities and the 2014 Moscow City Duma elections will show if the current level of civic activism can be maintained and if it can actually affect the course of Russian politics. It remains to be seen how the direct election of governors and the new political-parties law will affect the situation.

If there are more mass protests ahead, the form they take and their ability to impact established parties and the state will depend on the internal organization of Russia's civic sphere. If the disparate groups and individuals who first linked up during the 2011 and 2012 protests prove able to maintain and develop their work together, the prospects for democratic change in Russia will greatly improve.

Notes

1. Except where noted otherwise, the results presented throughout this paper come from nationwide public-opinion polls conducted by the Moscow-based Levada Center with a sample size of N = 1,600 respondents ages 18 and older, and a statistical error of 3.4 percent. The results of the Levada Center's polls are available at www.levada.ru.

2. Samuel P. Huntington, *Political Order in Changing Societies* (New Haven: Yale University Press, 2006), 37.

3. Based on two Levada Center polls: 1) poll carried out by the Committee for Fair Elections of participants in the 24 December 2011 protest on Sakharova Prospekt in Moscow (791 respondents, 4.8 percent margin of error), www.levada .ru/26-12-2011/opros-na-prospekte-sakharova-24-dekkabrya; 2) poll carried out on behalf of *Novaya Gazeta* of participants at the 4 February 2012 Yakimanka Street and Bolotnaya Square demonstrations in Moscow (1,346 respondents,

5.2 percent margin of error), www.levada.ru/13-02-2012/opros-na-mitinge-4-fevralya.

4. Lev Gudkov, "The Nature of 'Putinism,'" *Russian Public Opinion Herald*, no. 3, 2009, 11.

5. Havel borrowed this concept of "parallel structures" from Václav Benda. See Havel's discussion of it in his 1978 essay "The Power of the Powerless," section XVIII, available at http://vaclavhavel.cz/showtrans.php?cat5clanky&val572_aj_clanky.html&typ5HTML.

Critical Thinking

1. How does social mobilization arise in a tightly controlled political system?

2. How can such protests be developed "from the bottom-up"?

3. What has the Law of Treason, passed in 2012, accomplished to date?

Create Central

www.mhhe.com/createcentral

Internet References

After a Year of Protest, a Different Russia Beckons
http://articles.washingtonpost.com/2012-12-04/world/35624360_1_anti-putin-boris-dubin-levada-center

New Report: The Protest Movement in Russia 2011 – 2012
http://hro.rightsinrussia.info/archive/right-of-assembly-1/levada/report

Opposition Figures Walk Out of Putin's Protest Fines Debate
http://en.ria.ru/russia/20120524/173651905.html

Critics Say New Russia Treason Law Is 'Broad' and 'Dangerous'
www.foxnews.com/world/2012/11/14/controversial-treason-law-takes-effect-in-russia-despite-putin-promise-to/

Accountable Only to Putin, Russia's Top Cop Sets Sights on Protest Movement
www.foxnews.com/world/2013/03/28/accountable-only-to-vladimir-putin-russia-top-cop-sets-sights-on-protest/

DENIS VOLKOV is a researcher at the Yuri Levada Center, an independent Moscow-based organization devoted to the analysis of Russian public life. He comments frequently on politics in the Russian media and studies youth political engagement, the sources and limits of democratization, and the role of digital media in social and political change. This essay was translated from the Russian by Patrick Walsh.

Article

Prepared by: Caroline Shaffer Westerhof,
California National University for Advanced Studies

United Arab Emirates (UAE)—Government and Economy

EXPAT FOCUS

Learning Outcomes

After reading this article, you will be able to:

- Explain the economic dimensions of the United Arab Emirates as one of the fastest growing economies in the world.
- Explain Dubai's "Media Free Zone."
- Understand how and when the United Arab Emirates became a constitutional federation of seven emirates.

Government
The Supreme Council

Budgets and fiscal matters, international agreements and treaties, federal laws and decrees are dealt with by the Supreme Council. The Supreme Council is made up of the ruler of each of the individual emirates and it is from here the presidential elections are decided. The President and Vice-President both hold office for a term of five years after which time the Supreme Council reaffirms the existing posts or elects new presidents.

Council of Ministers

The Council of Ministers is headed by the Prime Minister and is the executive authority for the Federation. The 22 members manage all the foreign and internal affairs of the federation under the constitutional and federal laws.

The Federal National Council

Taking both a supervisory and legislative role the FNC is a member of the Arab Parliamentary Union and the International Parliamentary Union. Until recently the number of members an emirate had on the FNC were based on the size and population of the emirate and chosen by its ruler. The new election system that was put in place in 2006 is slightly more complex but has resulted in the election of a woman, for the first time ever, to the FNC. To be elected to the FNC members have to be literate, at least 25 years old and citizens of the emirate they represent.

The Federal Judiciary

The Supreme Court and the Courts of First Instance are included in the Federal Judiciary. The president and five judges of the Federal Judiciary are chosen by the Supreme Council of Rulers and decide if federal laws are constitutional. They mediate between emirates to solve problems and if any senior officials or cabinet ministers are involved in disputes they will be tried by the Federal Judiciary.

Local Governments

The seven emirates each have their own local government according to their size and population and all follow a general pattern of departments and municipalities. The Constitution lays down the rules between the federal and local governments but this is changing over time to meet the needs of this expanding country. Each emirate has considerable powers and holds control over its own revenues and mineral rights, particularly where oil is concerned.

Federal Government

The list of responsibilities of the federal government is very long indeed. It includes the following; extradition of criminals and delimitation of territorial waters, air traffic control, public health, communication services, currency, education, immigration and nationality issues as well as foreign affairs and security and defence.

Foreign Policy

The UAE believe that it is better not to interfere in the affairs of other countries but if necessary they will help towards finding peaceful solutions with the help of organisations such as the United Nations. As a country with a stable economy the UAE are very keen on helping with disasters around the world and have the Red Crescent Society, The Zayed Foundation and the Abu Dhabi Fund for Development. Many billions of dirhams are allocated as loans and grants to help others and at the last count 52 countries had received aid from the UAE.

The President

Having learned "the need for patience and prudence in all things" from his late father, HH Sheikh Khalifa bin Zayed Al Nahyan, Ruler of Abu Dhabi was elected in November 1971.

Sheikh Khalifa is a firm believer in re-structuring, not just in governmental terms but in the way his people help their own country and see their duties towards society.

Since taking up office Sheikh Khalifa has travelled extensively throughout the country and in particular the Northern Emirates. Here he has authorised the building of projects relating to social services, education and housing.

As the ruler of Abu Dhabi as well as the UAE president Sheikh Khalifa has made major changes to his own local government. A lot of time and money has been invested in his community to improve services and efficiency.

Sheikh Khalifa is also a member of the GCC, the Gulf Corporation Council and has exchanged visits with other leaders many times. He is firm believer that the GCC will enjoy success and achievement if the leaders set a good example.

Economy

The booming oil industry in the UAE has been attracting expats from all over the world for a number of years now and there are many job opportunities, not just with oil, but in banking, real estate or tourism. Many international companies have headquarters here and the income per head is one of the highest in the world.

Dubai is the most popular destination for expats with its free trading zone and international atmosphere. Outside of Dubai it is harder to get a foot in the door for companies as the law states a business must be at least 51% locally owned. The UAE is a young modern country with a strong economy and the expats and companies investing their time and money here can reap the rewards.

The UAE central bank projected 4% growth in 2012 and 2013 and despite the downturn of the economy globally the UAE is proving to be remarkably resilient.

Being the world's seventh largest oil producer probably helps contribute to this as well a huge increase in tourism, transport and trade. The emirates have solidarity among themselves and this with the restructuring of debts from high profile companies have all played a part in keeping the UAE stable.

The UAE is still considered to be one of the most politically secure and stable countries in the region and the troubles in the Middle East and North Africa have little or no impact, therefore making it an ideal place for investment and tourism.

Critical Thinking

1. Does an open economy equate to a democratic society?
2. Why does the United Arab Emirates Gulf intervention contrast sharply with Obama's Administration in responding to Egypt's military takeover?
3. Although within the United Arab Emirates there is a "Media Free Zone," how effective is the government ownership of radio and television?

Create Central

www.mhhe.com/createcentral

Internet References

United Arab Emirates - Central Intelligence Agency
www.cia.gov/library/publications/the-world-factbook/geos/ae.html

United Arab Emirates | World News | *The Guardian*
www.theguardian.com/world/united-arab-emirates

BBC News—United Arab Emirates profile—Overview
www.bbc.co.uk/news/world-middle-east-14703998

United Arab Emirates (UAE)—Expat Groups
www.expatfocus.com/expatriate-uae

UAE News and Information—United Arab Emirates
www.uaeinteract.com/

UAE History
www.sheikhmohammed.com/vgn-ext-templating/v/index.jsp?vgnextoid=15e504ee11a11310VgnVCM1000004d64a8c0RCRD

Article   Prepared by: Caroline Shaffer Westerhof,
                                    California National University for Advanced Studies

Foreign Talent and the Thriving Malaysian Economy

EXPAT FOCUS

Learning Outcomes

After reading this article, you will be able to:

- Understand why business leaders and investors are crucial to the health of Malaysia's economy and society.

- Understand why Coca-Cola has invested more than one billion Ringgit in Malaysia.

- Understand why the New Economic Model is important to the infrastructure of Malaysia.

D
ue to strong governance, the Malaysian economy has continued to thrive and grow despite global economic downturns in the rest of the Asian world. Expats are drawn to this success, viewing the economic performance of the country as a good indication of future growth and prosperity. Many credit the recent economic good fortune to a flexible form of governance that has been able to overcome problems that have beset other countries. As a successful manufacturing hub of Asia, Malaysia has more than ever before begun to appeal to expats from areas such as Europe, North America and Australia. By securing foreign talent, Malaysia's economy has expanded further, reaping beneficial foreign investment as well.

Slow and Steady Wins the Race

Malaysia's economy has been steadily increasing since the 1980s. While other countries were seeking instantaneous prosperity, the methods deployed for Malaysian growth shifted the country gradually from agriculture to industry. This transition radically changed the economy and gave the country a new, urban feel. Expanding into new areas over the years such as science, tourism and commerce, Malaysia recognizes the need for expats in order to continue the economic growth that it has enjoyed over recent years. For this reason, locals are extremely friendly and helpful to expats who choose to relocate here.

Implications of Economic Growth for Expats

The investment in the infrastructure and industries of Malaysia has driven the expat population up, continuing growth and development. The low cost of living and affordable, high quality medical facilities are just some of the financial benefits that expats can expect should they move to Malaysia. The large-scale movement of expats to the country has driven up property values and encouraged further growth and building. Thus, as much as expats are reaping the benefits of Malaysia's successful economy, they are also a catalyst for further growth and development.

A larger implication of Malaysian economic success is the establishment of an Expatriate Services Division (ESD). This is meant to encourage expats and their families to relocate to Malaysia to continue fueling the growth that cannot be sustained on local workers and existing expat workers alone. This program includes simpler visa regulations for highly skilled applicants. The idea is to encourage foreign talent by connecting them to local workers. By offering a more relaxed approach for workers willing and wanting to contribute, Malaysia is ensuring the further development of their society. This should be extremely appealing to expats seeking long-term employment and residence in this country.

In addition to the ESD program, the government has also revamped and restarted the Residence Pass-Talent (RP-T) work permit. This allows expats and their families to remain in the country for 10 years. Malaysian's Prime Minister views this as just part of the effort to integrate foreign and local people, adding to the economic dynamism that the country is coming to be known for.

Expat Contributions to the Malaysian Economy

Although the Malaysian economy is better than it has ever been, there is still room for improvement. This is a consideration that holds even greater value for expats in comparison to locals. Many experts state that there is still a need to speed up the country's progression towards greater productivity and efficiency. Incorporating higher quality technology can help with this as well. Expats are valuable insofar as they are able to help speed up this process, aiding the country and helping themselves through securing work. With so many expats seeking work in technology-related fields, the Malaysian economy is almost certain to continue improving over time. This offers an attractive option to expats and their families when considering a stable, profitable place in which to live.

The thriving economy of Malaysia is a system of mutual reciprocity. Expats seeking a low cost of living that still provides a high standard of life need to look no further than this Asian destination. In a country that desperately needs foreign talent to continue growth at a fast rate, expats are more likely to secure high-earning jobs in Malaysia. Additionally, the growing economy holds many positive benefits for expats, such as affordable healthcare. For whatever reason an expat may decide to move, they should definitely consider Malaysia as a new and upcoming location fit for them and their family.

Critical Thinking

1. How does Malaysia's education system improve Malaysia's workforce of the future?

2. How will the level of poverty in Malaysia change in the 21st century?

3. How is Malaysia embracing a leadership role in green technology?

Create Central

www.mhhe.com/createcentral

Internet References

The New Economic Model
hsudarren.files.wordpress.com/2010/03/the-new-economic-model.doc

Greater Kuala Lumpur
www.investkl.gov.my/upload/Greater%20Kuala%20Lumpur%20-%20A%20Regional%20Hub%20For%20Business,%20Innovation%20and%20Talent%20(simplified%20version).pdf

Singapore Economy | *Economy Watch*
www.economywatch.com/world_economy/singapore/?page=full

Chapter 2 — TalentCorp Malaysia
www.talentcorp.com.my/wp-content/themes/agenda/TC_Chapter2.pdf

What Does the New Economy Mean to Malaysian Tellers?
www.justlabour.yorku.ca/volume19/pdfs/03_khoo_press.pdf

Article   Prepared by: Caroline Shaffer Westerhof,
                                           California National University for Advanced Studies

The Technocrats and Tahrir

JAMES TRAUB

Learning Outcomes

After reading this article, you will be able to:

- Understand why the Egyptian government received a cash infusion from Saudi Arabia, the UAE, and Kuwait after Morsi was toppled.

- Understand why economic reform is so complicated in Egypt.

- Understand why Morsi was toppled, even though it was known that his election was won through the democratic process.

As part of my ongoing effort to find something positive to say at a moment when everything in the Middle East is objectively dreadful, I would like to introduce some of the members of the new Egyptian government: Prime Minister Hazem el-Beblawi, former director of Egypt's Export Development bank; Minister of Finance Ahmed Galal, former World Bank official and think tank scholar; deputy prime minister Ziad Bahaa el-Din, former head of Egypt's investment authority. The modern Arab world has probably never seen a governing apparatus as well-educated and professionally competent as this.

So what? No government erected on the ruins of Mohamed Morsi's Islamist regime will be deemed legitimate by the millions of Egyptians who believe that Morsy was toppled by a coup. Absent such legitimacy, no government can make its policies stick, however wise. Neither the military leaders who overthrew Morsy nor the secular forces who have now taken the reins show any recognition that a democratic state must include the millions of people who shared Morsy's Islamist vision. So who cares how many degrees and doctorates the new technocrats have?

I did say I was trying to be optimistic; hear me out. First of all, the new government has something that its predecessor did not have: $12 billion from Saudi Arabia, the UAE and Kuwait, who delivered a mountain of cash (and promises of oil) as a reward to Egypt for getting rid of the Muslim Brotherhood. This lavish gift will sow yet more bitterness among the Brothers, but it also averts a crisis that has been looming ever since Egypt's foreign currency reserves began dwindling towards zero. Egypt will not default on its foreign debt and will not suffer a run on

its currency—either of which would wreak havoc on the economy and make foreign investors head for the hills.

The cash infusion also ends, for the moment, Egypt's exhausting stand-off with the International Monetary Fund. The Morsy government, desperate for cash, had tried, and failed, to carry out the painful fiscal reforms the fund had demanded in exchange for a $4.8 billion loan. This ongoing melodrama had the effect of shrinking a very complicated discussion about economic reform into the very narrow confines of the IMF's terms. Ahmed Galal, the new finance minister, has said that while an IMF loan is "part of the solution" for Egypt—it would be a powerful signal for foreign investors—it can be laid aside for now. This seems, on balance, like a good thing.

Whatever ordinary Egyptians think of the new rulers, investors are paying close attention. Angus Blair, the head of Signet LLC, a Cairo-based research and investment firm, says that the mere appointment of the new team has begun to change the prevailing mood among both foreign and domestic investors. Blair points out that Egypt is a "cash-rich society" primed with $18 billion a year in remittances from abroad, and with little private debt. He argues that if the government demonstrates a willingness to take tough measures, Egypt can quickly return to the 6 percent growth it enjoyed from 2006–2009. Blair expects that, by the end of this month, the government will propose new policies—including, he hopes, paring the bureaucracy, moving against corruption, and reducing the budget deficit.

The problem is that any economic measures which inflict substantial pain require a high degree of social consensus, at least in non-autocratic states. The Islamist government quickly frittered away its store of post-revolutionary goodwill, so that when Morsy tried to comply with IMF demands by imposing a sales tax on consumer goods, furious demonstrations forced him to retreat just eight hours after the policy was announced. Egypt is now running an utterly unsustainable budget deficit equal to about 15 percent of gross domestic product. The el-Beblawi government will have to increase revenues and cut costs. That means raising taxes on the rich—Egypt's rates top out at 25 percent—and actually collecting tax revenue, which will be difficult enough. But the much harder part will be reducing subsidies on food and fuel, which now consume $20 billion a year, or one quarter of its budget. And the new interim government almost by definition cannot claim the popular mandate it would need to make those decisions stick.

Hosni Mubarak, for all his dictatorial powers, never had the courage to implement longstanding plans to reduce subsidies. Morsy tried, and balked. There is a plan on the table to provide direct cash payments to the poor to offset the loss of the fuel subsidy (no one is even talking about phasing out food-price supports), and to distribute smart-cards so that recipients can make direct purchases at stores and gas stations, cutting out the middle-men who take their own cut and often steal or divert oil and gas. It's the cutting-edge solution currently under consideration in Jordan, India, and elsewhere. And Egypt now has the money to fund such a program. But it still won't work absent "a major PR campaign," as Mohsin Khan, a former IMF director for Egypt, puts it. And that, he suspects, will be beyond the reach of the interim government, which is operating without a parliament, and so would have to issue rules by decree.

Of course technocratic solutions can't heal the vast breach which has opened up in the heart of Egyptian society. But it's also true that you can't satisfy elemental demands for social and economic justice without sound policy. And formulating policy is one thing the A-Team can do. Ashraf al-Araby, the planning minister—and a rare holdover from the Morsy government—has spoken of laying out an economic "roadmap" and making a start on the "structural reform" Egypt needs. Those reforms include changing budgetary priorities to focus on investments that enhance growth, such as infrastructure projects; pruning the vast tangle of regulations which inhibit private investment; targeting monopolistic control of sectors like telecom; and selling some grossly uncompetitive public-sector enterprises. None of the experts I spoke to even mentioned the imperative of reducing the military's giant role in the economy, presumably because they are practical people who do not tilt at windmills.

Even such sweeping changes won't touch the heart of Egypt's problem, which is the persistent failure to invest in its own people. This is no secret: The 2002 Arab Human Development Report identified low literacy rates, mediocre secondary schools and universities, a lack of intellectual creativity and openness, and above all the second-class status of women as the besetting problems of the Middle East. (Since then, Egypt and other states have made real progress on literacy rates, but little on the status of women or the quality of higher education.) With no oil wealth to fall back on, Egypt will remain locked in poverty until it can start producing citizens adapted to life in the 21st century. The current deadlock over identity and political representation only further postpones that day of reckoning.

It's yet another reason to wish for a leader that's less chauvinistic, provincial, and intolerant that the ones Egypt now seems to have.

The experts I spoke to were hardly blinded by the dazzling resumes of the new government. "Politics will trump any attempt at reform at least for a while," hazarded Alia Moubayed, senior economist for MENA at Barclay's Bank in London. "But the people who have been called to lead on economic policy management have enough credibility to devise proposals, though not implement solutions, in order to pave the way for the next elected government to drive reforms much faster and in a more coordinated fashion."

That assumes, of course, that there will be another elected government, and that it will be seen as broadly representative. If not, economic stagnation will be the least of Egypt's problems.

Critical Thinking

1. Will the present government in Egypt ever be able to implement solutions for peace? Explain.

2. Can the poor in Egypt ever be helped by offsetting the loss of the fuel subsidy? Explain.

3. Will the distribution of smart-cards be beneficial in Egypt so that recipients can make direct purchases, cutting out the middle-men? Explain.

Create Central

www.mhhe.com/createcentral

Internet References

The Rise of Egypt's Technocrats
www.salon.com/2013/07/14/the_rise_of_egypts_technocrats_partner

200K Egyptians Flood Tahrir Square Demanding Morsi Quit
forward.com/articles/179618/k-egyptians-flood-tahrir-square-dem

Riot Police Block Morsi Supporters from Marching on Tahrir Square
www.ktvu.com/videos/news/riot-police-block-mursi-supporters-from-marching/v6n6L

RealClearWorld—The Compass Blog
www.realclearworld.com/blog/egypt

JAMES TRAUB is a fellow of the Center on International Cooperation. Terms of Engagement for Foreign Policy.com runs weekly.

Unit 4

UNIT

Prepared by: Caroline Shaffer Westerhof,
California National University for Advanced Studies

The Executive: Accountability and Responsiveness at the Top

Responsiveness at the top: Accountability. How does the CEO of a nation-state, and his or her associates, balance responsiveness and accountability within the different institutions of government. How is policymaking handled? Does decision making depend on the behavior, integrity, public service of the actors? Is policymaking always effective at the top? Is it biased, depending on the actors, individually and collectively? How does their performance as institutions and in policymaking fare in the midst of the nation's political development? The institutions are the executive, the legislature, and the unelected officers of the judiciary, the military, and the bureaucracy. We address the political questions of when, why, how, and what regarding executives and their cohorts in policy and decision making.

We begin with the question, "Why executives?" The explanation may be found in theories of government, articulated by venerated political theorists such as John Locke, John Stuart Mill, Jean-Jacques Rousseau, and the framers of the U.S. Constitution: to achieve efficient and efficacious policymaking. Even if a community is small enough to allow everyone to partake in policymaking and implementation, it is inefficient to do so. Think about a community the size of a country and it becomes clear that it is prohibitive to have everyone partake in policymaking. Thus, citizens choose a representative government to make those policies on their behalf. The paradox is that the more diverse the society, the larger and more diverse the representative government becomes. That, in turn, progressively works against efficient policymaking. On the other hand, in a democratic, political system it makes for more people participating in the process.

CEOs and executives in political system tie the various units of the organization together, which can ease the burden of disagreement as well as enhance such, as we saw in October 2013 in the United States "budget shutdown." Depending on the political system, power, tyranny, decision making, consensus, and accommodation are all part of the process.

We witness how Hungary's former Prime Minister and the ruling Fidesz Party obtained a strong majority in the legislature and proceeded to rewrite the constitution; thus the new constitution redefined that states' institutional structures. Among the controls on the executive that are compromised is the significant restriction of the Constitutional Court's review of laws, giving the executive strong and institutionalizing power well into the future.

What does this mean? On the one hand, the political damage cannot be ignored when (1) the checks and balances to the executive are compromised or (2) checks fail to work. In Chile, the middle-class is disabusing the government of the notion that economic achievements will keep the citizenry happy and the government in office. Instead, the middle-class is making demands of the government to untie historic relations with businesses—all political parties are seen to have such ties—in order to provide stronger social programs in education, the environment, and other consumer rights. Likewise, in Singapore—where the ruling party has been in political power since 1969—citizens are clamoring for new constitutional counterweights to the authority of the government that may turn a largely ceremonial presidential position into one with more constitutional authority. As a supporter for one of the presidential candidates points out, "We are the people. Listen to us."

The lessons from Chile and Singapore are particularly instructive for other transitioning or less-democratic countries, such as Russia and China. In both countries, there is an adherence to the "letter" of democratic development but not its spirit. Until recently, it appeared that strong policy performance—particularly in terms of the economy—is a sufficient mark of executive excellence and enough to keep the executive in office. However, increasingly, it is clear that policy performance alone is not enough; as a country transitions economically, its people also transition politically. Given that economic performance is predictably unpredictable, political leaders have to do more to stay in office: They have to embrace and promote "social diversity" rather than choke it in order to demonstrate to the voters that they are responsive and accountable.

It becomes apparent that political choice is just that: "Conflict Is a Choice, Not a Necessity." When one recognizes the reality of such policy thought processes one recognizes that such is a reality determination, if one truly wishes to seek a global peace for both the West and the East. It is important, that for some executives, it becomes a power and character issue. Can leaders be blinded by cronyism, corruption, moral manipulation, and divisive policies? If they are, a horrendous backlash can occur by other nation-states. Yet we are witnessing the political networking of Chinese economic leaders in meetings with members of the Washington, D.C. political establishment. Thus, it is possible to avoid conflict, as we anticipate that the economic playing field will be leveled because of the decisions of particular senior management in diverse political systems.

Further, how do we define executive leadership in a dictatorial nation? Does one person control the entire arena, whether it be public policy, execution of individuals, or other issues? Is the Supreme Leader truly such? How do world leaders confront such individuals and situations? Is conflict a choice or a necessity? Who determines?

Prepared by: Caroline Shaffer Westerhof,
California National University for Advanced Studies

Article

The Future of U.S.-Chinese Relations

Conflict Is a Choice, Not a Necessity

HENRY A. KISSINGER

Learning Outcomes

After reading this article, you will be able to:

- Understand how the United States can be friendly with a country that sells nuclear weapons to some of our deep-seated antagonists.

- Understand the economy of China and why some 500,000 Americans are dependent upon their jobs in China.

- Understand the cultural and economic reasons why United States and China must have a postive relationship.

Dealing with the New China

(A) reason for Chinese restraint in at least the medium term is the domestic adaptation the country faces. The gap in Chinese society between the largely developed coastal regions and the undeveloped western regions has made Hu's objective of a "harmonious society" both compelling and elusive. Cultural changes compound the challenge. The next decades will witness, for the first time, the full impact of one-child families on adult Chinese society. This is bound to modify cultural patterns in a society in which large families have traditionally taken care of the aged and the handicapped. When four grandparents compete for the attention of one child and invest him with the aspirations heretofore spread across many offspring, a new pattern of insistent achievement and vast, perhaps unfulfillable, expectations may arise.

All these developments will further complicate the challenges of China's governmental transition starting in 2012, in which the presidency; the vice-presidency; the considerable majority of the positions in China's Politburo, State Council, and Central Military Commission; and thousands of other key national and provincial posts will be staffed with new appointees. The new leadership group will consist, for the most part, of members of the first Chinese generation in a century and a half to have lived all their lives in a country at peace. Its primary challenge will be finding a way to deal with a society revolutionized by changing economic conditions, unprecedented and rapidly expanding technologies of communication,

a tenuous global economy, and the migration of hundreds of millions of people from China's countryside to its cities. The model of government that emerges will likely be a synthesis of modern ideas and traditional Chinese political and cultural concepts, and the quest for that synthesis will provide the ongoing drama of China's evolution.

These social and political transformations are bound to be followed with interest and hope in the United States. Direct American intervention would be neither wise nor productive. The United States will, as it should, continue to make its views known on human rights issues and individual cases. And its day-to-day conduct will express its national preference for democratic principles. But a systematic project to transform China's institutions by diplomatic pressure and economic sanctions is likely to backfire and isolate the very liberals it is intended to assist. In China, it would be interpreted by a considerable majority through the lens of nationalism, recalling earlier eras of foreign intervention.

What this situation calls for is not an abandonment of American values but a distinction between the realizable and the absolute. The U.S.-Chinese relationship should not be considered as a zero-sum game, nor can the emergence of a prosperous and powerful China be assumed in itself to be an American strategic defeat.

A cooperative approach challenges preconceptions on both sides. The United States has few precedents in its national experience of relating to a country of comparable size, self-confidence, economic achievement, and international scope and yet with such a different culture and political system. Nor does history supply China with precedents for how to relate to a fellow great power with a permanent presence in Asia, a vision of universal ideals not geared toward Chinese conceptions, and alliances with several of China's neighbors. Prior to the United States, all countries establishing such a position did so as a prelude to an attempt to dominate China.

The simplest approach to strategy is to insist on overwhelming potential adversaries with superior resources and materiel. But in the contemporary world, this is only rarely feasible. China and the United States will inevitably continue as enduring realities for each other. Neither can entrust its security to the other—no great power does, for long—and each will continue to pursue its own interests, sometimes at the relative expense of the other. But both have the responsibility to take into account the other's nightmares, and both would do well to recognize that their rhetoric, as much as their actual policies, can feed into the other's suspicions.

China's greatest strategic fear is that an outside power or powers will establish military deployments around China's periphery capable of encroaching on China's territory or meddling in its domestic institutions. When China deemed that it faced such a threat in the past, it went to war rather than risk the outcome of what it saw as gathering trends—in Korea in 1950, against India in 1962, along the northern border with the Soviet Union in 1969, and against Vietnam in 1979.

The United States' fear, sometimes only indirectly expressed, is of being pushed out of Asia by an exclusionary bloc. The United States fought a world war against Germany and Japan to prevent such an outcome and exercised some of its most forceful Cold War diplomacy under administrations of both political parties to this end against the Soviet Union. In both enterprises, it is worth noting, substantial joint U.S.-Chinese efforts were directed against the perceived threat of hegemony.

Other Asian countries will insist on their prerogatives to develop their capacities for their own national reasons, not as part of a contest between outside powers. They will not willingly consign themselves to a revived tributary order. Nor do they regard themselves as elements in an American containment policy or an American project to alter China's domestic institutions. They aspire to good relations with both China and the United States and will resist any pressure to choose between the two.

Can the fear of hegemony and the nightmare of military encirclement be reconciled? Is it possible to find a space in which both sides can achieve their ultimate objectives without militarizing their strategies? For great nations with global capabilities and divergent, even partly conflicting aspirations, what is the margin between conflict and abdication?

That China will have a major influence in the regions surrounding it is inherent in its geography, values, and history. The limits of that influence, however, will be shaped by circumstance and policy decisions. These will determine whether an inevitable quest for influence turns into a drive to negate or exclude other independent sources of power.

For nearly two generations, American strategy relied on local regional defense by American ground forces—largely to avoid the catastrophic consequences of a general nuclear war. In recent decades, congressional and public opinion have impelled an end to such commitments in Vietnam, Iraq, and Afghanistan Now, fiscal considerations further limit the range of such an approach. American strategy has been redirected from defending territory to threatening unacceptable punishment against potential aggressors. This requires forces capable of rapid intervention and global reach, but not bases ringing China's frontiers. What Washington must not do is combine a defense policy based on budgetary restraints with a diplomacy based on unlimited ideological aims.

Just as Chinese influence in surrounding countries may spur fears of dominance, so efforts to pursue traditional American national interests can be perceived as a form of military encirclement. Both sides must understand the nuances by which apparently traditional and apparently reasonable courses can evoke the deepest worries of the other. They should seek together to define the sphere in which their peaceful competition is circumscribed. If that is managed wisely, both military confrontation and domination can be avoided; if not, escalating tension is inevitable. It is the task of diplomacy to discover this space, to expand it if possible, and to prevent the relationship from being overwhelmed by tactical and domestic imperatives.

Community or Conflict

The current world order was built largely without Chinese participation, and hence China sometimes feels less bound than others by its rules. Where the order does not suit Chinese preferences, Beijing has set up alternative arrangements, such as in the separate currency channels being established with Brazil and Japan and other countries. If the pattern becomes routine and spreads into many spheres of activity, competing world orders could evolve. Absent common goals coupled with agreed rules of restraint, institutionalized rivalry is likely to escalate beyond the calculations and intentions of its advocates. In an era in which unprecedented offensive capabilities and intrusive technologies multiply, the penalties of such a course could be drastic and perhaps irrevocable.

Crisis management will not be enough to sustain a relationship so global and beset by so many differing pressures within and between both countries, which is why I have argued for the concept of a Pacific Community and expressed the hope that China and the United States can generate a sense of common purpose on at least some issues of general concern. But the goal of such a community cannot be reached if either side conceives of the enterprise as primarily a more effective way to defeat or undermine the other. Neither China nor the United States can be systematically challenged without its noticing, and if such a challenge is noted, it will be resisted. Both need to commit themselves to genuine cooperation and find a way to communicate and relate their visions to each other and to the world.

Some tentative steps in that direction have already been undertaken. For example, the United States has joined several other countries in beginning negotiations on the Trans-Pacific Partnership (TPP), a free-trade pact linking the Americas with Asia. Such an arrangement could be a step toward a Pacific Community because it would lower trade barriers among the world's most productive, dynamic, and resource-rich economies and link the two sides of the ocean in shared projects.

Obama has invited China to join the TPP. However, the terms of accession as presented by American briefers and commentators have sometimes seemed to require fundamental changes in China's domestic structure. To the extent that is the case, the TPP could be regarded in Beijing as part of a strategy to isolate China. For its part, China has put forward comparable alternative arrangements. It has negotiated a trade pact with the Association of Southeast Asian Nations and has broached a Northeast Asian trade pact with Japan and South Korea.

Important domestic political considerations are involved for all parties. But if China and the United States come to regard each other's trade-pact efforts as elements in a strategy of isolation, the Asia-Pacific region could devolve into competing adversarial power blocs. Ironically, this would be a particular challenge if China meets frequent American calls to shift from an export-led to a consumption-driven economy, as its most recent five-year plan contemplates. Such a development could reduce China's stake in the United States as an export market even as it encourages other Asian countries to further orient their economies toward China.

The key decision facing both Beijing and Washington is whether to move toward a genuine effort at cooperation or fall into a new version of historic patterns of international rivalry. Both countries have adopted the rhetoric of community. They have even established a high-level forum for it, the Strategic and Economic Dialogue, which meets twice a year. It has been productive on immediate issues, but it is still in the foothills of its ultimate assignment to produce a truly global economic and political order. And if a global order does not emerge in the economic field, barriers to progress on more emotional and less positive-sum issues, such as territory and security, may grow insurmountable.

The Risks of Rhetoric

As they pursue this process, both sides need to recognize the impact of rhetoric on perceptions and calculations. American leaders occasionally launch broadsides against China, including specific proposals for adversarial policies, as domestic political necessities. This occurs even—perhaps especially—when a moderate policy is the ultimate intention. The issue is not specific complaints, which should be dealt with on the merits of the issue, but attacks on the basic motivations of Chinese policy, such as declaring China a strategic adversary. The target of these attacks is bound to ask whether domestic imperatives requiring affirmations of hostility will sooner or later require hostile actions. By the same token, threatening Chinese statements, including those in the semiofficial press, are likely to be interpreted in terms of the actions they imply, whatever the domestic pressures or the intent that generated them.

The American debate, on both sides of the political divide, often describes China as a "rising power" that will need to "mature" and learn how to exercise responsibility on the world stage. China, however, sees itself not as a rising power but as a returning one, predominant in its region for two millennia and temporarily displaced by colonial exploiters taking advantage of Chinese domestic strife and decay. It views the prospect of a strong China exercising influence in economic, cultural, political, and military affairs not as an unnatural challenge to world order but rather as a return to normality. Americans need not agree with every aspect of the Chinese analysis to understand that lecturing a country with a history of millennia about its need to "grow up" and behave "responsibly" can be needlessly grating.

On the Chinese side, proclamations at the governmental and the informal level that China intends to "revive the Chinese nation" to its traditional eminence carry different implications inside China and abroad. China is rightly proud of its recent strides in restoring its sense of national purpose following what it sees as a century of humiliation. Yet few other countries in Asia are nostalgic for an era when they were subject to Chinese suzerainty. As recent veterans of anti-colonial struggles, most Asian countries are extremely sensitive to maintaining their independence and freedom of action vis-à-vis any outside power, whether Western or Asian. They seek to be involved in as many overlapping spheres of economic and political activity as possible; they invite an American role in the region but seek equilibrium, not a crusade or confrontation.

The rise of China is less the result of its increased military strength than of the United States' own declining competitive position, driven by factors such as obsolescent infrastructure, inadequate attention to research and development, and a seemingly dysfunctional governmental process. The United States should address these issues with ingenuity and determination instead of blaming a putative adversary. It must take care not to repeat in its China policy the pattern of conflicts entered with vast public support and broad goals but ended when the American political process insisted on a strategy of extrication that amounted to an abandonment, if not a complete reversal, of the country's proclaimed objectives.

China can find reassurance in its own record of endurance and in the fact that no U.S. administration has ever sought to alter the reality of China as one of the world's major states, economies, and civilizations. Americans would do well to remember that even when China's GDP is equal to that of the United States, it will need to be distributed over a population that is four times as large, aging, and engaged in complex domestic transformations occasioned by China's growth and urbanization. The practical consequence is that a great deal of China's energy will still be devoted to domestic needs. . . .

Critical Thinking

1. Why are U.S. relations with China a complex combination of cooperation and contention?

2. How have the atrocities of the World Trade Center and the Pentagon devastation changed relations between the United States and China?

3. Why does Dr. Kissinger believe that "Conflict Is a Choice, Not a Necessity"?

Create Central

www.mhhe.com/createcentral

Internet References

The Future of U.S.-Chinese relations—Opinion—Al Jazeera English
www.aljazeera.com/indepth/opinion/2012/06/
201263143517185405.html

Henry Kissinger Addresses Yale Students on U.S.-China Relations and American Diplomacy

http://jackson.yale.edu/henry-kissinger-addresses-yale-students-us-china-relations-and-american-diplomacy

The Future of U.S.-China Relations—All Things Nuclear

allthingsnuclear.org/the-future-of-u-s-china-relations

Kissinger reflects on U.S.-China Relations Columbia Daily Spectator

www.columbiaspectator.com/2012/04/17/kissinger-reflects-us-china-relations

HENRY A. KISSINGER is Chair of Kissinger Associates and a former U.S. Secretary of State and National Security Adviser. This essay is adapted from the afterword to the forthcoming paperback edition of his latest book, *On China* (Penguin, 2012).

Kissinger, Henry A. From *Foreign Affairs,* vol. 91, no. 2, March/April 2012, pp. 44–55. Copyright © 2012 by Council on Foreign Relations, Inc. Reprinted by permission of Foreign Affairs. www.ForeignAffairs.com

Article

Prepared by: Caroline Shaffer Westerhof,
California National University for Advanced Studies

Disabling the Constitution
Hungary's Illiberal Turn

Miklós Bánkuti, Gábor Halmai, and Kim Lane Scheppele

Learning Outcomes

After reading this article, you will be able to:

- Understand the constitutional aspects of the Fidesz parliamentary supreme majority.

- Understand the "Fundamental Law" of Hungary and how it has fallen into the concept of "Illiberalism."

- Understand how the populace identifies with the opening words of the Constitution, "God Bless Hungarians."

I n Hungary's April 2010 general elections, former prime minister Viktor Orbán and his Fidesz party won an overwhelming majority of the seats in parliament. The elections gave voters a choice among the discredited Socialist Party (MSzP), which had governed for the preceding eight years; a new youth party of unclear aspirations (Politics Can Be Different or LMP); the neo-Nazi right (Jobbik); the center-right Fidesz; and a few smaller parties that did not muster enough votes to cross the 5 percent threshold into the unicameral, 386-seat Hungarian National Assembly.[1] Given that the bottom had fallen out of the economy on the Socialists' watch and that the party had been mired in scandal, it was not surprising that Fidesz won 53 percent of the popular vote. That was normal party politics. What happened next was a mistake of constitutional design.

During Hungary's transition away from communist rule in 1989 and 1990, the constitutional drafters had been worried about two things: a fractured parliament in which small parties would be unable to form stable majority coalitions, and a deeply entrenched constitution that would be too hard to change once the new democrats figured out how they wanted to design their political institutions. To allay the first of these worries, the framers opted for an election law that put its thumb on the scale in favor of larger parties—effectively using extra seat bonuses as a means of ensuring stable government. In order to address the second concern, the amendment rule in the new constitution allowed a single two-thirds majority of parliament to alter any provision of the constitutional text.

What happened in April 2010 amounted to a perfect storm battering Hungarian constitutionalism. The disproportionate election law translated Fidesz's 53 percent vote share into 68 percent of the seats in parliament. And with the easy constitutional-amendment rule, this two-thirds supermajority was big enough to change everything, which is what the ruling party set about doing. In its first year in office, the Fidesz government amended the old constitution twelve times, changing more than fifty separate provisions along the way. Many of these changes were designed to weaken institutions that might have checked what the government was going to do next, which was to impose upon Hungary a wholly new constitutional order using only ideas and votes from Fidesz.

One of the ruling party's first amendments removed the last restraint on a government with a two-thirds majority. In 1995, the constitution was changed to require a four-fifths vote of parliament to set the rules for writing a new constitution. But because the amendment rule to the constitution had not been altered to exempt the new four-fifths rule from its purview, the Fidesz parliament was able to use its two-thirds vote to eliminate the four-fifths rule from the constitution. With that rule out of the way, Fidesz could write a new constitution on its own.

Fidesz then attacked the Constitutional Court. For more than twenty years, the powerful Court had been the constitutional guardian and primary check on the government.[2] It might well have declared many of the Fidesz initiatives unconstitutional had it not first been disabled.

The government wasted no time in changing the constitution to alter the system for nominating constitutional judges.[3] The old constitution required a majority of parliamentary parties to agree to a nomination and then a two-thirds vote of parliament's members to elect the nominee to the Court. The Fidesz parliament simply amended the constitution to allow the governing party to nominate candidates and let its two-thirds majority elect judges to the Court. This gave Fidesz the power to name judges without needing multiparty backing.

The Fidesz government then restricted the Constitutional Court's jurisdiction. In order to plug gaping budget holes, the Fidesz government established a 98 percent retroactive tax on the customary departing bonuses of those who had left public employment in the preceding five years. The Constitutional Court, before it could be packed with a working majority of new judges, struck down this tax as unconstitutional.[4] Parliament responded by amending the constitution to take away the Court's power over fiscal matters.[5]

Now the Court can no longer review for constitutionality any laws about budgets or taxes unless those laws affect rights that are hard to infringe with budget measures (rights to life, dignity, data privacy, thought, conscience, religion, and citizenship). Conspicuously, the Constitutional Court is *not* allowed to review budget or tax laws if they infringe other rights that are much easier to limit with fiscal measures, such as the right to property, equality under the law, the prohibition against retroactive legislation, or the guarantee of fair judicial procedure. Sidelining the Court in this area enabled the Fidesz government to continue to roll out a series of unconventional economic policies. Among other measures, it effectively nationalized private pensions, which resulted in eight-thousand cases on the issue going to the European Court of Human Rights.[6] Meanwhile, the Constitutional Court remained silent.

To further establish its control over the Constitutional Court, the Fidesz government amended the old constitution to increase the number of judges, giving the party power to name seven of the fifteen judges on the Court in its first year and a half in office. Although the Court still exists, it has now largely disappeared from the political landscape. All these measures enacted within the first year of the Fidesz government—the new nomination procedure for judges, the limitation on judicial review of fiscal measures, and the expanded size of the Constitutional Court—were entrenched in the new constitution.

Majoritarianism Unleashed

In its early days in power, Fidesz brought the Election Commission under its control as well, prematurely terminating the mandates of members who were elected to serve through 2014. Under the old system, the Commission was divided so that five of its seats were filled by party delegates (one from each parliamentary party), while the other five were filled by mutual agreement between the governing and opposition parties. Fidesz immediately filled all the nondelegate seats on the Commission with its own members, giving the ruling party a dominant majority on the Commission. This mattered not only for election monitoring but also because the Election Commission must rule on proposals for referendums. Thus the Commission could thwart attempts by civil society groups to use referendums to derail aspects of the government's program. (Electoral Commission decisions can be appealed to the Constitutional Court, but that hardly matters since the Court, as we have seen, was disabled early on.)

Another early target of the Fidesz government was the mass media. Two major new laws restructured the Media Authority, the state regulatory agency, and created a five-member independent Media Council with powers to levy hefty fines on all media outlets for, among other things, failing to achieve "balanced" news coverage.[7] Orbán appointed a former Fidesz MP to a nine-year term as head of the Media Authority (a position whose occupant must by law now be the chair of the independent Media Council) and the parliament elected other Fidesz loyalists to every seat on the Council.

These media reforms faced heavy criticism from both the Council of Europe and the European Union, which forced Hungary to relax the rules slightly.[8] But the key features of the new Council system were left in place—most crucially, the power to interpret vague standards vested in a Council whose membership consists exclusively of affiliates of one party. As a result of a decision by the dying Constitutional Court in December 2011,[9] these restrictive content requirements no longer apply to the print and online press. But the media remain under pressure since the Council still controls the entire broadcast sector and has not foresworn its still-extant legal power to reregulate print and online media. A May 2012 Council of Europe analysis confirms that the changes made by the Hungarian government still do not meet European human-rights standards.[10]

Finally, under the old constitution, the president held a number of important powers that could keep the government in check. The president could exercise a suspensive veto by sending laws back to parliament for revision or could send a law of questionable constitutionality to the Constitutional Court for review. Without changing the laws, the Fidesz government changed the person. In 2010, parliament elected former Fidesz vice-chair Pál Schmitt to the office. Schmitt never hesitated to sign anything that the Fidesz government put before him; thus he provided no real check on the constitutional revolution either. (Schmitt was forced to step down amid a plagiarism scandal in April 2012, and János Áder, a cofounder of Fidesz and coauthor of the controversial new election law, was elected to replace him.)

These four actions—limiting the Constitutional Court, dooming the referendum process, asserting control over the media, and putting a Fidesz loyalist in the presidency—effectively created an opening through which the Fidesz government could then push a new constitution without challenge.

The key parts of the constitution-drafting process occurred behind closed doors. The two-stage process required first that a parliamentary committee adopt the basic principles of the new constitution and then that representatives draft the constitution following these principles. But when the parliamentary committee (which opposition members had boycotted because their proposals made little headway) announced the constitutional principles in December 2010, there was no debate or formal adoption of these principles. Instead, a March 2011 parliamentary resolution gave all MPs one week to come up with proposed draft constitutions "with or without" taking the principles into account.

In the end, only two proposals for a new constitution were offered. One came from an extraparliamentary committee consisting of three Fidesz members. Its head was József Szájer, a Fidesz member of the European Parliament. The other came from former National Assembly speaker and 2005 Socialist presidential candidate Katalin Szili. The Szájer draft was promptly introduced in parliament as a private-member's bill. Using this procedure, Fidesz could eliminate the preparatory stage required of all government bills that mandates consultation with the opposition and interested civil society groups. As a result, virtually no one outside Fidesz was given the chance to discuss the draft constitution as it was being constructed. Szili's draft was quietly dropped by parliament and never received a serious hearing.

The Szájer constitution was introduced in the National Assembly with one month for a public debate that never occurred. Parliament itself discussed the constitution in only nine sessions, during which about 180 amendments were offered. But the only alterations that had any chance of passage were those submitted by Fidesz. Democratic opposition parties, whose proposals were virtually all rejected, eventually walked out of the chamber and did not vote on the final constitution. Only the far-right Jobbik stayed and voted no.

In a party-line vote, with all Fidesz members in favor and everyone else either boycotting or voting no, the new constitution passed parliament by the requisite two-thirds vote and was signed by the president on 25 April 2011. The whole process was completed in a rush without even contemplating a public referendum to ratify the result. The new constitution went into effect on 1 January 2012,[11] along with many of the "cardinal laws" that the constitution required to fill in the specifics.

The New Constitutional Order

Both the old and the new constitution have at their core a parliamentary system with a unicameral parliament. But unicameral parliaments need checks if they are to avoid the potential abuses of majoritarianism. The old constitution had many checks. The new constitution has substantially weakened all of them.

The Constitutional Court had been the primary check on the power of government majorities, and we have already seen how Fidesz captured the Court prior to the new constitution's adoption. But in addition to changing the size of the Court, its jurisdiction, and the procedures for nominating judges to the Court, the new constitution also sharply limits access to the Court. Under the old constitution, *anyone* could challenge a law's constitutionality. This *actio popularis* jurisdiction was unusual in Europe and had become the most effective way in Hungary to keep the government in constitutional line.

The new constitution eliminates *actio popularis* review, substituting instead a constitutional complaint on the German model. In this new system, individuals may challenge laws only if the laws affect them personally. The ability of the Court to review laws in the abstract is further limited by the narrow list of officials who have competence under the constitution to take a case to the Court for abstract review. For example, the constitution requires 25 percent of the MPs to challenge a law. But given the current division of the opposition between the left (the Socialists) and the far right (Jobbik), it is unlikely that 25 percent of MPs will work together to organize such a challenge. The cumulative effect is that the Court will now hear primarily individual-level complaints alleging infringements of rights, but will not be able to reach many of the most disturbing aspects of the new constitutional order—issues related to separation of powers and institutional structure.

Other checking institutions that were important in the old constitutional order have also been seriously weakened. The ordinary judiciary has lost a great deal of its independence. Under the old system, lower-court judges were selected by panels of their fellow judges. Under the new system, the president of the newly created National Judicial Office has the power to select new judges, to promote and demote any judge, to begin disciplinary proceedings, and to select the leaders of each of the courts.[12] The person chosen by parliament with a two-thirds majority to fill this office is both a close friend of Prime Minister Orban and the wife of József Szájer, the principal drafter of the new constitution.[13]

In choosing new judges, the head of the National Judicial Office must pick candidates from a list prepared by local councils of judges, but she sets up the process through which candidates may apply and she may reject the judges' lists and start the process over again if need be. Hungary's president must sign off on all new judicial appointments, but with a Fidesz loyalist holding that position, the president is unlikely to object.

The Transitional Provisions to the Basic Law, enacted by parliament on 30 December 2011, give the president of the National Judicial Office the power to reassign specific cases from the courts where they are assigned by law to any other court in the country. In the first set of reassignments, made in February 2012, two of the nine cases moved to other courts had distinct political overtones, including the highest-profile corruption case that the public prosecutor has so far brought against MSzP officials as well as an appeal by a Fidesz party member from a criminal conviction for corruption.[14]

Between selecting the judges and being able to assign cases, the head of the National Judicial Office has extraordinary power. Moreover, when her nine-year term expires, she can be replaced only by a candidate who can muster a two-thirds vote of parliament. Should parliament be unable to agree on her successor, she may stay on until a new candidate wins the required legislative supermajority. The Council of Europe's Venice Commission (formally, the European Commission for Democracy through Law) recently condemned the new law on the judiciary for concentrating unheard-of powers in the hands of one person and for the extraordinarily long term of her office, among other issues.[15]

The new president of the National Judicial Office has had many judgeships to fill in her first months in office. Between lifting a moratorium that had blocked the selection of new judges until the new system could be set up and suddenly and abruptly lowering the judicial retirement age from 70 to 62, the government had about 10 percent of all judicial posts in the country to fill when the new constitution took effect. The European Union has brought an infringement action against Hungary for violating EU law by arbitrarily lowering the judicial retirement age. In the meantime, the newly opened judgeships are being filled quickly while the infringement procedure is pending.

Entrenching Fidesz

In addition to weakening the separation of powers and attacking judicial independence, the Fidesz government has also compromised accountability institutions that were once known for their independence and expertise. The old ombudsman system for monitoring human rights has been seriously weakened. In place of four separate ombudsmen with separate staffs and independent jurisdictions, the new system has only one "parliamentary commissioner for human rights" with two deputies operating under his direction and a much-reduced staff. The old data-protection ombudsman's office has been eliminated, and its functions have been transferred to a new office that is part of the government and no longer an independent body. The European Union has brought an infringement action against Hungary for violating EU law with this change in the status of the data-protection authority.

In the new constitutional order, the state audit office, once a bastion of independent expertise, has been granted additional powers to launch serious investigations into the misuse of public funds. But the new head of the state audit office, a former Fidesz MP who was elected to hold the audit post for twelve years by a two-thirds vote of parliament, has no professional auditing experience. The public prosecutor, elected by a two-thirds parliamentary majority for nine years, also has increased powers—for example, to assign any criminal case to any court of his choosing. Not surprisingly, the occupant of this office, too, has long been closely aligned with Fidesz. The long terms of the current head of the state audit office and the current public prosecutor mean that both will survive through multiple parliamentary election cycles, providing crucial veto points should any other party come to power in the meantime.

The new constitution also establishes a Budget Council with the power to veto any budget produced by parliament that adds even a single point to the national debt. The Budget Council consists of three officials, two elected by a two-thirds vote of parliament and one appointed by the president. All have terms of office that exceed a normal parliamentary cycle—six years for two of the members and twelve for the other. Thus this institution can exercise dead-hand control over future elected governments.

According to the new constitution, if parliament fails to agree on a budget by March 31 of each year, then the president may dissolve parliament and call new elections. Obviously, if the Budget Council, dominated by Fidesz loyalists, vetoes the budget on the eve of the deadline, the constitutional trigger may be pulled for new elections. If another party manages to gain power in a future election, this provision will hang like the Sword of Damocles over its continued term in office.

There are numerous other troubling aspects of this new constitutional order: the gerrymandering of election districts, which makes it hard for any other party to win an election in the foreseeable future; the removal of the statute of limitations for crimes committed during the Soviet period, which opens the door to selective prosecution of the political opposition; an unwisely large number of "cardinal" laws (that is, laws requiring a two-thirds vote in parliament) that fix details of state policy on issues such as taxes, pensions, and family protection; the troubling constitutional preamble, which gives constituent power to ethnic Hungarians both at home and abroad while leaving out all other citizens; the references to the historic constitution, which invite (among other things) revisiting the 1920 Treaty of Trianon (which set Hungary's borders after the Habsburg Empire was defeated in the First World War); the

sudden deregistration of more than three-hundred churches that had operated in Hungary for years; and incursions on the independence of the Hungarian Central Bank. We have focused on the core structural issues, however, because they reveal why it will be hard for any non-Fidesz government to govern, should such a government manage to be elected.

Assuming that there continue to be free and fair elections among competing parties in the future, it will be hard for any other party to come to power with this level of political control over all the institutions necessary for democratic elections. Even if another party defies the odds and manages to win an election, however, Fidesz loyalists are entrenched in every corner of the state—from the Constitutional Court, Budget Council, and National Judicial Office to the State Audit Office, Public Prosecutor's Office, and National Bank. These loyalists ensure that there will be multiple choke-points at which Fidesz can stop anything that deviates from its preferences.

In a September 2009 speech, Viktor Orbán predicted that there was "A real chance that politics in Hungary will no longer be defined by a dualist power space. . . . Instead, a large governing party will emerge in the center of the political stage [that] will be able formulate national policy, not though constant debates but through a natural representation of interests."

Orbán's vision for a new constitutional order—one in which his political party occupies the center stage of Hungarian political life and puts an end to debates over values—has now been entrenched in law. The new constitutional order was built with the votes of his political bloc alone, and it aims to keep the opposition at bay for a long time. Constitutions, though, often have a way of turning against their makers, as the new rules of the game are learned and used by those who were initially disadvantaged by them. Whether Orbán can keep his opponents down forever, then, remains to be seen.

Notes

1. Among these parties were the Hungarian Democratic Forum (MDF), the biggest winner of the 1990 elections, and the Alliance of Free Democrats (SzDSz), the most successful of the liberal parties since the transition. By 2010, both were near complete collapse.

2. Gábor Halmai, "The Hungarian Approach of Constitutional Review," in Wojciech Sadurski, ed., *Constitutional Justice, East and West, Democratic Legitimacy and Constitutional Courts in Post-Communist Europe in a Comparative Perspective* (The Hague: Kluwer International, 2002), 189–211.

3. Amendment to Law XX of 1949 on the Constitution of the Republic of Hungary, 5 July 2010, *Magyar Közlöny*, Issue 113 (2010).

4. Hungarian Constitutional Court, Decision 184/2010 (X. 28), *Magyar Közlöny*, Issue 165 (2010).

5. Law CXIX of 2010 on the amendment to Law XX of 1949 on the Constitution of the Republic of Hungary, *Magyar Közlöny*, Issue 177 (2010).

6. "Human Rights Court Inundated with Hungary Complaints," EurActive.com, 16 January 2012, available at www.euractiv.com/future-eu/human-rights-court-inundated-hungary-complaints-news-510155.

7. Law CIV of 2010 on the Freedom of the Press and the Fundamental Rules of Media Content and Law CLXXXV of 2010 on Media Services and Mass Media. The laws are translated at the website of the Center for the Study of the Media at Central European University at http://cmcs.ceu.hu/node/26249.

8. Center for Media and Communication Studies, Central European University Hungarian Media Laws in Europe: An Assessment of the Consistency of Hungary's Media Laws with European Practices and Norms (2011), available at http://cmcs.ceu.hu/sites/default/files/field_attachment/news/node-27293/Hungarian_Media_Laws_in_Europe_0.pdf. The criticism of the new media laws is collected at the website of the Center for the Study of the Media at Central European University at http://cmcs.ceu.hu/node/26249.

9. Hungarian Constitutional Court, Decision 165/2011 (XII. 20), *Magyar Közlöny,* Issue 155 (2011).

10. See *Expertise by Council of Europe Experts on Hungarian Media Legislation: Act CIV of 2010 on the Freedom of the Press and the Fundamental Rules on Media Content and Act CLXXXV of 2010 on Media Services and Mass Media,* 11 May 2012, available at www.coe.int/c/document_library/get_file?uuid=fbc88585.

11. The new Hungarian Basic Law is available in translation at http://lapa.princeton.edu/hosteddocs/hungary/Hungarian%20Constitution%20English%20final%20version.pdf.

12. For more detail on the state of the judiciary under the new laws, see Kim Lane Scheppele, "First Let's Pick All the Judges" at Paul Krugman's blog, *Conscience of a Liberal,* http://krugman.blogs.nytimes.com/2012/03/10/first-lets-pick-all-the-judges, 10 March 2012.

13. Joshua Rozenberg, "Meet Tunde Handó: In Hungary, One Woman Effectively Controls the Judiciary, and She Happens to be Married to the Author of Its Constitution," *Guardian,* 20 March 2012, available at www.guardian.co.uk/law/2012/mar/20/tunde-han-do-hungarian-judges.

14. Scheppele, "First Let's Pick All the Judges."

15. European Commission for Democracy Through Law (Venice Commission), *Opinion on Act CLXII of 2011 on the Legal Status and Enumeration of Judges and Act CLXI of 2011 on the Organisation and Administration of Courts of Hungary,* 19 March 2012, available at www.venice.coe.int/docs/2012/CDL%282012%29104-e.pdf.

Critical Thinking

1. How has the government, through the Constitution, become entrenched in its power and controlled by loyalists?

2. How does the concept of the constitution define its citizens?

3. Is it valid to define the nation as "intellectual and spiritual" and not "political"?

Create Central

www.mhhe.com/createcentral

Internet References

Eurozine—Towards an Illiberal Democracy
   www.eurozine.com/articles/2012-01-25-halmai-en.html

Safeguarding Democracy inside the EU
   www.transatlanticacademy.org/publications/safeguarding-democracy-inside-eu-brussels-and-future-liberal-order

Istvan Pogany 2013—The Crisis of Democracy in East Central Europe
   www.istvanpogany.eu

MIKLÓS BÁNKUTI is senior research specialist at Princeton University's Woodrow Wilson School. **GÁBOR HALMAI** is professor of law at Eötvös Lóránd Univerity, Budapest, and visiting research scholar at Princeton University. **KIM LANE SCHEPPELE** is the Laurance S. Rockefeller Professor of Sociology and Public Affairs at the Woodrow Wilson School and the University Center for Human Values at Princeton University as well as director of its Program in Law and Public Affairs.

From *Journal of Democracy,* July 2012, pp. 138–146. Copyright © 2012 by National Endowment for Democracy and The Johns Hopkins University Press. Reprinted with permission of The Johns Hopkins University Press.

Article

Prepared by: Caroline Shaffer Westerhof,
California National University for Advanced Studies

White House's Egypt Debate Heralds Shift

In Skirting Declaration on Whether Morsi's Overthrow Was a Coup, U.S. Seeks to Guard Its Limited Leverage over Generals

Adam Entous

Learning Outcomes

After reading this article, you will be able to:

- Understand why the United States is pulling away some, but not all, of its funding for Egypt.

- Understand why Saudi Arabia is supporting Egypt with billions in funding.

- Understand why Mohamed Morsi was overthrown by the military.

Washington—When Obama administration lawyers told top policy makers that they had come up with a way to avoid designating Egypt's military takeover a coup—a decision that would obligate the U.S. to freeze aid—some senior White House staffers voiced reservations about the message that would send.

But the plan was embraced by members of President Barack Obama's national security cabinet, who concluded unanimously that there was no other way to maintain limited U.S. leverage with Egypt's generals and avoid fueling further violence, said U.S. officials.

The debate came to a head last week, just days before Egyptian police gunned down at least 74 supporters of ousted President Mohamed Morsi. The decision shows that nearly a month after Mr. Morsi's overthrow, the White House is adopting a more "real-politik" approach that reflects the administration's adjustment to the aftershocks of the Arab Spring, with implications for other rocky democratic transitions.

A year after embracing Mr. Morsi, the White House is trying to manage the crisis following his ouster by subjugating immediate U.S. distaste about how he was brought down to the importance of preserving U.S. ties with generals who will decide how and when, and whether, Egypt restores democracy. The approach also aims to keep channels of communication open with the Muslim Brotherhood.

"What was driving this decision was what's in the best interest of the United States going forward and how can we have the most leverage to promote our interests in a very volatile situation," a senior administration official said.

In initial White House discussions about how to respond to Mr. Morsi's overthrow, State Department and Pentagon lawyers voiced skepticism that the U.S. could avoid calling it a "coup." Making such a determination about how Egypt's elected government was removed would have frozen some $1.5 billion in U.S. aid, barring a waiver from Congress. "This is a coup and this means everything is cut off. Period. Full Stop," an official said of the initial assessment.

That didn't go over well with top policy makers at the White House, the State Department and the Pentagon, who wanted to find a way to avoid an aid cutoff that would alienate generals who have other suitors competing for influence. Since the coup, Saudi Arabia, Kuwait and the United Arab Emirates have pledged billions of dollars to Egypt's interim government.

After Mr. Morsi's ouster, the Pentagon and the State Department drew up timelines showing what aid was set to be provided to the Egyptians and when. The White House wanted to decide on a case-by-case basis whether the aid should go through. The first item in the Pentagon's pipeline: four F-16 warplanes, slated to ship to Egypt last week.

Just two weeks earlier, Pentagon officials indicated publicly that they intended to go ahead with the shipment, a signal to Egypt's top military leader, Gen. Abdel Fattah Al Sisi, that Secretary of Defense Chuck Hagel wanted to keep aid flowing on schedule. Pentagon officials argued that the deliveries shouldn't be affected by a White House review of aid because the planes were part of a 20-plane package that had already been funded.

The disclosure of the Pentagon's plan to proceed with the deliveries, however, upset officials on the White House National Security Council, according to officials. The White House protested because it didn't want to "box in" Mr. Obama given the uncertain direction of events on the ground inside Egypt, these officials said.

In their nearly daily phone calls, Mr. Hagel cautioned Gen. Sisi against cracking down on the Muslim Brotherhood and urged him to allow observers in to see Mr. Morsi, who was jailed on the night of his ouster. Gen. Sisi listened to Mr. Hagel but was "noncommittal" about heeding U.S. advice, U.S. officials said.

With the F-16 shipment date fast approaching last week, the White House held another round of deliberations. One of the biggest concerns for policy makers was the "optics" of going through with a highly visible delivery of F-16s at a time when the military appeared to be readying a major crackdown on the Brotherhood, against U.S. wishes.

There wasn't a big debate inside the White House about freezing the plane shipment, according to meeting participants. Mr. Hagel agreed with the decision and conveyed that message to Gen. Sisi in a phone call. Mr. Hagel also made clear the F-16 delivery could be unfrozen if conditions improved.

That same week, the debate over whether to sidestep the "coup" designation came to a head at the White House.

The lawyers told top policy makers that U.S. law was written in such a way that it didn't obligate the administration to issue a coup-or-no-coup designation. So the U.S. could skirt the issue by not issuing a decision.

That formula didn't sit well with some senior White House staffers, including Deputy National Security Adviser Benjamin Rhodes, according to U.S. officials who took part in the talks.

These officials said Mr. Rhodes and other staffers at the White House felt "pretty strongly that this was in fact a coup" and should be labeled as such.

Mr. Hagel, Secretary of State John Kerry and the newly minted White House National Security Adviser, Susan Rice, supported not making a designation—arguing that making a determination one way or another would hurt U.S. interests, officials said.

Mr. Rhodes declined to comment on the concerns that officials said he and other staffers raised.

A senior administration official said it was normal for Mr. Rhodes and others to point out to policy makers what implications a decision will have. "That's their job," the official said.

Critical Thinking

1. Will the military in Egypt be successful in pushing out and controlling members of the Muslim Brotherhood? Explain.

2. How would you explain the identity crisis Egypt is now suffering politically and economically? Explain.

3. Do you deem the present government of Egypt as being legitimate? Explain.

Create Central

www.mhhe.com/createcentral

Internet References

U.S.'s Stance Was Product of Yearlong Shift—*Wall Street Journal*
http://online.wsj.com/news/articles/SB20001424127887324260204578585910863051042

Official: U.S. Plans to Curb Military Aid to Egypt—**I4U News**
www.i4u.com/2013/10/barack-obama/egypt-military-curb-plans-official-us-aid

Mideast Allies Press U.S. on Egypt
http://online.wsj.com/news/articles/SB10001424127887323980604579029371599427840

U.S. Allies Thwart America in Egypt
http://online.wsj.com/news/articles/SB10001424127887323423804579023213295900596

Anti-U.S. Hostility Ramps up in Egypt
http://online.wsj.com/news/articles/SB10001424127887323838204579000830652806204

ADAM ENTOUS is national security correspondent for *The Wall Street Journal*.

Article

Prepared by: Caroline Shaffer Westerhof,
California National University for Advanced Studies

Chile's Middle Class Flexes Its Muscles

Patricio Navia

Learning Outcomes

After reading this article, you will be able to:

- Understand how Chile's middle class is pressuring successfully for greater economic security.

- Understand the concept of democracy in Chile.

- Understand the success and *debits of* what is referred to as a social market economy.

Chileans can live their entire lives without much interaction with a state institution. A middle class woman, born in a private clinic paid for by her parents' private health insurance, will attend a (government-subsidized) private voucher school. She will graduate from a private university paid for with government-subsidized student loans. If the young professional joins the mining sector, she likely will work for one of the private companies that control 70 percent of Chile's copper production. Her mandatory retirement contributions will be sent directly from her employer to the private retirement management fund of her choice. In all likelihood she will have private health insurance. She will send her children to private school. She'll pay her utilities to private companies, obtain a mortgage from a private bank, and even drive on privately operated highways in the capital city of Santiago.

Since the end of the Augusto Pinochet dictatorship in 1990, Chile has grown robustly and steadily. For 20 years, a center-left coalition, Concertación, led an impressive period of development. Poverty declined from 40 percent of the population in 1990 to 15 percent in 2009. Child obesity has replaced malnutrition as a leading public health concern. Primary and secondary education is now universal. And almost 60 percent of college-aged Chileans are enrolled in higher education institutions. More than 70 percent of them are first-generation college students.

Having regained their rights as citizens in 1990, Chileans increasingly are exercising their rights as consumers. Larger and more diverse, the middle class is testing its political muscle as it demands that social policies be redesigned to fit its needs. Indeed, Chile's new middle class has developed a sense of vertigo, fearing vulnerability and at the same time seeking to fly even higher. The social safety net, designed to aid those at the lowest 40 percent of the income ladder, is set too low for the next 40 percent. The high-flying middle class wants a safe place to land in case times get rough. But because the tax structure is not sufficiently progressive, the government lacks resources to fund programs for the middle class. Many Chileans thus want tax reforms to fund the expansion of government assistance, especially in higher education.

After the Protests

The student protests that rocked Chile in 2011 fueled claims that the country's market-friendly model is crumbling. However, opinion surveys show that Chileans remain optimistic that their middle-class expectations will materialize. Chileans do not want to make a left turn in the elections scheduled for next year. They want to continue moving forward, faster and more securely.

The recent social mobilizations in favor of education, the environment, gay rights, consumer rights, and other post-materialist demands, far from suggesting political decay, show a vibrant civil society committed to democracy. After remaining steadily in the middle of the 50 percent range for about a decade, support for democracy among Chileans surpassed 60 percent in recent years, according to a Latinobarómetro poll. In a recent Diego Portales University survey, 78 percent of respondents said they believe future economic conditions will improve for their families. Education (32 percent) and crime (29 percent) rank atop the main national problems. Employment (8 percent) and inflation (2 percent) are at the bottom of the list.

However, Chileans increasingly worry that opportunities are insufficient and the playing field is not level. Historically low levels of trust in political institutions (10 percent trust political parties and the legislature) are now affecting the government generally (down from 33 percent in 2010 to 21 percent in 2011), according to Latinobarómetro. Even trust in the Catholic Church has declined—from 43 percent to 24 percent from 2010 to 2011—as a result of pedophilia scandals. Trust in private companies declined from 20 percent to 16 percent in the same period.

In 2009, a conservative businessman, Sebastián Piñera, won the presidential election on a message of change in the context of continuity. He promised to more efficiently lead Chile into the promised land of development. The social protests and active student movement of 2011 highlighted the caveats of Chile's successful experience of economic development. The protests also sunk Piñera's approval ratings to the lowest observed since democracy was restored. Some critics of the market-friendly model have prematurely declared the end of Chile's social market experiment. A more reasonable assessment suggests the need for increased effort to foster social inclusion and expand opportunities.

Two problems stand out. First, inadequate regulation and government oversight tilt the balance in favor of providers against consumers. Business concentration is high in several sectors of the economy. Private companies that provide formerly public services—utilities, health insurance, education, and private roads—often abuse their position and impose excessively high fees and penalties on consumers who miss payments. In some cases they even abuse consumers who pay on time.

Chileans want government institutions to step up their involvement and provide better consumer protection. Several of the grievances behind last year's student protests have to do with the government's inability—or unwillingness—to adopt stricter regulations to guarantee quality education and control skyrocketing university tuition costs. Chileans perceive that political parties side with business interests, and that democratic institutions do not represent people's interests well. Still, when asked about their political identification, a majority identify themselves as moderates. Chileans do not want to throw out the democracy- and market-friendly baby with the bath water.

Chileans do not want to throw out the democracy- and market-friendly baby with the bath water.

The second problem is an insufficient safety net. Successive center-left governments focused on earmarking social programs and subsidies to the poorest 40 percent, leaving the middle class unprotected. Because the safety net is inadequately funded, expanding existing programs to the middle class would not suffice. The public sector tax take is slightly over 20 percent of GDP. Without a more progressive tax code, little progress can be made to strengthen the safety net and expand opportunities for the middle class.

As a candidate, Piñera campaigned on leveling the playing field for the middle class. Though he has lost favor with the public, his initial message remains popular. Meanwhile, the Concertación opposition is divided among those who defend their 20-year government legacy of moderation and pragmatism and those who seek to follow the leftist populist model found elsewhere in Latin America. If the Concertación stays in the middle, calling for moderate reforms that will strengthen individual rights for citizens and consumers, it will likely retake power in 2013.

Rising Expectations

Twenty days after his inauguration, Piñera bluntly encouraged higher expectations when he declared—mocking previous Concertación governments—that "what others failed to do in

20 years, we already did in 20 days." The spectacular rescue of 33 trapped miners in October 2010 underlined the message of efficacy. If Piñera could successfully rescue the miners, he could also address education, health care, and other pending—and admittedly difficult—challenges that Concertación governments failed to tackle.

Piñera's clumsy handling of the 2011 student protests has distracted attention from progress on other issues—including social programs; maternity leave reform; and electoral reform to make registration automatic, which will incorporate millions of previously excluded Chileans into the voting rolls. When he took office, Piñera successfully freed the right of its Pinochet authoritarian legacy and seized the social market economic model from the Concertación. Moderation, gradualism, and pragmatism are no longer Concertación trademarks. The center-right will remain electorally competitive if it sticks to Piñera's centrist policies. Even if he achieves little else, Piñera already has transformed the Chilean political landscape.

Last year's student protests tested his ability to deliver on his promise of expanding opportunities for the middle class. But the protests also showed that the middle class, having consolidated its electoral dominance, seeks to transform the social market economy into a more inclusive market-friendly model.

Critical Thinking

1. Why is the center-right coalition government responding to the demands of a reformed social market economy?
2. Why is the Chilean government responding to the middle class demands?
3. Is Chile on the road to sustaining a political system that we identify as a "democracy"?

Create Central

www.mhhe.com/createcentral

Internet References

Chile: Protest for the "Promised Land"
www.opendemocracy.net/patricio-navia/chile-protest-for-%E2%80%9Cpromised-land%E2%80%9D
Chile Seeks Developed Status, Meets Soaring Energy Costs
www.bloomberg.com/news/2013-01-15/chile-seeks-developed-status-meets-soaring-energy-costs.html
Chile after the Elections
clas.uchicago.edu/page/chile-after-elections
Do Segregated Schools in Chile's Capital Stunt Mobility?
http://santiagotimes.cl/do-segregated-schools-in-chiles-capital-stunt-mobility

Patricio Navia teaches at the Center for Latin American and Caribbean Studies at New York University and is a professor of political science at Diego Portales University in Santiago.

Article

Prepared by: Caroline Shaffer Westerhof,
California National University for Advanced Studies

Singapore Poll Energizes Voters

Enlivened Presidential Campaign Is Seen as Move toward Improved Democratic System.

Chun Han Wong

Learning Outcomes

After reading this article, you will be able to:

- Explain why Singapore has been a major economic success for the last 50 years.

- Examine the political changes that are slowly taking place in Singapore.

- Examine the dominance of the political party in Singapore.

Singapore—An unexpectedly fierce contest for Singapore's largely ceremonial presidency is turning into a test of the country's tightly controlled political system, energizing the movement toward a more competitive democracy in the city-state.

The vote Saturday will mark only the second time in Singapore's history that more than one candidate has competed for the job, which has gone to individuals with strong ties to the ruling People's Action Party that has dominated Singapore since it became a nation in 1965. It follows a landmark general election in May in which the PAP retained power but saw its vote share fall to the lowest level since independence, spurring talk about a new era of a more-plural democracy after decades of highly centralized governance.

If the PAP's preferred candidate—former Deputy Prime Minister Tony Tan—wins by a wide margin, it would serve as a vote of confidence in the party, whose policies have helped to raise Singapore from a relatively poor trade post in the 1960s to one of the richest countries in the world. PAP leaders have promised modest reforms since the party's relatively poor showing in May, including steps to ease housing costs and review government salaries amid concerns over a widening gap between rich and poor.

But if any of the other three candidates prevail—or force a slim margin of victory for Dr. Tan—it would serve as another rebuke to the ruling party and could push it to consider more populist policies to win back support. The result could also lead to livelier debate about issues such as immigration, housing and transportation policies, and create another check on the PAP's power, analysts say.

Regardless of what happens Saturday, the ruling party will still hold a dominant parliamentary majority. The vigorous campaigning, however, signals an evolution of the political system in Singapore, with a further dilution of the electorate's deference to the political establishment.

Analysts point to the diminishing grip of PAP's old guard—led by 87-year-old Lee Kuan Yew, Singapore's first and longest-serving prime minister—and the success of online media in blunting the opinion-shaping power of traditional news sources.

"A new generation, better educated than the last, no longer subscribes to the notion that sacrifices must be made today for survival tomorrow, nor are they so easily convinced that the PAP has all the answers," said Alex Au, a prominent political blogger. "These are secular trends, and therefore the change in political climate will not be short-lived or reversed."

Already, some of the candidates are using the election to promote the idea of a more assertive president with more influence than officially prescribed in Singapore, which has a parliamentary system of government currently headed by Prime Minister Lee Hsien Loong.

Under constitutional amendments enacted in 1991 that made the post a directly elected office, the presidency has no executive authority, though it has certain veto powers over the use of Singapore's foreign-exchange reserves, government budgets and key public-office appointments.

While the office is theoretically nonpartisan—candidates can't be current members of political parties—three of the contenders have premised their campaigns on the need for a political counterweight to the PAP, while expressing views on a host of issues—from socioeconomic policies to capital punishment to Singapore's internal-security laws—that traditionally fall outside the bounds of the job.

"What's the problem with bringing [issues like the death penalty and Singapore's casinos] up for debate," Tan Jee Say, a candidate with no ties to the ruling PAP, said last week in a presidential debate organized by independent website the Online Citizen. "Let's have a proper debate, a mature debate, a contest of ideas between president and prime minister on matters of conscience."

A PAP spokesman didn't respond to a request to comment.

The calls for a more assertive presidency have resonated with many voters, who have swarmed the candidates during campaign stops this week.

"The president is supposed to speak up for us. I will not feel very comfortable if the president and the government are on very good terms," said James Lee, a youth counselor who in his 30s will vote in his first presidential poll. "It is much easier for someone independent, with no ties with the PAP, to ask tough questions."

Singapore bars opinion polling during campaigning periods. But analysts say the results on Saturday could be close, and would send a message.

"A second political setback after the rap on the knuckles the government received [in May] would clearly encourage more Singaporeans to assert themselves politically," said Derek da Cunha, a Singapore-based political analyst. "The government will simply have to make more gestures to the electorate to mollify it or risk its unpopularity growing."

The ruling party already has taken steps in recent months to rebuild confidence following its historically low 60.1 percent share of the vote in May. The prime minister announced a cabinet reshuffle, and pledged broad reviews of social policy and ministerial pay. While unveiling this month fresh plans to tackle high housing costs and to slow foreign-worker arrivals, Prime Minister Lee also promised greater engagement and consultation with the public.

But whether these gestures underpin a more thorough reform agenda remains unclear.

Unlike previous polls, the government has declined to openly endorse a candidate, but battle lines have formed between an establishment candidate and his challengers.

Tony Tan, who was most recently deputy chairman of Government of Singapore Investment Corp., has implicit backing from government leaders, including Prime Minister Lee. His campaign has emphasized the president's fiduciary role amid current global economic turmoil. "Some people argue that the president must take a public stand on current issues . . . [or] must oppose the government. People interested in such roles should run for Parliament," Dr. Tan said last week in a televised speech. "The president stands for all Singaporeans. He has to be independent and above politics."

In contrast, his rivals promise a more outspoken head of state unburdened by ideological baggage from years in top government ranks.

Former lawmaker and medical doctor Tan Cheng Bock, and Tan Kin Lian, ex-chief executive of insurer NTUC Income,

have fostered reputations for speaking up against the government despite their background as former PAP members.

Tan Jee Say, an investment adviser and former senior civil servant, contested May's election as a member of the opposition Singapore Democratic Party but failed to win a seat.

Crowds as large as 30,000 people have attended the presidential-candidates' rallies, offering boisterous cheers in scenes reminiscent of the intense campaign for May's election.

"I used to be a keyboard warrior, but I've decided to do what I can to make a difference," said Daniel Chua, a 52-year-old realtor who this week started backing Tan Jee Say. "Even if we lose, if the margin is small, it'll send a signal to the government: We are the people, listen to us."

Critical Thinking

1. How and why has Singapore become a dominant economic power in Asia?

2. How have the Singapore presidential candidates sought to expand the executive branch of government?

3. What has been accomplished by Singapore directly increasing public input?

Create Central

www.mhhe.com/createcentral

Internet References

Voter Turnout Data for Singapore
www.idea.int/vt/countryview.cfm?CountryCode=SG

Singapore Elections Department - Non-Voters
www.eld.gov.sg/voters_compulsory.html

The Strike That Rattled Singapore: A WSJ Investigation
http://blogs.wsj.com/searealtime/2013/08/26/the-strike-that-rattled-singapore-a-wsj-investigation/

Modelling the Singapore Elections II: Are Singaporeans Stupid Voters?
http://akikonomu.blogspot.com/2011/05/modelling-singapore-elections-ii-are.html

Singapore Poll Energizes Voters
http://online.wsj.com/news/articles/SB10001424053111904279004576525850411219490

CHU HAN WONG is a Staff Reporter at *The Wall Street Journal*.

Prepared by: Caroline Shaffer Westerhof,
California National University for Advanced Studies

Article

North Korea

The New York Times

Learning Outcomes

After reading this article, you will be able to:

- Examine whether Kim Jong-un has been successul in implementing free education for another year.

- Examine the political and business relationships between North Korea and South Korea.

- Examine the use and results of electronic media, such as cellphones and DVD players, by some of the populace in North Korea.

North Korea is the last Stalinist state on earth, and in 2006 it became the latest country to join the nuclear club. Over the past two decades, it has swung between confrontation and inch-by-inch conciliation with South Korea, its neighbor, and the United States, in an oscillation that seems to be driven both by its hard-to-fathom internal political strains and by an apparent belief in brinksmanship as the most effective form of diplomacy.

The uncertainty surrounding the actions of Pyongyang, the North's capital, deepened with the announcement by state media on Dec. 19, 2011, that its ailing ruler, Kim Jong-il, had died of a heart attack on a train on Dec. 17. Kim Jong-un, the youngest and previously least-known son of Kim Jong-il, was declared to be the country's next leader.

North Korea said the "great successor," as the younger Mr. Kim has been called, will faithfully follow his father's songun, or "military-first," policy, which has raised tensions with Washington and Seoul.

In his first six months as leader, Mr. Kim quickly alienated the Obama administration and put North Korea on track to develop a nuclear warhead that could hit the United States within a few years. By October 2012, North Korea claimed to have missiles that can reach the American mainland.

Most surprising, though, is how Mr. Kim has thumbed his nose at China, whose economic largess keeps the government afloat. For example, shortly after Mr. Kim took over, a Chinese vice minister of foreign affairs, Fu Ying, visited Pyongyang, North Korea's capital, and sternly warned him not to proceed with a ballistic missile test. The new leader went ahead anyway.

After Kim's Takeover, Average North Koreans See Few Gains

In the 10 months since Kim Jong-un took the reins of this desperately poor nation, North Korea—or at least its capital, Pyongyang—has acquired more of the trappings of a functioning society, say diplomats, aid groups and academics who have visited in recent months.

But four North Koreans—who were interviewed by The New York Times in Dandong, China—said that at least so far, they have not felt any improvements in their lives since the installment of their youthful leader. It was a sentiment that activists and analysts say they have also heard. In fact, the North Koreans said, their lives have gotten harder, despite Mr. Kim's tantalizing pronouncements about increasing people's livelihoods that have fueled outside hopes that the nuclear-armed nation might ease its economically ruinous obsession with military hardware and dabble in Chinese-style market reforms.

Food prices have spiked, the result of drought and North Korea's defiant launching of a rocket in April that shut down new offers of food aid from the United States. Development organizations also blame speculators who have hoarded staples in anticipation of reforms that have yet to materialize. The price of rice has doubled since early summer, and chronic shortages of fuel, electricity and raw materials continue to idle most factories, leaving millions unemployed.

What has become clear in recent months is that Mr. Kim is intent on a new leadership style—allowing more women to dress in Western wear that had long been branded a capitalist affectation, and breaking with tradition by publicly admitting a failure when the much ballyhooed rocket launch went awry. What is less clear is whether he will allow more than the baby steps toward economic reform that he is reported to have taken.

Those changes include a pilot project that North Korean defector groups say was introduced in the spring of 2012 that aims to let farmers keep 30 percent of their yield. The government has reportedly begun a guest-worker program, with the goal of giving thousands a chance to earn foreign currency in and around Dandong, China, a booming city that taunts hungry North Koreans across the Yalu River with its neon-lit barbecue restaurants.

Among the four North Koreans who were interviewed, though, optimism was in short supply. Emaciated beggars haunt train stations, they said, while well-connected businessmen continue to grow rich from trading with China and government officials flourish by collecting fines and bribes.

In two days of interviews with the North Koreans, a thinly concealed disgust over inequality that has risen in recent years—and a realization that the national credo of juche, or self-reliance, was a carefully constructed lie—was striking. While such feelings appear to be fed by the creeping availability of at least some information from the outside world, disillusionment mounted last spring after the government's promised era of prosperity, slated to begin in April, went unfulfilled. The discontent seemed to solidify with the government's rare admission of the failed rocket launching.

Escaping hunger by illegally crossing into China appears to be less viable since Mr. Kim came to power. According to South Korean officials, the number of defectors who arrived there after traveling through China had dropped to 751 during the first six months of 2012, a 42 percent decline from the same period last year.

Such figures do not tell the whole story, since it can take months or even years for refugees to earn enough to travel to South Korea, but rights advocates say the border has become increasingly impenetrable. The North Korean government has recently erected miles of electrified fencing at the border and sent as many as 20,000 additional guards, according to Open Radio for North Korea, which is based in South Korea, but has contacts in the North. In recent months, the Chinese government has also begun a crackdown on defectors who live in the three provinces closest to North Korea. Rights advocates say those caught are deported to North Korea, where they often face imprisonment.

Claims That Missiles Can Reach U.S. Mainland

In October 2012, North Korea claimed to have missiles that can reach the American mainland, and it said that the recent agreement between the United States and South Korea to extend the range of the South's ballistic missiles was increasing the risk of war on the Korean Peninsula.

Estimating the missile capabilities of a country as secretive as North Korea is notoriously difficult. But military experts and South Korean government officials have said that the North has already deployed ballistic missiles capable of reaching targets as far away as Guam, the American territory in the Pacific.

In addition, North Korea has repeatedly conducted what it calls satellite launchings that American and South Korean officials, as well as the United Nations Security Council, have condemned as a cover for developing and testing intercontinental ballistic missile technology. In 1998, the North sent up a rocket called the Taepodong-1 that flew over Japan and crashed into the Pacific. In 2006, the North launched the Taepodong-2, which exploded seconds after liftoff. It launched yet another long-range rocket, the Unha-2, in 2009; its first two stages appeared to work, but according to American and South Korean officials, the third stage never separated.

In April 2012, the Unha-3 rocket disintegrated in midair shortly after liftoff, a failure that the new government in Pyongyang publicly acknowledged.

But the North claimed to have successfully placed satellites into orbit in 1998 and 2009. The country has also conducted two nuclear tests, the first in 2006 and the second in 2009, although it remains unclear whether it can make a nuclear warhead small enough to fit atop a missile. Robert M. Gates said in early 2011, while he was the American defense secretary, that North Korea was within five years of being able to strike the continental United States with an intercontinental ballistic missile.

According to Jeung Young-tae, a military analyst at the government-run Korea Institute for National Unification in Seoul, the North's most recent strident statement was driven in part by a domestic political need to highlight the supposed threat from the United States and its allies. On Oct. 7, 2012, South Korea announced that it had reached a deal with Washington that would allow it to nearly triple the range of its ballistic missiles to 800 kilometers, or 500 miles, to better cope with the North's growing missile and nuclear capabilities.

Background: Self-Imposed Isolation and Poverty

Since the end of the Korean War in 1953, the North has not attacked its neighbor, South Korea, but to this day keeps large concentrations of troops and artillery focused on Seoul, and has regularly engaged in provocations like kidnappings, submarine incursions and missile tests over the Sea of Japan. In the 1990s, North Korea took steps toward warmer relations with South Korea, before questions about its nuclear ambitions plunged it back into isolation. More broadly, North Korea has taken a consistent anti-Washington line since its creation in 1948, denouncing South Korea as a puppet of the United States.

Internally, North Korea's problems continue to mount. A ham-handed currency revaluation in 2009, aimed at reasserting central control over the economy, was reported to have badly backfired, producing unrest and disaffection with the government. At the same time, the spread of cellphones and DVD players has broken the North's self-imposed isolation, giving many of its citizens a sense for the first time of how poor and backward their country has become.

Signs of hardship are evident even in the capital, Pyongyang. Commuters cram into decrepit electric buses, and pedestrians bow under huge bundles stuffed with goods for trade in private markets, which have eclipsed the ill-supplied state stores. Power shortages occur frequently. The pyramid-shaped, 105-story Ryugyong Hotel remains a shell nearly 25 years after construction began. Outside the city, other abandoned construction projects scar roads.

Away from the capital, North Korea is a land of shuttered factories and skimpy harvests. Residents, especially in northern provinces, report that child beggars haunt street markets, families scavenge hillsides for sprouts and mushrooms and workers at state enterprises receive nominal salaries, at best.

Although malnutrition has improved in the past decade, one in three North Korean children is stunted, and nearly one in five is underweight, according to the World Food Program. With paltry harvests, inflation of food prices is a chronic problem.

Food shortages have also been caused by years of economic mismanagement and underinvestment, and have been made worse in 2011 by poor weather and a reduction of food imports from China and South Korea.

In October 2011, Valerie Amos, the United Nations' humanitarian chief, said that North Koreans, especially children, urgently need outside aid to fight "terrible levels of malnutrition."

In November 2011, South Korea authorized the World Health Organization to resume the distribution of medical aid for malnourished North Korean children. The decision "was based upon our belief that purely humanitarian support for the young and vulnerable in North Korea should continue," a senior South Korean Unification Ministry official told reporters.

The Legacy of Kim Jong-Il

Called the "Dear Leader," Kim Jong-il had been the hereditary and eccentric ruler of North Korea, which was founded by his father, Kim Il-sung, from the time his father died in 1994. The two Kims had been the only leaders their country has known.

Under Kim Jong-il, North Korea became a nuclear power. It also became the world's most isolated state, one in which unknown numbers starved during recurrent famines, while money flowed to the country's military programs.

Kim Jong-il was considered an eccentric playboy who invariably appeared in platform shoes and a khaki jumpsuit. In 2008, Mr. Kim disappeared from sight for several months, and it was later revealed that he had suffered a stroke. After that, he became increasingly reclusive and began taking actions to transfer power to his son, Kim Jong-un, who in September 2010 was appointed a four-star general in the People's Army. In February 2011, he named his son vice chairman of the National Defense Commission, the country's most powerful body led by his father.

A Series of Provocative Actions

After setting off its first atomic device in 2006, the secretive, heavily militarized and desperately poor country slowly moved away from confrontation—and then slowly moved back toward it. In 2009 it successfully conducted its second nuclear test, again defying international warnings. Another international crisis was sparked by the sinking in March 2010 of a South Korean warship, the Cheonan, by a North Korean torpedo.

American intelligence officials said they were increasingly convinced that Kim Jong-il had ordered the sinking of the ship to help secure the succession of Kim Jong-un. Relations between North and South deteriorated to their worst point in many years, as South Korea's president, Lee Myung-bak, recast North Korea as its "principal enemy"—a designation dropped during inter-Korean detente in 2004—and the North retaliated by severing its few remaining ties with the South. The Obama administration announced that it would impose further economic sanctions against North Korea.

In November 2010, in the most serious clash in decades, North and South Korea exchanged artillery fire after an estimated 175 shells fired from the North struck a South Korean island near the countries' disputed maritime border. The North asserted that the South had fired first.

A Calculated Propaganda Message

When Kim Jong-il died, the younger Mr. Kim was such an unknown that the world did not even know what he looked like until his ailing father began grooming him as a successor in 2010. But the biggest enigma may be whether he will be able to hold onto power in this last bastion of hard-line Communism, much less prevent its impoverished economy from collapsing.

News of Kim Jong-il's death was kept secret for roughly two days, perhaps a sign that the leadership was struggling to position itself for what many believed could be a perilous transition.

For South Korean and American intelligence services to have failed to pick up any clues about Kim Jong-il's death attests to the secretive nature of North Korea, a country not only at odds with most of the world but also sealed off from it in a way that defies spies or satellites.

As the United States and its allies negotiate a leadership transition in North Korea, the closed nature of the country greatly complicates their calculations. With little information about Kim Jong-un, and even less insight into the palace intrigue in Pyongyang, much of their response has necessarily been guesswork.

Question of the Military's Allegiance

When Kim Jong-un was unveiled as his father's heir in 2010, he was given two powerful military titles: four-star general and vice chairman of the Central Military Commission. With his father's death, the support of the military is crucial if Kim Jong-un is to consolidate power.

To that end, on Dec. 21 North Korean television showed senior military leaders saluting the young Mr. Kim as he received mourners at the Kumsusan mausoleum, where his father lay inside a glass case for public viewing.

Three days later, state-run media showed footage of the top military brass flanking Kim Jong-un as they paid their respects to Mr. Kim's father and vowed their allegiance to his chosen successor. Among the officials there was Jang Song-taek, Mr. Kim's uncle and a vice chairman of the powerful National Defense Commission, whose role as the young successor's caretaker has been magnified during the transition. Mr. Jang, 65, wore a general's insignia.

On Dec. 28, the day of Kim Jong-il's funeral, Kim Jong-un walked alongside the hearse through snow-covered downtown Pyongyang, leading a procession that provided early glimpses of those serving as guardians of the young untested leader. Mr. Kim's two elder brothers, Kim Jong-nam and Kim Jong-chol, were nowhere to be seen.

Most prominent among those leading the funeral alongside and behind Mr. Kim were Jang Song-taek, Mr. Kim's uncle and a vice chairman of the powerful National Defense Commission, and Vice Marshal Ri Yong-ho, chief of the general staff of the Korean People's Army.

Mr. Ri, a relatively unknown figure during most of Kim Jong-il's rule, rose to prominence in 2010 and was widely seen as one of Mr. Kim's most trusted mentors. But in mid-July 2012, the state-run Korean Central News Agency startled Pyongyang watchers with the announcement that Mr. Ri had been removed from all posts because of "illness." The Politburo of the Central Committee of the Workers' Party of Korea also dismissed him.

With Mr. Ri's dismissal, some analysts say, one thing at least is clear: Mr. Kim is wielding his family's favorite tool of control—using and discarding the senior officials around him like pawns on a chess board.

No Official Condolences from Seoul or Washington

A day after Mr. Kim's death was announced, officials in Seoul and Washington issued coordinated statements. They were careful to direct their "sympathy" or "prayers" to the "North Korean people," not to the government, in contrast to Beijing and Moscow, which sent official condolences to the authorities in Pyongyang, the capital.

In response, North Korea urged South Korea on to "show proper respect" over the death of Kim Jong-il, calling the South's decision to express sympathy for the North Korean people but not to send a government delegation to Mr. Kim's funeral "an unbearable insult and mockery of our dignity."

South Korean officials said that while they were careful to avoid any hints of approval for Mr. Kim's legacy, they wanted to relay hopes for a more productive relationship with the North.

Though South Korea sent no official mourners, a private delegation of prominent South Koreans traveled to North Korea and met with Kim Jong-un. The meeting with the private delegation, which included Lee Hee-ho, the widow of former President Kim Dae-jung, and the chairwoman of Hyundai Asan, Hyun Jeong-eun, which had business ties with North Korea, appeared to be cordial.

The Seoul government said that Ms. Lee and Ms. Hyun were reciprocating for the North Korean delegations that visited Seoul to express condolences over the deaths of President Kim and of Chung Mong-hun, the former Hyundai chairman.

No Shift in Stance toward the South

When Ms. Lee met with the delegation in Pyongyang, Kim Yong-nam, president of the North Korean Parliament, called for the implementation of the inter-Korean summit agreements, which would have brought massive South Korean investments had the South Korean leader, Lee Myung-bak, not scuttled them.

Kim Jong-il held summit meetings with President Kim in 2000 and with his successor, Roh Moo-hyun, in 2007. Both meetings produced promises of large South Korean investments. Both South Korean leaders believed that boosting economic exchanges would ease military tensions on the divided Korean Peninsula and reduce the cost of an eventual reunification of Korea.

But that approach was reversed when President Lee, a conservative, came to power in early 2008. He demanded that the North first abandon its nuclear weapons program. North Korea has since denounced Mr. Lee as a "national traitor" and demanded that the summit agreements be reinstated. Its recent military provocations against the South were seen as efforts to win concessions.

Pyongyang's demand concerning the summit agreements provided an early sign that Kim Jong-un was not shifting the North's basic stance on South Korea.

Indeed, on Dec. 30, the National Defense Commission, North Korea's highest decision-making body, announced that there would be no change in its policy toward South Korea under its new leader, Kim Jong-un. The statement struck a characteristically hostile posture with a threat to punish President Lee Myung-bak of South Korea for "unforgivable sins." It marked the country's first official pronouncement to the outside world since the regime upheld Mr. Kim as its supreme leader on Dec. 29.

By returning swiftly to typical bellicose form after two weeks of mourning, North Korea appeared to demonstrate a confidence that the transition of power in Pyongyang was going smoothly. But the strident rhetoric was also a sign that the government, as it often has, was using perceived tensions with the outside world to rally its military and people behind the new leader.

Kim Jong-un Declared 'Supreme Leader'

In April 2012, the Workers' Party declared Kim Jong-un to be "supreme leader" and awarded him the title of first secretary during a party conference, the country's first major political gathering in one-and-a-half years. The inevitable elevation of Mr. Kim to the top defense commission post will complete his rise to the pinnacle of party, military and state leadership, at a speed that analysts in the region said reflected the insecurity of the young leader's status as much as it did the secretive leadership's need to have a solid power center in place immediately.

The Worker's Party conference gives the young leader—or the senior power elite surrounding him—an opportunity to shuffle party and military leaderships, gradually retiring old stalwarts from his father Kim Jong-il's days as leader and elevating younger loyalists.

Such a generation change has been unfolding since Mr. Kim was officially designated as his father's successor in the last party meeting, held in September 2010. More signs of the shift came on April 10, when the Korean Central News Agency revealed that Vice Marshal Kim Jong-gak, a key military political officer widely believed to be Mr. Kim's promoter among the military elite, was made People's Armed Forces Minister, a title equivalent to defense minister.

Two other senior officials said to have been hand-picked by Mr. Kim's father to help engineer the transfer of power to his son—Choe Ryong-hae and Hyon Chol-hae—were promoted to vice marshal ahead of the party meeting, the news agency said. The rise of Mr. Choe was particularly significant, according to analysts. At 61, he is relatively young among the top North Korean hierarchy, which has been filled with people in their 80s and 70s.

Mr. Choe's rise also showed that the dynastic transfer of power in Pyongyang was not just for the Kim family but was often for the rest of the elite class as well—a factor that analysts often cite to help explain the cohesion of the Kim rule. Mr. Choe's father fought alongside Kim Il-sung when he was leading a group of Korean guerrillas during the Japanese colonial rule from 1910 to 1945. The families of many of those guerrillas remained key members of the top ruling class.

Kim Jong-il never achieved the revered status of his father. The party decided to leave the previous top post—general secretary—vacant, designating Kim Jong-il "eternal general secretary." Similarly, when Kim Il-sung died in 1994, he was upheld as "eternal president" of the country.

The move illustrated the long shadows of his forefathers under which the young leader, Kim Jong-un, must operate.

Seeds of Foreign Enterprise

Ever so slowly, North Korea is opening to foreign investment. A focus of its strategy is developing previously created "free trade and economic zones" on the borders that have languished.

An example can be found in the remote northern port towns of Rajin and Sonbong. About 30 miles from China, the combined towns, called Rason, are central to the new push. Since designating Rason a special zone in 1991, North Korean officials have tried on occasion to attract investment there, with poor results. Some foreign analysts and businesspeople remain skeptical, saying the country's investment climate is still too unstable, but others argue that North Korea could be establishing here the kind of laboratory that the Chinese Communist Party set up in the fishing village of Shenzhen in 1980 to help move China forward.

On the surface, Rason is an unlikely site for a boomtown. It is a three-hour drive on a rutted dirt road from the Chinese border. In the surrounding countryside, green with cornfields and pine trees, men ride horses and ox carts while women dry cuttlefish on rooftops. The area, home to 200,000, suffers from blackouts. In the town center, bicyclists navigate dirt tracks. There are few cars, stores or restaurants.

But Rason's port remains ice-free, a rarity in Northeast Asia, and officials there see shipping as a pillar of economic growth, along with seafood processing and tourism. They say they also want foreign-run assembly plants and high-technology factories. As inducements, they say they would offer tax breaks, full foreign control and minimum monthly wages set at $80 per worker, lower than in China.

The central question is whether the ideologies of the current regime will allow for long-term reforms to spur economic growth.

Nuclear Program

The United States came close to military action against North Korea in 1994, as President Clinton weighed the idea of air strikes against its nuclear sites. Instead, in a last-minute deal, North Korea agreed to shelve its nuclear program. In 2002, President Bush included Pyongyang in the "axis of evil," and American officials charged later that year that North Korea had violated the earlier agreement. Pyongyang declared the agreement void and expelled international nuclear inspectors.

North Korea agreed in September 2005 to abandon its nuclear programs in exchange for economic assistance and diplomatic incentives from other parties to the six-party talks, which include China, Japan, Russia and South Korea, in addition to North Korea and the United States.

But the agreement collapsed in a dispute over how thoroughly North Korea should reveal its nuclear activities and subject its nuclear facilities to outside inspections. North Korea's continuing nuclear activities, its testing of missiles and the lethal shelling of the South Korean island—as well as the sinking of the South Korean naval vessel—all added to the chill in relations.

In November 2010, the North revealed a vast facility built secretly and rapidly to enrich uranium. The Obama administration concluded that the North's plant to enrich nuclear fuel uses technology that is "significantly more advanced" than what Iran has struggled over two decades to assemble.

In January 2011, former Defense Secretary Robert M. Gates warned that North Korea was within five years of being able to strike the continental United States with an intercontinental ballistic missile, and said that, combined with its expanding nuclear program, the country "is becoming a direct threat to the United States."

In late August 2011, Kim Jong-il went to Russia, where he met with President Dmitri A. Medvedev. During their meeting, Mr. Kim agreed to consider a moratorium on nuclear weapons tests and production, and said he wanted to return to the stalled talks on the nation's nuclear program.

In January 2012, North Korea said that it was open to further negotiations over a deal to halt its uranium enrichment program, an agreement that seemed within reach before the death of Kim Jong-il in December 2011.

In late February, North Korea agreed to suspend nuclear weapons tests and uranium enrichment and to allow international inspectors to verify and monitor activities at its main reactor, as part of a deal that included an American pledge to ship food aid to the impoverished nation. The agreement came after two days of talks with American officials in Beijing.

North Korea also agreed on a moratorium on launches of long-range missiles, and to resume the six party talks. Both South Korea and Japan welcomed the deal as an important first step, though they cautioned that they would wait to see whether North Korea would faithfully implement it.

Indeed, the agreement was imperiled only two weeks later, when North Korea announced that it planned to launch a satellite into orbit in April, testing a technology that the United States and the United Nations Security Council have condemned as a cover for developing and testing long-range intercontinental ballistic missiles.

Group Says North Korea Resumes Building Reactor

In May 2012, an American-based institute said that North Korea had resumed construction of a nuclear reactor, citing satellite imagery of the building site.

Commercial satellite imagery, including photography taken in April 2012, showed that North Korea had resumed building work in its main nuclear complex in Yongbyon, north of Pyongyang, after months of inactivity and that the country was close to completing a reactor containment building, according to an analysis posted at 38 North, a Web site run by the U.S.-Korea Institute at Johns Hopkins University.

"Over all, it may take another one to two years before the new facility becomes operational," the organization said in a statement.

Analysts warned that the failed satellite launching might cause North Korea to ramp up its uranium enrichment in an effort to regain leverage in talks with Washington.

Following the humiliating satellite launch, North Korea accused South Korea's government and news media of slandering its leadership and threatened "special actions" by the military—a sharp escalation of the bellicose statements that have accompanied the rise of Kim Jong-un.

Forging a Different Leadership Style from His Father

The world knows precious little about Kim Jong-un, including exactly how old he is, the best guess is in his 20s. But figuring out what he might be thinking is critical to determining how much of a threat he, and the nuclear program he inherited, poses to his neighbors, and North Korea's enemies in the West.

During the summer of 2012, analysts puzzled over photos of women sporting miniskirts and heels in downtown Pyongyang, a stunning change from the years when Western wear was mostly shunned in favor of billowy traditional dresses or drab Mao-style work uniforms.

Then, Mr. Kim himself was shown on state TV giving a thumbs up to a girl band featuring leggy string players performing for him and his generals, and the debate over deeper meaning began in earnest.

In a political system that tightly choreographs its messages, could short skirts—along with the appearance of Mickey Mouse and a film clip of Sylvester Stallone as Rocky Balboa at the same concert—indicate some rethinking of the North's attitudes toward the West? Or was the fashion statement decidedly less weighty: perhaps another short-lived attempt to divert the attention of an unhappy populace?

So far, the puzzle pieces leave little doubt that Mr. Kim is trying to forge a very different leadership style from his father. Kim Jong-un, by comparison, appears to be more approachable (photos show him hooking arms with factory workers and soldiers); less threatened by foreign cultures and apparently more willing to admit failure (he told the nation of a botched rocket launch in April 2012).

But there is also ample evidence that Mr. Kim does not plan to veer far from his father's and grandfather's governing policies on most issues, including maintaining a strong military and nuclear arms program and issuing frequent, florid threats against South Korea and the United States. Mr. Kim launched the rocket in April despite the likelihood that it would kill a new food aid agreement with the United States, which it did, and annoy the North's last true ally, China, which had urged restraint.

North Koreans Learn They Have a First Lady

In July 2012, North Korea's state-run news media ended weeks of speculation about the identity of a young woman seen with Kim Jong-un at various public events, announcing that she is his wife.

The North's Central TV showed Mr. Kim attending a ceremony honoring the completion of an amusement park in the capital, Pyongyang, with the woman, and identified her as "Comrade Ri Sol-ju, wife of Marshal Kim Jong-un," South Korean officials said.

The images were a major shift for North Korea. During the rule of Mr. Kim's father, most ordinary North Koreans had never seen their first lady on television; many defectors in that era did not know her name or those of any of the leader's children. By revealing Kim Jong-un's marital status, North Korean media was broadening his appeal and emphasizing his maturity, analysts said.

Another photo showed Ms. Ri with something most North Korean women have never heard of, much less owned: a Christian Dior handbag.

South Korean journalists were quick to point out that its going price in Seoul is about 1.8 million won, or $1,600. That is about 16 times the average monthly wage of a North Korean worker in the Gaeseong industrial park, a joint venture between North and South Korea that provides some of the best-paying jobs in the impoverished North.

The South Korean news media also noted the apparent "belly fat"—or is it a baby bump?—that Ms. Ri has developed. The South Korean spy agency believes that Ms. Ri and Mr. Kim already have a child.

A Deepening Reliance on China

Mr. Kim called for building a "prosperous country" in a major policy guideline published on Aug. 3, 2012, a day after he told a visiting Chinese delegation that he was focused on "developing the economy and improving people's livelihoods."

The statements were the latest in a series that Mr. Kim has issued in which he sounded more focused on tackling North Korea's moribund economy than his father, Kim Jong-il, who championed a "military-first policy" that lavished resources on the armed services.

Mr. Kim made the statements after meeting with the head of the Chinese Communist Party's International Liaison Department. China's help is crucial to an economic revitalization program that analysts believe Mr. Kim is pursuing, including a reported agreement to allow thousands of North Koreans to work in China on a guest-worker program as a way of building foreign currency reserves.

North Korea's reliance on China has deepened as international sanctions have tightened and outside aid has dwindled following the country's nuclear and long-range missile tests in recent years. China's trade with North Korea grew rapidly in the past several years as North Korea bolstered exports, mainly minerals, to China and imported more food and other Chinese goods to make up for losses in trade and aid from countries like South Korea and Japan. For years, Chinese leaders have urged North Korea to follow their route to economic reform. But so far, the country has only dabbled in such experiments.

North Korea's poverty is so deep, and its economy so dysfunctional, that two-thirds of its people are estimated to be suffering from chronic food shortages.

While analysts have noted the apparent change in tone from Mr. Kim, some suggest caution in reading too much into it just yet.

North Korean Leader in Beijing

On Aug. 17, 2012, the uncle of the North Korean leader met in Beijing with President Hu Jintao and Prime Minister Wen Jiabao of China, indicating his growing influence as a key adviser to the young Mr. Kim.

China's official media said the trip could be a prelude to the leader's first visit, but the official focus was economic development. The meetings between the uncle, Jang Song-thaek, and the top leaders came toward the end of his six-day trip to China, during which the government in Beijing promised to help North Korea develop two special trade zones near the Chinese border. Such zones, if successful, would provide the Pyongyang government with badly needed money as it tries to revive its staggering economy.

Mr. Jang, who is widely seen as Mr. Kim's point man to oversee the development of the zones, is the most powerful North Korean official to visit China since Kim Jong-il went there in August 2011. South Korean analysts consider him a significant influence in Mr. Kim's recent efforts to tame his military and implement his economic revitalization program, which, according to South Korean news media, includes allowing farmers to own part of their annual yield as an incentive.

Beginning Talks with Japan

Japan and North Korea ended their first direct talks in four years on Aug. 31, 2012, with an agreement to meet again, apparently in a sign of the North's desire to reduce tensions with Japan, and by extension, the United States.

Japanese analysts have said that the talks in Beijing, which began on Aug. 29, may be a signal that the North's new ruler, Kim Jong-un, wants to improve his nation's destitute economy by reaching out to Japan, America's most important Asian ally. They said Mr. Kim might also be trying to reduce his country's economic dependence on China, which supplies the North with fuel and food.

Disagreements over issues like the fate of Japanese citizens abducted by North Korean agents decades ago had led Japan to cut off all trade and ties with the North. The top

Japanese government spokesman, Chief Cabinet Secretary Osamu Fujimura, said the abduction issue would be on the agenda when the two nations meet again.

While the North's overtures might represent a new openness, North Korea has reached out to countries it considers adversaries before, only to break agreements and lash out in anger.

The talks began as a meeting to discuss Japan's retrieval of the remains of some of the 21,000 Japanese who died at the end of World War II in what is now North Korea, which at the time was part of a Japanese colony. But the meeting broadened into a discussion of an agenda for future talks between the two nations.

Leaders Promise Improvements in Education

North Korea's leadership ended a rare second session of Parliament in a single year on Sept. 25, 2012, without making the announcements on economic reforms that many analysts had expected.

The one-day session ended instead with an announcement of changes to the isolated country's educational system, including adding a year of free education that analysts saw as potentially popular with the North Korean people.

It is unclear what the silence on economic reforms means. Recent reports by the South Korean press and Seoul-based websites that rely on sources in North Korea have said that Kim Jong-un was considering a series of important changes to try to jump-start the moribund economy, including giving more incentives to farms and factories to increase productivity.

The country has begun economic reforms in the past, but then backtracked.

Analysts in South Korea said that in putting education at the center of the first policy changes made public under his leadership, Mr. Kim was trying to reinforce the public's faith in the country's dynastic regime.

The move would seem to fit with Mr. Kim's attempts in recent months to at least appear to be open to change and attuned to his people's needs. The North Korean education system has been in ruins since a famine in the 1990s deprived most schools of heating fuel, adequate food rations and school supplies, deprivations that some analysts believe continue today.

The rubber-stamp legislature extended compulsory education to 12 years from 11, promised more classrooms and said that teachers would be given priority in the distribution of food and fuel rations, according to the North's official Korean Central News Agency.

The Supreme People's Assembly also pledged to end the "unruly mobilization of students" for activities outside school. The official report did not elaborate on this; however, since famine struck North Korea in the mid-1990s, mobilizing students to gather firewood and human and animal waste for fertilizer has become a common practice in the country's schools, and a major parental grievance, according to defectors.

The report did not say how the North would finance the first major overhaul of its educational system in four decades, and it is unclear how far the government will be willing to go in changing an education system that defectors say focuses much of its time on state propaganda.

Critical Thinking

1. Can the relationships between North Korea and South Korea be truly normalized? Explain.
2. Can China's liaison to North Korea be a positive influence in decision making within the Pacific Rim? Explain.
3. If the farmers in North Korea are allowed to keep more of their fair yield, will famine be reduced among the very poor? Explain.

Create Central

www.mhhe.com/createcentral

Internet References

North Korea—*The New York Times*
   http://topics.nytimes.com/top/news/international/countriesandterritories/northkorea

North Korean Leader Tightens Grip with Removal of His Top General
   www.nytimes.com/2013/10/11/world/asia/north-korean-leader-tightens-grip-with-removal-of-top-general.html?_r=0

Korea News—Gateway to Korea
   www.korea.net

UN Panel Urges International Action on North Korean Human Rights Abuses
   www.nytimes.com/2013/09/18/world/europe/un-panel-urges-action-on-north-korean-rights-abuses.html

North Koreans Launch Rocket in Defiant Act
   www.nytimes.com/2012/12/13/world/asia/north-korea-rocket-launching.html

North Koreans See Few Gains below Top Tier
   www.nytimes.com/2012/10/15/world/asia/north-koreans-say-life-has-not-improved.html

Article   Prepared by: Caroline Shaffer Westerhof,
                        California National University for Advanced Studies

Wang, Yang Make the Rounds in DC

CHEN WEIHUA

Learning Outcomes

After reading this article, you will be able to:

- Understand your interpretation of the major breakthrough for China and the United States to agree to begin "substantive negotiations."

- Understand the importance and meaning of negotiations on the bilateral investment treaty (BIT).

- Understand the benefits, activity, and outcome of networking by Chinese Vice Premier Wang and State Councilor Yang.

Chinese Vice-Premier Wang Yang and State Councilor Yang Jiechi, who co-chaired the 5th round of the China-US Strategic and Economic Dialogue (S&ED), wasted no time in implementing the consensus reached by both sides to enhance high-level exchanges.

On Friday morning, Wang met with U.S. Commerce Secretary Penny Pritzker and US Trade Representative Michael Froman, both of whom just took office in late June.

Wang said that the S&ED July 10–11 had achieved its expected outcome. Both sides had reached consensus on a number of key issues, such as entering a substantive stage of negotiation on a bilateral investment treaty.

Wang, who assumed his post in March, said both sides should redouble their efforts in implementing the consensus from the dialogue.

"China hopes to take the S&ED as a fresh start to further expand consensus and narrow differences and to elevate China-US economic relations to a higher level," Wang said.

Froman and Pritzker praised the S&ED as a great success. They said that the goodwill on both sides in resolving problems and boosting cooperation had laid a solid foundation for further bilateral economic and trade cooperation, including the China-US Joint Commission on Commerce and Trade (JCCT) session to be held later this year.

The outcome document of the S&ED's economic track, which was made public on Friday, said China and the US recognize that a bilateral investment treaty that sets high standards, including openness, non-discrimination, and transparency, would be important to both sides.

It also said that after nine rounds of technical discussions, China would enter into substantive BIT negotiations with the U.S.

The same morning, Wang went to the Capitol Hill to meet a bipartisan group of Congressional leaders, including Senate Majority Leader Harry Reid, a Democrat from Nevada; Republican Senator John McCain of Arizona; Senator Tim Kaine, Democrat from Virginia and Senator Kelly Ayotte, Republican from New Hampshire.

Their talk touched on a wide range of economic and security issues, such as cyber security, denuclearization of the Korean Peninsula, Iran's nuclear program, and Syria.

That same day, State Councilor Yang, a former foreign minister and ambassador to the US, met with Defense Secretary Chuck Hagel in the Pentagon.

Yang said China will continue to strength military-to-military exchanges with the US in order to increase strategic trust and avoid misunderstanding and miscalculations.

Hagel echoed Yang's words, saying the US will earnestly implement the consensus reached at S&ED and the one by the two heads of state in Sunnylands, California, a month ago to deepen dialogue, exchange and cooperation with the Chinese military and to increase mutual understanding and trust and push forward a bilateral military relationship.

The outcome document from the strategic track of the S&ED, also made public on Friday, identified 91 areas for further cooperation, including a commitment to strengthen the military-to-military relationship and to make efforts to raise the relationship to a new level.

It reaffirms the visit to the US by China's Minister of National Defense in 2013 and a reciprocal visit to China by the US Secretary of Defense at a mutually convenient date in 2014.

Both sides also decided to actively explore a notification mechanism for major military activities and to continue discussions on the rules of behavior on military air and maritime activities, including at the next Military Maritime Consultative Agreement (MMCA) plenary.

Also on Friday, Yang met US National Security Advisor Susan Rice. Yang said that the consensus reached by Presidents Xi Jinping and Obama to build a new type of major-country relationship has pointed a clear direction and mapped out a blueprint for a bilateral relationship. Rice, who took office on July 1, said that President Obama and the US government are committed to the promise of developing relations with China. She also expressed her satisfaction at the outcome of the S&ED.

Last Thursday, Obama met Wang and Yang in the Oval Office, during which Wang delivered a letter from President Xi, who expressed his confidence in the prospect of China-US relations. That same day, Wang met with US Agriculture Secretary Tom Vilsack.

Critical Thinking

1. Is it realistic to believe that President Obama and the U.S. government and China's Vice Premier Wang and State Councilor Yang and the government of China will deepen their dialogue regarding discussions on Chinese military, thus promoting a bilateral military relationship? Explain.

2. Are there complex issues that can disrupt the China–U.S. relations? Explain.

3. What is to be accomplished bilaterally by China accepting a U.S. invitation to participate in the 2014 Rim of the Pacific Conference (ROMPAC)? Explain.

Create Central

www.mhhe.com/createcentral

Internet References

China–US Focus
www.chinausfocus.com/china-news/constructive-mood-at-sino-us-talks

Obama Applauds China-US High-Level Talks—*China Daily*
www.chinadaily.com.cn/business/2013-07/12/content_16768979.htm

Dialogue Important to Accelerate Development & Co-op
www.chinadaily.com.cn/business/2013Sino-UStalk/2013-07/11/content_16762836.htm

---

CHEN WEIHUA is the Chief Washington Correspondent of *China Daily* and Deputy Editor of *China Daily USA*.

Article

Prepared by: Caroline Shaffer Westerhof,
California National University for Advanced Studies

U.S., China Hopeful of BIT after Talks Reignited

CHEN WEIHUA

Learning Outcomes

After reading this article, you will be able to:

- Understand why the Bilateral Investment Treaty is considered a priority for United States and China.

- Understand how the China-United States BIT will affect the global economy.

- Examine the effects if the BIT talks between China and United States were disrupted.

If Chinese and United States leaders hammer out and agree on their long-discussed investment treaty, Chinese officials and observers believe the deal will further encourage Chinese outbound investment in the US.

With Chinese outbound direct investment rising dramatically, leaders from both nations reignited negotiations on the Bilateral Investment Treaty at the just-concluded China-US Strategic and Economic Dialogue in Washington.

"The two sides agreed to enter a more substantive stage of negotiation as soon as possible,"said Chinese Minister of Commerce Gao Hucheng on Thursday in Washington.

Talks on a BIT have gone through nine rounds of preliminary discussions between the two countries, drawing a great deal of attention from business communities in both China and the US. Gao described the previous talks on a BIT as "technical negotiations" that laid a foundation for more substantive talks.

China was the world's third-largest outbound investor last year. Its direct investment into the US reached $20 billion, compared to $70 billion in US direct investment within China. In recent years, Chinese outbound investment has been rapidly growing.

"This requires us to establish a better legal framework with our partners that will better protect the interests of Chinese investors," Gao said.

He predicted that in the next three to five years, the amount of Chinese outbound investments will exceed US investments into China.

Gao said leaders stepped up negotiations on a BIT as a result of the consensus reached a month ago by Chinese President Xi Jinping and US President Barack Obama in Sunnylands, California.

He said investment is an important part of the China-US economic and trade relationship.

"It requires creative thinking to build a cooperative and mutually beneficial environment," he said.

A senior official from the US Treasury Department hailed the discussion on the BIT at the S&ED, applauding some of the concessions from China, especially involving the service sector.

"A high-standard US-China BIT is a priority for the US and would work to level the playing field for American workers and businesses by opening markets for fair competition,"said US Treasury Secretary Jack Lew in a statement on Thursday afternoon.

Orville Schell, director of the Center on US-China Relations at the Asia Society, said if the two countries are serious about cementing better relations, it is essential that Chinese FDI in the US be explicitly welcomed.

"By helping the US to capture more of the significant new investment capital now starting to seek exit from China, a US-China BIT would serve a critical purpose. One can only hope the treaty will find early agreement and lead to a more cooperative atmosphere that enables other more intractable, but even more important, bilateral issues to resolutions," Schell said.

While the US claims it offers the most open environment for foreign investors, many Chinese feel that Chinese FDI within the US has been unjustly targeted.

Besides a possible BIT, a wide range of economic and trade issues were discussed over the two-day S&ED. China raised its concerns over US restrictions on high-tech exports to China and the US' review process of Chinese FDI into the US. Both sides also discussed trade protectionism.

Critical Thinking

1. How will the success of the BIT benefit global economic issues?
2. Why is China media calling for "de-Americanising" after U.S. shutdown?
3. Would BIT talks be affected because China's September 2013 growth is slower?

Create Central

www.mhhe.com/createcentral

Internet References

China, US Explore New Treaty
usa.chinadaily.com.cn/epaper/2013-07/12/content_16767835.htm

Change Drives China-US Talks
http://usa.chinadaily.com.cn/business/2013-07/17/content_16789180.htm

Economy—*China daily US Edition*
usa.chinadaily.com.cn/business/economy_9.html

World Trade Online
insidetrade.com

Shanghai Daily
www.shanghaidaily.com

CHEN WEIHUA is the Chief Washington Correspondent of *China Daily* and Deputy Editor of *China Daily USA*.

Unit 5

UNIT

Prepared by: Caroline Shaffer Westerhof,
California National University for Advanced Studies

The Legislature: Is Representation Also Representative?

The concept of representation focuses on legislatures' role in the political process: how they balance democratic responsiveness and accountability with effective policymaking; how continuous reelection, serving some 20 or more terms is effective representation; and how their performance as institutions and in policymaking may run up against political development. To that effect, we systematically address the questions of "why, what, and how" regarding the legislature. Legislatures demonstrate and capture representation of their constituents in government and serve to check against the excesses of executives or they may become the stronghold of representation for autocratic leaders. It is possible that where the executive imposes the "discipline" of a single policymaker in lawmaking, the legislature aims at representing the range of citizens' responses and needs in policy and legislation making while balancing the tyranny of the single executive decision-maker. Ideally, the legislature may be a small replica of the citizenry in all its diversity. One of the most important tasks of legislators is to represent. In an authoritarian regime the legislature becomes the "mouthpiece" for the tyrannical leader.

How important is it that the legislature performs as a representative institution? One way to answer that question is to consider the alternative: what happens when legislatures fail to represent. Such can lead to "tyranny of the majority;" which is not measured in numbers, but the concept of majority is registered as "Who holds the power?" The Party of Freedom (PVV) in The Netherlands makes it clear that the only real guard against widespread negative stereotypical views against minorities and xenophobia is to ensure that legislatures truly represent that concept.

In Israel we witness the power and control of Israel's minority ultra-religious groups, being now challenged by new electoral rules. Of course, even when the role is embraced by legislators, realization of representation is often not so easy. Underrepresentation of minorities tends to be the norm, because countries often embrace electoral systems that privilege the majority. Why? Part of the problem may be the electoral system. For example, most countries embrace the single-member district electoral system. In the single member district, candidates with the most votes often win the seat as legislative representative. In practice, single-member district electoral systems also skew, rather than ensure, representativeness.

In parts of India we see political party dissension coming to the forefront as voters try to push for changes through their elected representatives. Such changes include a demand for separate statehood. In the United States, also, one must go through Congress to change state boundaries or create a new state. Political party dissension and voting results have come to the forefront in polls in certain parts of India as in the United States. Pakistan is in crisis. Can Pakistan be stabilized through changing personalities and political party representation in its legislature?

Specifically, with increased representation, the legislature strengthens as a representative institution and, hence, provides more stability through representation. However, with increased representation, the legislature also becomes more competitive, as parties—large and small—gain seats into the legislature. With such a broad array of parties, the ability to unify and guard against the excesses of the president as executive is concurrently reduced while the ability of the prime minister and cabinet as executive to formulate policies and implement them is also reduced. Institutionally, the executive is structured in one of three ways: as president in a presidential system; as prime minister and cabinet in a parliamentary system; as president and prime minister in a presidential-parliamentary hybrid system. In a presidential system, the executive—the president—is independently elected to office. Many voters, particularly in the United States, may independently vote for the president from one party and elect representatives from another party. Such can make for negotiations between the president and the representative body in trying to develop legislation. In a parliamentary system, the executive—generally a reference to the prime minster, but more accurately applied to the entire cabinet—is chosen by the elected legislature or parliament. In parliamentary systems, there is no independent election for the executive. In a presidential-parliamentary hybrid system, also known as the semi-presidential system or mixed system, the president is elected independently, while the prime minister and cabinet are chosen by the legislature. The mixed system is becoming the political system of choice in emerging democracies: at last count in 2002, there were 25 nations with mixed systems, up from only three in 1946.[1]

The mixed systems maximize efficiency in policymaking but provide some guard against executive authority.[2]

Of course, this means that the representational and institutional roles of the legislature remain at the fore in emergent democracies. In this regard, representation must be measured by more than physical symbol. To truly represent a constituency, a legislator must achieve successful policymaking, not populist appeals. Indeed, the legislator's role is to actively avoid such populist appeals, since these provide springboards for individual political careers but do nothing in terms of the enhancing the political or economic infrastructure that will improve the people's lives.

It is important to note that legislators do not have to initiate policies in order to support or oppose them. What legislatures must do in order to demonstrate representation in policymaking is to pass or decline legislation, which entails the essential tasks of discussing, examining, and debating the policies introduced, doing so with an eye on the big picture of economic and political development in the country. In principle, the aggregation of all legislators' input ensures that proposed legislation captures or is amended in the end product to contain the diversity of citizens' responses and needs or the affirmation of the autocratic leader.

This brings us full circle to the importance of citizens' participation, particularly at the polls. Lack of participation at the polls, regardless of whether in emergent or mature democracies, undermines the political process and its development. Insofar as the lack of representativeness affects participation, many of the potential barriers to representation from electoral systems may be relatively easy to remedy. For instance, transparent campaign finance laws have helped address the disadvantages faced by minority or women candidates. What is clear is that the representativeness of legislature is not merely a political principle but a means to ensuring political stability or to affirming the decisions of the dictatorial leader, whether acknowledged or not.

Notes

1. See José Antonio Cheibub and Svitlana Chernykh. 2008. "Constitutions and Democratic Performance in Semi-Presidential Democracy." *Japanese Journal of Political Science* vol. 9 no 3: 269–303.

2. See Michael Sodaro, *Comparative Politics: A Global Introduction* (*3rd edition*). New York: McGraw-Hill (2007).

Article

Prepared by: Caroline Shaffer Westerhof,
California National University for Advanced Studies

The Famous Dutch (In)Tolerance

"Variations of Geert Wilders's xenophobic message are shared by the majority of the political parties represented in the Dutch parliament."

Jan Erk

Learning Outcomes

After reading this article, you will be able to:

- Understand the concept of the "tyranny of the majority."

- Examine why the Party of Freedom in the Netherlands has made discrimination acceptable.

- Explain the concept of xenophobia.

The Dutch have long enjoyed a reputation for tolerance, and they are indeed a tolerant people: They are tolerant of the anti-immigrant sentiment that has engulfed their country's politics over the past decade. Part of the political partnership running the Netherlands today is a party whose agenda includes ethnic registration, a tax on Muslim headscarves, repatriation of Dutch criminals of immigrant origin, a blanket ban on the construction of mosques, and outlawing the Koran.

To a large extent, this situation is a side effect of the fact that anti-Muslim discourse has encountered growing acceptance in recent years. Such discourse has allowed anti-immigrant sentiment—in the Dutch case, sentiment against the people of Moroccan and Turkish derivation who constitute a majority of the country's immigrants—to become palatable to mainstream sensibilities.

In fact, the far-right Party of Freedom (PVV) could never have gained inclusion in the political coalition governing the nation had it continued using the race-based rhetoric associated with xenophobic parties of the past. Instead, the PVV employs anti-Islam rhetoric. The words do not carry the same anti-immigrant overtones as race-based rhetoric, but they have the same effect.

In June 2010, national elections resulted in a major electoral success for the upstart PVV, which had been formed only four years before by Geert Wilders. Afterwards the PVV became a coalition partner of the Christian Democrat Appeal (CDA, a Christian Democrat party) and the People's Party for Freedom and Democracy (VVD, a right-liberal party). Leaders of the three parties unveiled a new coalition program on September 30, a cabinet was put together in the following weeks (though the PVV gained no ministerial portfolio), and the government was sworn in on October 14.

Not long before this, Wilders had tried to take his party's message to the United States, joining in the opposition to the planned construction of a Muslim community center near the former site of the World Trade Center in New York City, but he failed to attract much media interest in North America. Wilders managed to create more interest in Australia, where in an interview he called Islam a "retarded and violent" religion.

The PVV's membership in the governing coalition will likely help Wilders increase his international profile beyond Europe, where he is already well known. But how did his party, in a country renowned for its progressive politics, become a governing partner?

The Anti-Islam Norm

A simple but misleading narrative seems to dominate media reporting on the rise of the xeno-phobic right in the Netherlands. According to this narrative, a single party led by the colorful populist Wilders broke ranks with The Hague–based Dutch political establishment and stood up to the left-liberal media, thereby shaking the country's progressive foundations. This picture is clear and compelling. It is very kind to the Dutch political establishment. It is also incorrect.

Wilders's peroxide blond hair, his offensive outbursts, and his clownish antics comport with the image that the media have painted for him, that of the outsider. But in fact, variations of Geert Wilders's xenophobic message are shared by the majority of the political parties represented in the Dutch parliament. Put simply, Wilders is a product of the Dutch political system and his message is not confined to the fringes of the political spectrum. His message is disguised in anti-Islam language, which makes it more palatable than is naked xenophobia to mainstream sensibilities.

Although no member of the PVV holds a ministerial portfolio, the party's influence over the formation of the cabinet last year was recently exposed when it became clear that certain posts—including that of the minister of integration—had had to be vetted by Wilders.

Moreover, the governing coalition's program includes a number of priorities that defined the PVV's 2010 electoral campaign. The government proposes to ban the face-covering Islamic burqa. Residence without a permit is to be made a criminal act, and arranging family unification for immigrants will become harder. The governing coalition plans to halve the number of people allowed to immigrate to the Netherlands from so-called non-Western countries, and to require those who are allowed in to participate in stricter and more expensive integration courses.

Some of the PVV's anti-Islam positions are concealed in ambiguous wording. One example is the rather bizarre goal of cutting unemployment and social security benefits to those "whose clothing is not suitable for finding work"—which potentially could become a means for denying benefits to Muslims who wear traditional garb.

To be sure, not all components of the government's program necessarily represent realistic proposals. For example, this author has never seen anyone in the Netherlands wearing a burqa, so the ban against it is more a coded message to supporters than a piece of public policy. Yet this only accentuates the fact that the coalition program, while highlighting symbolic issues, has failed to address many pressing problems in the economic realm. The government has made a few selective cuts in public spending, but it has proposed no structural reform of the economy, no reform of the housing market, and no relaxation of the country's rigid labor market.

Meanwhile, immigration has become the top political issue in a country that—compared to other nations across the Western world—does not have a very large immigrant population. The four biggest immigrant communities in the Netherlands are Turks, Moroccans, Antilleans, and Surinamese; together they total just under 1 million people, in a country of 17 million. Yet these Dutch citizens now find themselves living under a coalition government that has adopted specific policies targeting them.

Margin to the Middle

This picture of Dutch politics probably clashes with the impression of the Netherlands that most foreign visitors to Amsterdam take home with them. The Netherlands is of course bigger than the old city center of the capital, and the rest of the country has always been more socially conservative than its biggest city, which among its tourist attractions offers (sanitized) vice.

In any case, Dutch people's tolerance of soft drugs, pornography, and prostitution is not the same as social permissiveness. The Dutch word that refers to the decriminalized provision of vice, *gedogen,* merely suggests that those who infringe against collective morality will be tolerated and granted tacit immunity from prosecution. Such tolerance implies no endorsement, and this is nothing new.

What is new is the acceptance of a far-right xenophobic party as a bona fide governing partner. Parties with similar agendas have appeared on the Dutch landscape in the past. These, however, not only were politically marginalized—they were pursued by magistrates for promoting discrimination.

For example, the far-right Dutch People's Union entered the parliament in 1977, but immediately became a target of prosecutors, and was banned the following year (although a

complicated legal process followed). The Center Party (CP) was another such party, entering parliament in 1982. Internal splits spawned offshoots such as the Center Democrats (CD), the Center Party '86 (CP'86), the New National Party (NNP), and the Dutch Bloc. CP'86 was banned in 1996 and was dissolved by magistrates the following year for advocating discrimination and endangering public order. The same year the veteran leader of the CD (who had started his career in the CP) was found guilty of inciting racial hatred.

It is important to recall that these far-right outfits operated on the margins of Dutch mainstream politics. Yet now the two largest center-right parties in the parliament maintain a political partnership with Wilders—and they do so even though, coincident with the formation of the coalition government, Wilders was the subject of a court case that involved inciting racial hatred against Muslims. (Prosecutors themselves, who had brought the case to court partly because they had come under criticism from antiracism activists for doing too little regarding Wilders, declared their opinion that he was not guilty.)

The PVV's status as the third-largest party in the parliament might not appear to justify all the attention it has received—but the Dutch electoral system is based on the principle of proportional representation, and it lacks the nationwide vote threshold that is a feature of most other proportional systems. In Germany, for example, political parties must gain at least 5 percent of the nationwide vote to gain seats based on their proportion of the votes cast.

The absence of such a threshold in the Netherlands means that the Dutch parliament is composed of a multitude of parties ranging from the Party for Animals, with 2 seats, to the right-liberal VVD, with 31. In this context, the PVV's 24 seats give Wilders major clout within the ruling partnership. By themselves, the CDA with its 21 seats and the VVD with its 31 seats would have fallen short of a governing majority in the 150-seat parliament. With the PVV included, a parliamentary majority was achieved.

Word Games

So what explains the acceptance of the xeno-phobic PVV in mainstream Dutch politics? First, Wilders's position on Islam is shared by the majority of Dutch parties in the parliament—there is nothing preposterous or marginal about his message in the contemporary Netherlands. Wilders's immoderate language and attention-seeking antics might annoy some of his political partners, but his party's message is not alien to mainstream Dutch politics.

Second, while the xenophobic far-right parties of the past explicitly targeted immigrants, which created problems for them, Wilders's PVV has found a way around this by targeting a religion, Islam, instead of immigrants themselves. Voters need not feel they are targeting their Muslim immigrant compatriots; they are just manning the barricades to protect Western freedoms from onslaught by an intolerant, backward, Eastern culture. Of course, anti-Islam language need not in every national context equal anti-immigrant xenophobia—but the majority of Dutch immigrants are Muslims, and the connection is obvious.

The Dutch media, and Wilders himself for that matter, prefer as a descriptive prefix for his party the term "anti-Islam" (and not "anti-Muslim"). "Anti-Islam" suggests that the PVV opposes the values and teachings of the religion at an abstract, ideological level. The term attempts to obscure the fact that, in the Netherlands, the targets of anti-Islam sentiment are bound to be individual followers of Islam—that is, Dutch Muslims. The difference between "anti-Islam" and "anti-Muslim" might at first glance seem minor and semantic, but this choice in labeling has played a key role in bringing anti-immigrant sentiment into the mainstream, acceptably cloaked.

The Dutch public was already receptive to such a message. A 2005 survey by Pew Global Attitudes found that 51 percent of respondents in the Netherlands held an unfavorable opinion of Muslims living in their country—a number much higher than in other Western nations. (In the United States the number was 22 percent; in Britain it was 14 percent.)

Among younger Dutch people, the anti-Islam current is particularly pronounced. The 2009 International Civic and Citizenship Education Study, which reported on attitudes among secondary-school pupils in 39 countries, found that Dutch students (and Dutch-speaking Flemings in Belgium) held the most negative views regarding immigrants. Dutch students tended more than others to oppose the idea of granting equal rights to immigrants.

Meanwhile, labor market statistics show tendencies indicating immigrant marginalization. The analyst Peter Kee's findings on native-immigrant wage differentials (published in *Oxford Economic Papers*) reveal structural discrimination: The average nonimmigrant Dutch worker earns 35 percent more than the average Antillean-Dutch, 41 percent more than Surinamese-Dutch, 54 percent more than Turkish-Dutch, and 44 percent more than Moroccan-Dutch.

The pervasiveness of anti-Muslim sentiment goes a long way toward explaining how political parties, to varying degrees, have adopted into their programs anti-Islam views, the somewhat more intellectually acceptable sibling of anti-Muslim sentiment. But it is not clear what a Dutch political party can expect to achieve by adopting such a position. Unless Muslims somehow convert *en masse* to Christianity, demonizing Islam can only increase Muslim isolation from Dutch society while intensifying Muslims' solidarity. Worse, it could fan Islamic fundamentalism.

Unless Muslims somehow convert en masse to Christianity, demonizing Islam can only increase Muslim isolation and solidarity.

Political discussions about Islam in the Netherlands tend to lump all Muslims into one category. There are no secular or religious Muslims; no left or right; no radicals or moderates; no working class or middle class; no Shiites or Sunnis; no Turks, no Arabs, no Albanians, no Indonesians, no Iranians—just Muslims. One immediate outcome of lumping all Muslims

together has been to achieve precisely that: Muslims in the Netherlands have become more unified.

Secular, liberal Muslims, especially among the Turkish-Dutch, have been pushed toward finding common cause with their conservative coreligionists. Different ethnic communities have been brought closer together. An example is the Moroccan-Dutch and Turkish-Dutch, who had remained separate from one another since their arrival in the Netherlands. Today they are accepting the one-size-fits-all Islamic label.

It should have been self-evident that painting an entire religion as oppressive and its followers as backward could only exacerbate the ghettoization of Dutch Muslims. Then again, measures announced by the coalition government to facilitate the integration of immigrants were perhaps designed as disincentives for Muslims to remain in the Netherlands. Such measures, however, are unlikely even to bring about that outcome.

Measures to facilitate the integration of immigrants were perhaps designed as disincentives for Muslims to remain in the Netherlands.

The segments of Moroccan-Dutch and Turkish-Dutch populations that have not already integrated into Dutch culture and language will likely continue to live, mentally and physically, in ethnic ghettos. The well-integrated and aspirational segments of these two communities, on the other hand, are more likely than those in the ghetto to feel increasingly unwanted. If younger, educated, and better-integrated individuals start leaving the country, the Netherlands will be left with those who lack that option, thereby ensuring the perpetuation of a marginalized and disenchanted minority.

On January 10, 2010, leading figures of the Turkish-Dutch community published an open letter in the daily *Volkskrant* on precisely this issue, voicing their concerns about the increasing isolation of the young. As the educated start showing tendencies to leave, discrimination is making the remainder particularly susceptible to radical Islam.

It's Murder

Wilders did not create the anti-Islam sentiment that now pervades the ranks of the majority of the political parties and their voters—including some on the left. That trail was blazed by other, mainstream Dutch politicians before him. In fact, Wilders's success marks the culmination of a pattern evident since the late 1990s.

The first mainstream politician to court the anti-immigrant vote was a senior member of the VVD, Frits Bolkestein. The author Ian Buruma, in his 2006 book *Murder in Amsterdam: The Death of Theo van Gogh and the Limits of Tolerance*, recounts that Bolkestein told him: "One must never underestimate the degree of hatred that Dutch feel for Moroccan and Turkish immigrants. My political success is based on the fact that I was prepared to listen to such people."

Bolkestein was later appointed a commissioner of the European Union. In that post, he was able to take his anti-Islam crusade to the European level, warning against the Islamization of Europe and celebrating what he believed was a Christian, European victory against Muslim Turks in Vienna in 1683. (Bolkestein perhaps did not know that the Ottoman army then besieging Vienna included Hungarians under the prince of Transylvania, Imre Thököly; the Moldovan army under Prince George Dusak; and Romanian and Bulgarian units, as well as a number of smaller Christian contingents. His historically creative narrative in any case fit the mood of the times.)

While Bolkestein was reminiscing about medieval battles, dour mainstream politics in the Netherlands was shaken by the appearance of a flamboyant and charismatic character who challenged the very foundations of the Dutch political establishment. Pim Fortuyn suddenly emerged in the early 2000s with a style and message that contrasted markedly with the cliquish political culture of The Hague. His main message entailed criticism of Islam and calls for tighter restrictions on immigration. But Fortuyn was more than a one-dimensional, anti-immigrant politician; he held a broadly libertarian collection of views on all aspects of politics.

Fortuyn was murdered by an animal-rights activist in 2002. This, the first political murder in the history of the Kingdom of the Netherlands, produced a nationwide shock wave. Collective disbelief and outrage reached a new high with the murder of Theo van Gogh, a contrarian author/actor/director and equal-opportunity offender whose controversial missives had targeted both Jews and Muslims. He was stabbed to death by a Moroccan-Dutch man in 2004. A note left by the murderer warned Ayaan Hirsi Ali, van Gogh's high-profile collaborator and a former Labor politician who had by then joined the VVD, that she was next in line.

Hirsi Ali, an enterprising young female Dutch politician of Somali origin, played perhaps the key role, due to her Muslim origins, in bringing anti-Islam xenophobia into the mainstream. Hirsi Ali and her carefully crafted personal story eased the lingering discomfort some felt about the targeting of Muslim immigrants: If this Muslim immigrant woman of color herself warns us about the dangers of Islam and its practitioners, it surely cannot be xenophobia; this is instead a clash between (our) democratic freedoms and (their) backward and oppressive religion.

Ruthless, Incompetent

The ranks of the VVD included another such enterprising politician, Rita Verdonk, who had raised her profile in national politics by becoming a vocal proponent of the anti-Islam viewpoint. Verdonk, who had to compete for media attention with other VVD members like Bolkestein, Hirsi Ali, and Wilders (who used to be a VVD member), managed the astonishing feat of becoming—despite being an anti-immigrant politician—the minister of immigration and integration. This allowed her to peddle her message to a bigger audience.

One of Verdonk's suggestions, as part of her 2006 proposal for a "national code of conduct," was to outlaw on the streets the use of languages other than Dutch. Also that year she managed to add her name to the "Hall of Shame" of the international monitoring group Human Rights Watch, when she tried to deport homosexual Iranian asylum seekers back to Iran.

Verdonk's anti-immigrant campaign was not an unadulterated success. In a 2006 poll, her parliamentary colleagues voted her the nation's worst politician, one who somehow managed to combine ruthlessness and incompetence. Nonetheless, her anti-Islam message resonated well with the public.

In the 2006 election she received the highest number of preference votes, surpassing VVD party leader Mark Rutte. Verdonk then tried to unseat Rutte from the party leadership. Failing to achieve that goal, she established her own party, Proud of the Netherlands, in 2008. Verdonk's popularity has not matched her ambitions, however, and her party has failed to enter parliament.

In the meantime, Rutte has shown that he can continue disseminating anti-Muslim ideas in the VVD without Verdonk and Wilders. In a 2008 interview, Rutte stated that Islam has nothing valuable to bring to the Netherlands—other than couscous. If we assume Rutte is aware that the Koran does not include recipes involving semolina granules, we can reason that his comment was not meant to attack Islam as a religion, ideology, or culture, as he might claim, but instead to attack the Muslim citizens of the Netherlands.

As Islamophobia took hold in the political mainstream, Muslim Dutch fled other parties and ended up bolstering the performance of the Dutch Labor Party in 2007 local elections. This, however, was not a welcome development as far as the Labor leader Wouter Bos was concerned. Following the election, Bos in an interview expressed unease about having immigrant representatives among municipal councilors because he viewed Muslim political culture as incompatible with Dutch values. Trying to distance his party from its growing Muslim support, Bos declared that the election results did not mean that Labor had become the party of immigrants.

Bos's message was taken up as well by the leader of the Labor party in the Amsterdam municipal council, Hannah Belliot. In an interview she sent a message to immigrants: "At home you can say whatever you want. . . . But as an economic migrant you must work, make as little use of welfare as possible, and keep quiet."

The chair of the Labor Party organization, Lilianne Ploumen, offered further support for Bos. In language that would have been unthinkable a few years before, Ploumen led calls to do away with what she saw as the failed model of tolerance. In a position paper for the Labor Party in 2008 Ploumen stated that "the criticism of cultures and religions should not be held back due to concerns about tolerance. . . . Government strategy should bring our values into confrontation with people who think otherwise." The Labor Party chair then told "newcomers to avoid self-designated victimization."

To the left of the Labor Party sits the Dutch Socialist Party (SP), which itself has not been impervious to the growing anti-immigrant mood in the Netherlands. The SP did not join the anti-Islam currents right away, but following the Bulgarian and Romanian accession to the European Union in 2007—a time when the Dutch working class was worried about a potential influx of migrants from Eastern Europe—the Socialists flirted with anti-immigrant sentiment by opposing the free movement of labor within the EU. (To be fair, some of the SP's positions can be traced to the early 1980s, when the party opposed immigration as a capitalist ploy to break working-class solidarity and bring down pay.)

Few Dissenters

Widespread Dutch acceptance of an anti-Muslim message is a little surprising in a country that not so long ago was an unwitting accessory in the massacre of around 8,000 Bosnian Muslim men and boys. In the summer of 1995, Dutch troops transferred control of the United Nations safe haven of Srebrenica to a Bosnian Serb militia besieging the town. Dutch troops then helped the Serbs separate fightingage males from the others. Women and children were moved to a nearby town, while over the following days the militia organized the systematic execution of the males. The incident was Europe's worst mass killing since World War II. The fact that the Bosnian Serb militia claimed it was protecting Christendom against Islam shows the sinister potential of such language.

Some of Wilders's ideas would be comical, on account of their bizarre reasoning and internal inconsistency, were the political stakes of his message lower. Wilders claims to stand for freedom of expression, but he wants to ban the Koran. He believes Islam and its holy book have no place in Europe—or in Western civilization—because the Koran is a fascist work identical to *Mein Kampf*. Maybe Wilders himself has not read these two books and cannot remember which region of the world spawned fascism, but of course it is not the veracity of his claims that matters. The PVV, as a far-right party seeking to expand its appeal, must make sure to disown the heritage of European fascism.

During a December 2010 official visit to Israel, Wilders called for that country to annex and settle the West Bank. He of course is not the only far-right European politician to court Israel. Filip de Winter of the Belgian party Vlaams Belang and Heinz-Christian Strache of Austria's Freedom Party have also taken their anti-Islam message there. Their professed pro-Israel views do not please all Israelis, however. Following Wilders's visit, the daily *Haaretz* portrayed these European visitors as extremists "who after trading in their Jewish demon-enemy for the Muslim criminal-immigrant model are singing in unison that Samaria is Jewish ground."

Indeed, the far right's frequent invocations of the need to defend Judeo-Christian Europe against Islam, its declarations of support for Israel, and its habit of associating Islam with fascism are tools for severing the visible links between the far right of today and that of yesterday. This helps make such parties appear more acceptable as political partners (and potentially helps restrict international criticism).

The far right's declarations of support for Israel and its habit of associating Islam with fascism are tools for severing the visible links between the far right of today and that of yesterday.

One would have expected Wilders's ideas to be scrutinized and criticized by mainstream Dutch politicians, but the majority seems either to be on the same wavelength or simply to tolerate his views. One important exception is a small minority within the CDA. The first sign of party dissent regarding partnership with the PVV was the resignation of the deputy coalition negotiator, who also quit his parliamentary seat.

More CDA unease was exposed when the new coalition program was presented to the party congress for approval. During this process, it became clear that the deputy negotiator was not the only Christian Democrat with reservations about joining forces with the far right. While there was no sign of large-scale, open dissent, 32 percent of CDA members—including some senior members—voted against the coalition agreement (while the VVD supported the agreement unanimously).

A particularly interesting split exists now within the liberal political family: While the VVD assumed the lead in bringing about the new political partnership with Wilders, the left-liberal Democrats 66 party (D66) has not shied away from voicing its dislike of Wilders and its disapproval of the governing partnership. Preceding the announcement of the new coalition program, a couple of VVD members switched allegiance to their left-liberal siblings.

While the right-liberal VVD and the left-liberal D66 share roots in the continental European liberal heritage and see eye to eye on many issues such as support for a liberal market economy, a small state, and individual rights and freedoms, it is on the issue of Islamophobia that these two liberal parties have adopted opposite positions. Meanwhile, D66's lone ally in combating anti-Muslim sentiment has been the Green-Left party, which has moved from being a single-issue environmentalist party to one that leans toward left-liberal positions on other issues.

Questioning Loyalty

Of course, no guarantee exists that the partnership among the CDA, the VVD, and Wilders's PVV will be a smooth one, or that it will last. The early days of the governing coalition were shaken by revelations that six PVV members of parliament had concealed their criminal records—including violent, sexual, and financial offenses ranging from improper relations with subordinates in the military to head-butting critics to abusing the social insurance system. These have taken some credibility away from the PVV's strong law-and-order message.

Anti-Islam sentiment might be the lowest common denominator among these parties, but in a time of economic difficulties, the parties over the coming months will have to negotiate a complex political minefield. An early example of this has been a hapless effort by Prime Minister Rutte to contain criticism of the appointment of a minister of dual Dutch-Swedish citizenship to the new cabinet. Opposition to dual citizenship has been a longstanding PVV position; Wilders had objected to the inclusion of Turkish-Dutch and Moroccan-Dutch members of parliament in the previous cabinet, stating that "even if [the Moroccan-born junior minister of social affairs] had a blond mop and a Swedish passport, I would still want to see him go."

A March 2007 parliamentary motion by the PVV that questioned the loyalty of ministers with dual citizenship was supported by the right-liberal VVD. But following the swearing-in of the new cabinet in October 2010, the media reported on the dual citizenship of the new junior health minister. Rutte's response was that the Swedish citizenship of the minister was not a problem; however, it would have been different had the minister held Turkish citizenship.

The fact that Wilders himself has Indonesian immigrant roots and that he dyes his hair blond might be interesting avenues for studying the underlying psychological reasons for his xenophobic proclivities, but that is beyond the scope of this essay. What the preceding discussion shows is how changes in political discourse can make traditional xenophobia appear to be a bona fide point of view about clashing civilizations, cultures, and values.

Wilders is not the populist voice of the disen-franchised, questioning the elitist political establishment. He is part of the mainstream politics of the Netherlands, a mainstream in which the majority of the parties use the same anti-Islam language that he uses. And no matter how they try to obscure the reality, the inevitable targets of anti-Islam sentiment are individual Muslim immigrants. The message is not in fact anti-Islam. It is anti-Muslim.

Critical Thinking

1. How can discrimination be acceptable in The Netherlands, which is a country that permits interracial relationships?

2. Is The Netherlands a positive influence in Europe, having paid all its World War II debts?

3. Why are many in The Netherlands capitalizing on anti-immigration issues?

Create Central

www.mhhe.com/createcentral

Internet References

Migration Information Source
www.migrationinformation.org

Erk, Dr. JG—Social and Behavioural Sciences—Leiden University
http://socialsciences.leiden.edu/politicalscience/organisation/faculty/erk-dr-jg.html

On the (In)Famous Dutch (In)Tolerance: Anti-Immigrant Fringe Becomes Mainstream
http://citation.allacademic.com/meta/p_mla_apa_research_citation/4/8/5/3/5/p485354_index.html

JAN ERK is senior lecturer at Leiden University, The Netherlands.

Article   Prepared by: Caroline Shaffer Westerhof,
California National University for Advanced Studies

Israel's Unity Government: A Bid to Represent the Majority

For decades, Israel's system of representation gave tiny parties an outsized voice, particularly on the issue of settlements. The unity government now has a chance to prioritize majority views.

Joshua Mitnick

Learning Outcomes

After reading this article, you will be able to:

- Examine the concept of majority rule as it affects those who hold the power but also are in the minority in numbers.

- Examine the clashes between the Jewish ultra-religious groups and secular Jews.

- Examine the degree and spirit of democracy within the political system in Israel.

Benjamin Netanyahu's new unity government arrives with the implication that there is something even more fundamental and pressing for Israel than peace with its Arab neighbors: fixing an electoral system responsible for political instability and outsized influence of minority groups like ultra-religious Jews.

Electoral reform was one of the four key goals that Mr. Netanyahu and his rival-turned-ally, Kadima leader Shaul Mofaz, in explaining their stunning 11th hour agreement to join forces in a unity coalition that averted near finalized plans for an election in September.

Symptoms of electoral dysfunction include a decades-old exemption allowing ultra-religious men to opt out of army service, and the inability of the government to evacuate settlement outposts built on property which even the government admits is on Palestinian land.

The culprit is Israel's system of proportional representation. Experts say it has given rise to a tyranny of the minority that rewards narrow-interest parties representing ultra-Orthodox Jews, Israeli settlers, or Russian immigrants with veto on policy by threatening to implode coalition governments.

"This means that the majority is under-represented in government and the minority is over-represented," says Amnon Rubenstein, a law professor and former Justice Minister for the left-wing Meretz Party who is pushing a plan to reform Israel's system. "This causes cynicism and loss of belief in democracy."

Seven Elections in 20 Years

The power of the smaller parties has created notoriously unstable governments. In the past 20 years, Israel has been forced to hold seven general elections. And the last time an Israeli government finished out its term was in 1988. At the same time, support for mainstream big tent parties like Netanyahu's Likud Party and the Labor Party have suffered a drop-off in support, and are more vulnerable to pressure.

That has created a situation in which Israeli prime ministers are more involved in the politicking necessary to keep their coalitions together rather than policy making or strategic planning.

"Government needs to be able to implement policy in a much more vigorous manner. An American president knows he's going to be in power for four years, he doesn't have to waste enormous energies the whole time on simply staying in power," says Jonathan Rynhold, a political scientist at Bar Ilan University. "[Israeli] Politicians spend much too much time going to bar mitzvahs. They spend too much time on politics than policy. The public thinks they're being cynical, but there's no other way to govern."

Israel uses a form of extreme democracy, giving parties with as little as 2 percent of the general vote seats in the parliament.

The upside to the system is that gives expression to the country's mosaic of ethnic, religious, and ideological groups in the parliament, and then forces them to govern via coalition.

In practice, however, Israel's parliament has become a jumble of small and medium size parties representing small population segments which have become the coalition kingmakers in the rivalries between bigger mainstream parties.

Ultra-Orthodox Priorities

That's how the ultra-Orthodox, or Haredi, parties have been able to get government money to keep kids in religious seminaries and out of the compulsory draft or the work force. They've also been able to get government funding for autonomous school systems which have smaller class sizes and follow an independent curriculum that omits core subjects.

"The wholesale exemption of the Haredim [from military service] is a consequence of Israel's distorted electoral system. The two issues are intertwined," says Yossi Klein Halevy, a fellow at the Shalom Hartman Institute in Jerusalem. "It's our dysfunctional coalition system that allows a separatist minority to dictate policy to the mainstream. These are the issues that have to be unlocked."

There are a myriad of proposals floating around to reform Israel's electoral system. In the 1990s, Israel experimented with instituting a direct vote for prime minister alongside the contest between the parties to make the chief executive less dependent on small parties. But the number and diversity of small parties grew anyway. The system was eventually scrapped.

"We have to find measures for minority groups to be represented in larger political vehicles," says Ofer Kenig, a fellow at the Israel Democracy Institute, a think tank which has also called for reform. "In the UK you don't have a Pakistani immigrant party, they find their way to the Labor or Conservative party, and this is because of the electoral system that doesn't make it possible for them to compete independently."

If Israeli politicians and experts find the right formula, experts say, it should encourage a more inclusionary brand of politics that will result in policies to better integrate the ultra-Orthodox and Israeli Arabs into the mainstream through programs like national service.

Implications for Palestinians

It should also weaken the ability of the Jewish settlers in the West Bank to block steps toward a political settlement with the Palestinians.

"They would still have power, but it would be lessened," says Mr. Rynhold. "You would cease to see new settlements popping up every Wednesday and Friday."

As a result the reaction has been mixed to Prime Minister Benjamin Netanyahu's mammoth unity coalition with more

than three fourths of the parliamentary deputies. Some see it as more cynical coalition politics to survive for a year and a half. Others hope that not having to rely on the small parties will enable him to push through big reforms.

"Israel has a stable government with an enormous secular majority . . . we finally have a government that represents the Israeli majority which no sectoral party can extort," wrote Ari Shavit in the liberal Haaretz newspaper. But "if this was the maneuver of the decade to win one more year in the Prime Minister's residence, it's all over for him. The public will not forgive or forget."

Critical Thinking

1. *What is the realism of President Netanyahu's speech* in the United Nations attacking the language of the Iranian president, Hassan Rouhani, at the last United Nation General Assembly meeting (October 1, 2013)?

2. How is the ultra-religious right taking control of the political order within Isrel?

3. If there are clashes between the ultra right religious groups and secular Jews, how can there be political unity in Israel?

Create Central

www.mhhe.com/createcentral

Internet References

How Netanyahu's 'Unity' Government May Affect Palestinians, Iran
www.csmonitor.com/World/Middle-East/2012/0508/How-Netanyahu-s-unity-government-may-affect-Palestinians-Iran

Israel's Ultra-Orthodox Soldiers under Fire
http://online.wsj.com/news/articles/SB100014241278873245225045790000660630783386

Ithaca College
urpasheville.org/proceedings/ncur2011/

U.N. Peacekeeping Unit to Exit Israeli Border Area
http://online.wsj.com/news/articles/SB100014241278873233844804578528834124646470

JOSHUA MITNICK is a correspondent, Christian Science Monitor.

Article

Prepared by: Caroline Shaffer Westerhof,
California National University for Advanced Studies

Non-Telangana Ministers, MPs Oppose Division of Andhra Pradesh

INDIA TODAY

Learning Outcomes

After reading this article, you will be able to:

- Examine why some believe a separate Telangana state is important.
- Examine why some citizens consider a united Andhra Pradesh crucial.
- Examine the position of Prime Minister Singh.

As Congress and UPA government appear to be veering towards formation of a separate Telangana state, ministers and MPs from Andhra and Rayalaseema regions on Saturday met Prime Minister Manmohan Singh opposing any division of Andhra Pradesh.

Union ministers M M Pallam Raju, K S Rao, Chiranjeevi and D Purandeshwari (all hailing from coastal Andhra) and MPs Bapiraju and Anantarami Reddy met Singh in a delegation and favoured maintaining a united Andhra Pradesh.

Sources said the delegation conveyed to the Prime Minister that creation of a Telangana would not be in the interest of the state and the country.

On Friday, there were high-level discussions between the Congress leadership and the state Congress leadership on the demand for creation of Telangana.

AICC general secretary in charge of Andhra Pradesh Digivijaya Singh and his predecessor Ghulam Nabi Azad held separate discussions with chief minister N Kiran Kumar Reddy, PCC chief Botsa Satyanarayana and deputy chief minister Damodar Rajanarasimha.

The two leaders are understood to have conveyed to the state leadership that the party has made up its mind on creation of Telangana and it was only a matter of time before it is announced.

The discussions were followed by deliberations held in the core group meeting held at the residence of Prime Minister Manmohan Singh. Congress president Sonia Gandhi chaired the meeting which was also attended by senior cabinet ministers A K Antony, P Chidambaram and Sushil Kumar Shinde.

Sources said the party and the UPA government was in favour of a division of the state, which could be decided after the completion of the local bodies elections this month end.

The decision could be announced in the first week of August and may be formalised at a meeting of the Congress working committee (CWC) after which the issue could go to Parliament for passage of a bill for the purpose.

Bapiraju said the delegation told the Prime Minister that formation of Telangana will create problems in many states including Maharashtra, Uttar Pradesh and Madhya Pradesh where there are demands for separate statehood.

He said the PM gave a patient hearing to the leaders.

Critical Thinking

1. How do the responsibilities for a separate state affect the populace?
2. Why does the government of India rule out "going back" on the decision to carve a separate state of Telangana from Andhra Pradesh?
3. How will the decision of Parliament affect the position of prime minister?

Create Central

www.mhhe.com/createcentral

Internet References

Telangana Fallout: Seemandhra Ministers Firm on Resignations
www.hindustantimes.com/India-news/Telanganathetroubledstate/
Telangana-fallout-Seemandhra-ministers-firm-on-resignations/
Article1-1131940.aspx

Telangana Issue: Jaganmohan Reddy ups the Ante with Hunger Strike As He Protests Bifurcation of Andhra Pradesh
www.dnaindia.com/india/report-telangana-issue-jaganmohan-reddy-
ups-the-ante-with-hunger-strike-as-he-protests-bifurcation-of-andhra-
pradesh-1898110

FirstPost Politics
www.firstpost.com/politics/live-gom-to-consider-srikrishna-committees-
telangana-report-1150673.html

Cyclone Looms, but No End to Telangana Storm in AP
www.hindustantimes.com/india-news/telanganathetroubledstate/cyclone-
looms-but-no-end-to-telangana-storm-in-ap/article1-1132850.aspx

Article

Prepared by: Caroline Shaffer Westerhof,
California National University for Advanced Studies

BJP Will Achieve Record Breaking Results in Lok Sabha Polls: Advani

INDIA TODAY

Learning Outcomes

After reading this article, you will be able to:

- Explain why BJP leader Advani noted that since Congress has failed to destroy corruption, the opportunity is favorable for the opposition.

- Explain why there is much criticism of BJP as a party lacking its own vision.

- Explain the philosophy of the BJP party and the role of Sonia Gandhi.

Senior BJP leader L.K. Advani on Saturday said the political atmosphere in the country is ideal for the party to get "record breaking results" with the Congress-led government failing to tackle corruption and price rise, creating a favourable condition for the main Opposition.

At the BJP Scheduled Caste Front National Executive in New Delhi, he said the political situation prevailing in the country today were never more favourable for BJP in the past.

"Looking at the confidence of the SC Morcha workers here, I am sure that we will achieve record breaking results in the Lok Sabha elections," Mr. Advani said.

Referring to the opinion polls published in some newspapers on Saturday, he said usually such polls are "prejudiced" against BJP but this time, even these surveys show that the party will win the elections.

Predicting early polls, the BJP leader said the Lok Sabha and Assembly polls due this year would be over by April 2014.

"We have not experienced so many elections—in six-seven states and the Lok Sabha elections—in such a short span," he said.

"Keeping the weather conditions and other factors in mind, the Election Commission will also want early elections, whether the government wants it or not. The government may also want early polls. But whenever the elections are (to be) held, you should start preparations without speculating about the time," Mr. Advani said.

Mr. Advani asked the party cadre to take achievements of BJP governments in various states to people to improve the party's electoral prospects.

He said Congress has ensured that corruption, price rise, need for people-friendly governance and honest administration would be the issues in the forthcoming Lok Sabha elections.

Taking a jibe at Congress, Mr. Advani said, "The amount of effort that Congress has made in the last three years to make BJP win the next Lok Sabha elections, nobody else has."

However, Mr. Advani made no mention of Gujarat Chief Minister Narendra Modi, the rising star of the BJP, whom many party workers see as their biggest vote catcher and a Prime Ministerial probable.

Critical Thinking

1. Compare the political party dissension in India to the political party infighting in the United States.

2. How has the present economic turmoil in India affected the next elections?

3. Why will the 2014 election be so traumatic?

Create Central

www.mhhe.com/createcentral

Internet References

Modi Gets BJP Crown, but Advani Remains a Thorn
www.business-standard.com/article/politics/modi-gets-bjp-crown-but-advani-remains-a-thorn-113091300838_1.html

LK Advani to Skip Narendra Modi's Rally in Patna on October 27
http://ibnlive.in.com/news/lk-advani-to-skip-narendra-modis-rally-in-patna-on-october-27/427851-3-232.html

The Times of India
timesofindia.indiatimes.com/topic/2014

2014 Lok Sabha Elections: Rahul Gandhi Calls for Dalit Empowerment; Latest Reactions on 'Escape Velocity' Analogy
www.ibtimes.co.in/articles/512253/20131008/rahul-gandhi-dalit-community-jupiter-comment-video.htm

Advani vs Modi: Instead of Backroom Intrigues, BJP Should Hold . . .
http://articles.timesofindia.indiatimes.com/2013-09-13/edit-page/42040011_1_pm-candidate-l-k-advani-narendra-modi

Article

Prepared by: Caroline Shaffer Westerhof,
California National University for Advanced Studies

Pakistan 2020

A Vision for Building a Better Future

Hassan Abbas

Learning Outcomes

After reading this article, you will be able to:

- Identify the strength and the means of Pakistan's power structure.

- Examine and identify the continuing crisis within Pakistan.

- Examine the violence in Pakistan that hinders the nation's stability.

Executive Summary

In recent years, Pakistan has stumbled from one crisis to another. A number of political and socioeconomic challenges threaten to further destabilize a country that already is reeling from insurgencies along its northwestern border. Pakistan's newest democratic government is struggling to maintain control over parts of its territory where militant religious groups are intent on challenging its authority and legitimacy. The country's conflict with India over Kashmir, now in its seventh decade, appears as intractable as ever, and the war in neighboring Afghanistan has deepened instability throughout Pakistan. The transition from a near-decade-long rule under a military dictatorship is slow and complicated, as rampant corruption and politicization of the bureaucracy present huge obstacles to the state-building process.

Although Pakistan's vibrant civil society, relatively open media, and the rise of an independent higher judiciary provide some glimmers of hope, poor economic and development indicators coupled with worrying demographic trends pose serious challenges to the well-being of millions of Pakistanis. Energy shortages have worsened in recent years, and the destruction caused by the floods of 2010 has exacerbated the country's many strains. In short, how Pakistan manages these challenges in the coming years will have great consequences for its future prospects.

While recent reform efforts in the higher judiciary and constitutional amendments to strengthen democratic institutions and expand provincial autonomy signal a positive trajectory for the country, sustaining democratic governance is complicated by radicalization and violence perpetrated by an intolerant and extremist minority in the country. Terrorist attacks on respected and cherished Sufi shrines throughout Pakistan and high-profile assassinations—including the January 2011 killing of Salman Taseer, the governor of Punjab, and the assassination of Shahbaz Bhatti, Pakistan's only Christian cabinet minister, in March 2011—illustrate the lengths to which religious extremists in Pakistan will go to silence opposition voices in the country. And rather than condemning these acts of vigilante justice as un-Islamic, the government's slow and timid response to the violence has allowed voices of intolerance to gather strength.

Preventing Pakistan from further deterioration will require a sustained, long-term commitment from the government of Pakistan, the United States, and other international stakeholders to promote genuine reform in the coming decade. This commitment must be enshrined in a comprehensive package of policies aimed at promoting sustainable constitutional democracy, credible and effective rule of law and law enforcement, a significant expansion and improvement of the education and health sectors, and a peaceful resolution of the conflict with India. Economic growth and foreign investment in Pakistan arguably will follow such progress.

In Pakistan, there is a growing consensus about the need for reform, but the resources and will that are required to plan, support, and implement such an agenda remain elusive. In this context, the role of private and public sector media in preparing Pakistani society and the state for competition in the global economy and in creating a culture of innovation cannot be overlooked.

For this report, the Asia Society Pakistan 2020 Study Group focused on seven core issues that are essential to realizing a sound future for the country by 2020: (1) strengthening democratic institutions; (2) strengthening the rule of law; (3) improving human development and social services, especially in health and education; (4) developing the energy infrastructure; (5) assisting the victims of the 2010 flood in their recovery; (6) improving internal security; and (7) advancing the peace process with India. This report is not meant to represent a consensus among all the members of the Pakistan 2020 Study Group. Rather, it presents the findings and conclusions reached by the project director and the report's principal author, Hassan Abbas, through consultations with Study Group members. While individual members may disagree with parts of the report, the Group broadly supports the overall set of recommendations.

Civil-Military Relations and Democracy

The democratic leadership of Pakistan is struggling to consolidate and strengthen civilian-led democratic institutions in a country that has been ruled by military generals for half of its existence as an independent state. In this context, one of the most important challenges facing Pakistan is the military's dominance of the country's fiscal priorities and strategic calculus. For civilian institutions to take root and flourish over the next decade, the process of democratization must continue. The following course of action should be pursued to strengthen democratic governance in the country:

- A strict adherence to term appointments for armed forces personnel by the civilian leadership will support the professionalization of the Pakistani military.
- Making the expenditures of the Pakistani military more transparent is critical and will require enacting parliamentary legislation through a legislative process similar to those followed by many governments worldwide.
- Civilian supremacy in the Pakistani army can be established through the development of internal mechanisms, for example, by emphasizing democracy in military academies, making the Pakistani military's budget transparent, and involving civilians in strategic decision-making processes.
- The interests of the United States and other important allies of Pakistan will be better served by giving priority to strengthening relations with the democratic leadership and institutions of the country.
- Achieving stability in Pakistan and strengthening democratic traditions in the coming decade will require all major Pakistani political parties to hold regular elections and enact term limits for their leaders, limit the areas where candidates can contest an election to their home constituencies, and establish a transparent mechanism by which funding can be provided to low-income candidates.

Rule of Law and the Judiciary

The weaknesses of Pakistan's judicial system not only pose a serious challenge to access to justice, but also hinder the fight against terrorist groups. In the most basic sense, the rule of law in Pakistan must aim to protect the rights of citizens from arbitrary and abusive use of government power. A functioning judiciary is a fundamental element of any society's rule of law. Expanding reform efforts from higher to lower judicial levels of the system will be critical for Pakistan in the coming years.

The following measures should be carried out to strengthen the rule of law in Pakistan over the coming decade:

- The 2002 Bangalore Principles of Judicial Conduct—which stipulate that, in addition to independence, the values of impartiality, integrity, propriety, competence, diligence, and equal treatment of all before the courts are essential to proper judicial conduct—must be followed.
- Respecting the separation of powers enshrined in the constitution, as well as placing reasonable limits on the Supreme Court's use of *suo moto* powers, will contribute greatly to the enhancement of the rule of law in Pakistan.
- Security for judges, especially for those in lower courts hearing sensitive cases such as those concerning blasphemy and terrorism, must be enhanced.
- The United Nations Convention on the Elimination of All Forms of Discrimination Against Women needs to be ratified without delay.
- The National Judicial Policy should be implemented, with an emphasis on provisions calling for oversight, disciplining corrupt and inefficient judicial officers, setting a timeline and establishing special benches for prioritizing cases that can be fast-tracked, and funding courtroom construction and the hiring of judicial officers and administrative staff.
- In the Federally Administered Tribal Areas, the Pakistan government and Supreme Court must establish as a matter of priority a functioning judicial system with civil and criminal courts and a reformed legal code to replace the outdated and irrelevant Frontier Crimes Regulation.

Human Development

Poor governance and weak institutions have eroded the Pakistani public's confidence in the government's capacity to address their everyday needs. Pakistan currently ranks 125th (out of 169 countries) on the United Nations Development Programme's Human Development Index. The government is investing little in socioeconomic development, which also is hindering the growth potential of Pakistan's economy and depriving people of opportunities to live a satisfying life.

Education

Given the dire crisis in education in Pakistan today, the country will not achieve universal primary education by 2015, as set forth in the United Nations Millennium Development Goals. The focus should be on getting as close to the goal as possible by 2015, with a renewed commitment to achieve universal primary education by 2020. As a first step, Pakistan must immediately raise its public expenditures on education from less than 1.5% to at least 4% of gross domestic product, and by 2020, the expenditures should be set to at least 6%. Without making this minimal commitment, a reversal of the worrying trends in the education sector is unlikely to occur. An immediate increase in public expenditures on education to at least 4% of gross domestic product should target the following priority areas:

- Devising and implementing an accountable and predictable system of teacher recruitment, hiring, payment, retention, and training, as well as promotion based on merit, achievement, and outcomes will greatly improve the quality of education and teacher performance in Pakistan.
- The introduction of curriculum reform focusing on a life-skills-based approach to education will promote real-world applications of creative thinking and analytical reasoning.
- Developing a robust central regulatory system will contribute to the maintenance of standards and the collection of timely data on service delivery, operations, infrastructure availability, fiscal flows, learning achievements, teacher performance, and school outcomes in the education sector.
- A dynamic set of institutionalized relationships should be established between the central regulatory mechanism and the autonomous and independent subnational government units responsible for service delivery.
- Separating the higher education function completely from the primary education function and enacting legislation to provide specialized management and authority over higher education institutions will ensure greater regulatory control.
- Madrasa reform can be achieved through strategies for curricular improvement. Public school curricula should be devised, designed, and monitored by provincial governments and combine religious and secular education.
- The government of Pakistan can fulfill its education reform plans if foreign donors and international agencies focus their aid efforts on establishing a single coherent approach to providing significant budget support in this sector.

Health

Pakistan is in need of deep-rooted reform in its health care system, which must include systems of governance outside the public health sector that affect the performance of health systems. While universal access to basic public health facilities is an ambitious goal that many Pakistanis desire, investments now must begin to build a strong infrastructure by 2020 to make this goal attainable. Immediate action in the following priority areas should begin to address health needs in Pakistan:

- Proactive steps to improve health governance will be greatly enhanced by the development of a national consensus on a health reform agenda.
- In addition to devolving service delivery responsibilities from the federal level to the provincial and district levels, capacity building at the provincial level will allow for the planning, evaluation and implementation of alternative service delivery and financing mechanisms.

Key national functions for health should be retained by the federal structure.

- Collecting, analyzing, and swiftly scaling up successful best practices from existing examples of public service delivery reengineering at the primary health care and hospital levels will contribute greatly to health sector improvement in Pakistan.
- Separating policy-making, implementation, and regulatory functions in the health sector, as well as adopting market-harnessing regulatory approaches, will lead to an improvement in service delivery.
- Concrete steps for increasing public financing in health must begin alongside measures to improve utilization and limit pilferage. Strengthening essential services, enhancing social protection for the informally employed, and pooling insurance for the unemployed are priority areas for any increase in revenues in the health sector.
- An innovative system of private–public, employer- and sponsor-subsidized, and pooled group health insurance can be introduced nationwide, especially for low-income groups.
- Investments must be made to leverage the full potential of health information technology in mobile health systems, with the aim of improving transparency in procurements, increasing philanthropic subsidies, enhancing quality assurance, and promoting access to medical education. Technology such as telemedicine can help bridge the gap between rural and urban access to quality health care.
- Collecting, analyzing, and disseminating health information for shaping policy and planning at the decision-making level can be achieved through the development of an apex institutional arrangement.
- By adopting market-harnessing regulatory approaches, the first point of contact in primary health care will be broadened while enabling equitable access and the purchase of health care for many Pakistanis.
- Strengthening government oversight and regulations in private sector health care delivery will prevent and check problems such as malpractice and facilitate public–private collaborations in health delivery.

Energy Infrastructure

Pakistan faces chronic infrastructure challenges when it comes to energy sources. In addition to nurturing social and political instability, Pakistan's poor energy infrastructure imposes enormous economic costs in the form of unemployment and loss of revenue. An uninterrupted supply of energy to fuel the nation's economy should be the highest priority for Pakistan's economic managers. To meet its current and future energy demands, the government of Pakistan should invest a minimum of $5 billion in energy production by 2020. Additionally, the following measures in the energy sector should be implemented:

- Pakistan must enhance its capacity to cultivate more power from renewable energy sources, particularly by improving its ability to harness wind energy along its southern coast and by making use of solar power.

- Along with proper upkeep and maintenance of existing hydropower dams, more dams are needed to meet current and future energy requirements in Pakistan. This can be achieved by directing investments toward the construction of a very small number of large dams (Kalabagh dam is one project that has been stalled) or a larger number of small reservoirs. At the same time, these plans must be integrated into a broader strategy to improve water resources management throughout the country. Additionally, Pakistan can dispel the impression that big dam projects will benefit only larger provinces by exploring ways to reach a consensus among all the provinces on its water infrastructure and providing provinces with legally binding guarantees.
- Energy efficiency in Pakistan can be improved if government-owned power generation infrastructure is refurbished technologically and power infrastructure is upgraded with a modern efficient grid.
- Foreign donors can play a key role in building Pakistan's energy capacity by providing expert advice to the public and private sectors in Pakistan on energy development and management. The United States, in particular, should explore investing in a large energy infrastructure project in Pakistan, which will not only deepen strategic ties with Pakistan but also create goodwill in the country.

The Floods of 2010

The massive floods in Pakistan during the summer of 2010 set back all development indicators in the country. The enormity of the humanitarian crisis caused by the floods requires concerted planning and a seamless transition to the rehabilitation and reconstruction phase. Securing resources for the post-relief phase continues to be a challenge, but every effort should be made in the next two to three years to ensure that reconstruction in Pakistan proceeds effectively. The following steps should be taken to ensure that Pakistan fully recovers from the flood and is adequately prepared for future disasters:

- Pakistan's vulnerability to disasters can be addressed by immediately implementing sound building regulations, starting land rehabilitation, de-silting canals and waterways, and constructing dikes.
- Integrating climate change scenarios into the Pakistan government's annual development plans will help develop a well-coordinated strategy to address the impacts of global climate change in the country while ensuring progress toward meeting the Millennium Development Goals targets for poverty reduction.
- Regional as well as global support for reconstruction in flood-hit areas is critical. To improve its credibility and potentially attract more funds for reconstruction, Pakistan must be fully transparent about the use of international funds.
- Stabilizing and improving access to steady, affordable, and nutritious food supplies in Pakistan is essential, especially for the 6 million people most affected by the floods.

- Enhancing access to health services and medicines for flood-affected areas has to be a government priority, in addition to evaluating and addressing the health risks caused by the flood, including the spread of waterborne diseases.
- The losses incurred by displacement, migration, or damage to income-generating assets as a result of the floods highlight the need for introducing alternative mechanisms for flood survivors to reestablish their source of livelihood, especially for those whose primary source of income has been obliterated. Future asset-protection mechanisms need to be introduced concurrently—for example, through livestock insurance and weather-indexed crop insurance.
- Developing a comprehensive management framework for disaster prevention and mitigation in all aspects of national planning will help reduce Pakistan's vulnerability to natural calamities. The National Disaster Management Authority needs to be strengthened and properly resourced to function as a national focal point. In this context, Pakistan must follow the Kyoto Convention's recommendations on disaster prevention and management diligently.

Internal Security

Achieving internal security is of paramount importance to ensuring a stable and prosperous future in Pakistan. The significant rise in terrorist activity throughout the country, besides being a serious threat and demoralizing fact for its people, has dampened economic growth in Pakistan. At the core of internal security is the creation of a capable, well-resourced, structurally coherent, and institutionally autonomous police and law enforcement infrastructure. At the same time, any strategy must include measures that tackle the root causes of insurgency and violence in the first place, such as poverty, illiteracy, a sense of injustice, and a widely held perception that "external forces" are attacking Pakistan.

The following steps should be taken to ensure internal security in Pakistan:

- De-radicalization programs and the effective use of law enforcement backed by military force must be enhanced to reduce religious militancy.
- The Pakistan government will have to confront the multiple insurgent and terrorist groups operating simultaneously in the country and prevent these groups from establishing a sanctuary.
- Establishing an efficient, professional, and accountable law enforcement infrastructure will require fully implementing the 2002 Police Order to reorganize the police into a politically neutral force and discarding the controversial amendments made in 2004. Police safety commissions—already provided for under the new law—should be empowered to monitor police performance. An efficient police force can be created by devising and implementing procedures and policies aimed at improving conditions for police officers,

- establishing citizen–police liaison committees, and enhancing police and intelligence services cooperation.
- Military and civilian intelligence agencies must follow guidelines provided by law when gathering information and conducting interrogations. Human rights violations, especially in Baluchistan, where reports of abductions of political activists by security forces are common, must end.
- A robust witness protection program that also protects investigators, prosecutors, and judges—particularly in major criminal and terrorism cases—can be created through amendments in the Criminal Procedure Code.
- Rigid and impartial enforcement of the law will help ameliorate ethnic strife and sectarian killings in cities, especially in Karachi. This strategy will require revising the curriculum in public schools, as well as in madrasa networks, in ways that encourage pluralism and deter any dissemination of intolerance.
- Curricular improvement in Pakistan along scientific lines can be modeled on similar efforts in Indonesia and other countries. In this context, progressive religious scholars who challenge violent extremists must be provided full security as well as state support for their independent research work and publications.
- Internal security can be achieved if the international community directly targets its assistance toward helping Pakistan in this area. Half of U.S. funding allocated for counterterrorism and counterinsurgency support in Pakistan, for example, can be directed toward supporting scientific investigations and enhancing forensic capabilities in law enforcement. Additionally, the rules of engagement of coalition forces and policies on drone attacks should be reassessed.

Relations with India and Neighbors

Pakistan's development is almost impossible without regional cooperation, and China and India play a very important role in this context. An optimistic scenario in the next 10 years would be for Pakistan's economy to grow at a rate of approximately 5% annually, which would provide a cushion so that the country could begin investing in long-term human capacity development. However, without a sustainable peace deal with India that includes an amicable resolution of the Kashmir dispute, this is unlikely to happen. There is a growing realization in India that a failed Pakistan is not in its best interest. Peace in South Asia is attainable if Pakistan, its neighbors, and international stakeholders focus on the following measures:

- Pakistan must set a goal of increasing annual direct bilateral trade with India to more than $5 billion by 2020, as increased economic interactions will expand the space for peace constituencies in both states. As a first step, India should unilaterally lower nontariff barriers to trade with Pakistan. In turn, Pakistan can accord India most-favored-nation trade status.
- Reforming the visa issuance process will help support and strengthen people-to-people contact from both countries, as will further encouraging contacts between civil society groups and student exchange programs in both countries.
- Enhancing energy cooperation between India and Pakistan is a potential avenue of dialogue between the two countries. Cooperative energy projects, such as joint natural gas pipelines, joint electricity-generation projects, and the development of a common grid system, will go a long way toward demonstrating that the people of both countries can benefit from improved relations.
- The governments of Pakistan and India should place a moratorium on the expansion of their nuclear weapons programs. Pakistan's military leaders must realize that more nuclear weapons will neither improve the country's nuclear deterrence capabilities nor help in its fight against terrorism. Furthermore, Pakistan must ensure the safety and security of its nuclear materials.
- By reposturing militarily and becoming less Pakistan focused, India can help ease Pakistan's insecurity. War doctrines such as "Cold Start" should be reviewed and Pakistan's apprehensions about Indian interference in Baluchistan need to be addressed. At the same time, Pakistan must dismantle all armed groups focused on Kashmir.
- Pakistan, India, Afghanistan, and other external powers must recognize that terrorism is by no means a state-specific problem; the entire region will have to confront it together. Cooperation between civilian law enforcement agencies in South Asia should be institutionalized.
- The United States cannot promote an amicable resolution of the differences and disputes between India and Pakistan by supporting one side or the other; it must remain objective. In the case of Afghanistan, a more proactive role for the United States must include bringing all the regional stakeholders to the table, ideally under a United Nations umbrella and with the aim of ending the India–Pakistan rivalry and proxy war in Afghanistan.

Pakistan faces enormous challenges in the years ahead. But the people of Pakistan have shown a remarkable resilience in addressing some of these challenges, and there is a high potential for reform and development in the country. Progressive and constructive policy shifts, as suggested here, are what truly matter in the long term. Moreover, internal and regional factors will define and drive Pakistan's path toward reform, and the international community, especially important allies such as the United States, must play a supportive role.

Critical Thinking

1. Can Pakistan be stabilized? Explain.

2. What do you anticipate Pakistani politics and security to be like in 2020? Explain.

3. Do you believe that Pakistan will be the central foreign policy challenge during the last few years of the Obama administration? Explain.

4. Will the global war against terrorism within the Pakistan-Afghanistan region, as its epicenter, be a continuing tragedy? Explain.

Create Central

www.mhhe.com/createcentral

Internet References

Stabilizing Pakistan through Police Reform—Asia Society
asiasociety.org/files/pdf/as_pakistan_police_exec_sum.pdf

Logic is Variable
http://logicisvariable.blogspot.com/2013/02/pakistan-2020-vision-for-building.html

Pakistan 2020—Asia Society
http://asiasociety.org/files/pdf/as_pakistan%202020_study_group_rpt.pdf

Voice of America
www.voanews.com/content/musharraf-says-pakistan-can-play-critical-role-in-stabilizing-afghanistan/1593660.html

The Frontier Post
www.thefrontierpost.com/article/26471/

HASSAN ABBAS (Project Director), is Bernard Schwartz Fellow, Asia Society; Quaid-i-Azam Professor, Columbia University's South Asia Institute.

Unit 6

UNIT

Prepared by: Caroline Shaffer Westerhof,
California National University for Advanced Studies

Unelected Government Office: Judiciary, Military, and Bureaucracy in Everyday Politics

We describe the workings of the unelected branches of the government—the judiciary, military, and bureaucracies—to show their impact on policymaking. There is a clear ambivalence regarding these branches of government. In particular, as unelected officers, these officials are able to exert considerable influence as administrators and interpret if and how laws are carried out. Consequently, they have significant influence on the institutional effects over politics and society.

Such analysis reveals that where the executive or judiciary may be dragging its heels on policymaking—on issues ranging from counterterrorism to environmental protection—the judiciaries across a range of countries have executed clearer and more consistent policies in these areas. A look at these judicial decisions reveal that the claim that unelected officers are displacing elected ones is untenable: The judiciaries are ruling in areas where the executives and legislatures have failed to pursue clear policy options. The reality, then, is that the judiciary is expanding "policy space" to facilitate decision making rather than angling for a part as a policymaker. In doing so, the judiciary is engaging the other branches of government—the executive and the legislature—by applying the interpretation of foreign and international laws to cases, or stepping in to give voice to those unrepresented or poorly represented, such as following the Civil War in the United States and during the rise of fascism in Europe.

Such has been recently noted by Alan Dershowitz, one of the United States' most well-known constitutional scholars, who stated on CNBC that "there is no right to an abortion in the (U.S.) constitution. "I can't find anything in the constitution that says you prefer the life of the mother, or the convenience of the mother if it's an abortion by choice, over the potential life of the fetus...." He was referring to the U.S. Supreme Court Case of *Roe v. Wade,* decided in 1973. Thus, this is the type of policymaking framed by the decisions of the United State Supreme Court, whose justices are nominated by the president and confirmed by the vote of the U.S. Senate. We note that the judiciary tends to "make policy" by its decisions, whether in a democratic or authoritarian society.

In the intelligence community in the United States, in the political role of the military in democratic countries, in authoritarian nations, and in the political transition in Egypt, we note that unelected officials are not accountable; they may also behave in ways that destabilize the country. This is the case for transitioning countries such as Egypt, that is, where the military was and is considered an important ally and essential for political stability. The political transition in Egypt took place in part due to the military's withdrawal of support from the previous authoritarian regime; however, since the transition, the military has also established a firm role in politics. This role of the military in Egyptian politics was reduced in August 2012 through changes introduced by Egyptian President Mohammed Morsi; the changes included reversing constitutional decrees issued by the Supreme Council of the Armed Forces (SCAF) that reduced the powers of the presidency in Egypt. In reversing the SCAF's decrees, President Morsi appeared to have restored some oversight of the military and reestablished "civilian control over politics." The military continues to pose a destabilizing threat to civilian power that is likely to be asserted if civilian authorities fail to make the political, social, and economic performance necessary for popular support.

Nor is unaccountability limited to the unelected military and bearer of arms. If the global economic crisis provides any insights, those who wield the pen pose problems as well. Thus, on one side of the Atlantic in the United States, conservatives and liberals alike—although for different reasons—fault the Federal Reserve bureaucracy and the government for the crisis. On the other side, the European Central Bank (ECB) has provided a total of 1.7 trillion euros to ailing banks in the European continent and, consequently, undergirded the European Union. Whether such bureaucratic authority is good or otherwise depends on one's perspectives. Thus, from Germany's perspective, the ECB's policy is tantamount to easy money that delays real solutions such as public administration and wasteful spending; from the perspective of other European leaders, such as in Spain or Italy, the policy helps them compete against economic powerhouses such as Germany.

Can some positions be constitutionally changed and become elected positions? Are there clear advantages for continuing the practice of keeping branches of government unelected? In reviewing unelected officials, it is worthwhile to pay heed to the following argument on accountability:

"Horizontal accountability" (a concept developed by scholars such as Guillermo O'Donnell and Richard Sklar) refers to the capacity of governmental institutions—including such "agencies of restraint" as courts, independent electoral-tribunals, anticorruption bodies, central banks, auditing agencies, and ombudsmen—to check abuses by other public agencies and branches of government. (It is distinguished from, and complements, "vertical accountability," through which public officials are held accountable by free elections, a free press, and an active civil society.)[1]

Clearly, democratic progress in any country must build on both vertical and horizontal accountability. Like all other branches of government, these agencies or branches should not displace policymaking. Instead, an essential may be oversight or checks, so that the influence of these unelected officials do not exceed elected ones. When these unelected officials are countenanced with constraints, they stand as additional venues for citizen access. Then, they are not generally "runaway" policymakers; instead, they potentially fill in for government failures or oversights. At that level, perhaps the question is not whether they should have influence but, rather, why not.

Senegal has been a bastion of stability and democracy on a continent where such is a regional exception. Here we see that the president and its cohorts offer stability and economic growth. Such can only happen because the president recognizes that the bureaucracy is a vital part of a stable political system. Yet Tunisia and Egypt are linked together because of similarities. Massive demonstrations, as in Egypt and in Tunisia, are polarizing these countries, as we well know. Who forces the issues of quelling these demonstrations? It is the military—the unelected forces of power—that use weapons that kill when the demonstrators do not turn back.

The bureaucracy, also known as agencies within public administration, play a pivotal role in government policymaking. In the United States, many congressional legislators look to the agencies within the administration to write the bills that are sent to the president, after both houses have passed such. It is important to recognize that members of the bureaucracy have lengthy years of service, probably tenure, and therefore know the history and background of issues that warrant the potential of new legislation. Thus the bureaucrats are silently in the forefront of helping elected legislators to write the bills.

The military and the intelligence communities have played a pivotal role, both in stable and unstable political regimes, as unelected power and political actors. "The black bag job" is a "silent part of the Central Intelligence Agency, in the United States; it is the clandestine operations of surveillance of various actions. In war games designed by the military, the question is still asked, " . . . what forces are adequate to the problem of loose nukes?" Then the questions are raised that " . . . will Central Command decline?" How can they when another foreign policy expert writes, "Don't be too sure there won't be another U.S. war in the Middle East?"

Note

1. Harald Waldrauch of the Institute for Advanced Studies (Vienna), and the editors of the International Forum for Democratic Studies Report on the Third Vienna Dialogue on Democracy on "Institutionalizing Horizontal Accountability: How Democracies Can Fight Corruption and the Abuse of Power," 6-29 June 1997, co-sponsored by the Austrian Institute for Advanced Studies (Vienna) and the National Endowment for Democracy's International Forum for Democratic Studies (Washington, D.C.). Available at www.ned.org/forum/reports/accountability/report.html

Article

Prepared by: Caroline Shaffer Westerhof,
California National University for Advanced Studies

The CIA's New Black Bag is Digital

When the NSA can't break into your computer, these guys break into your house.

MATTHEW M. AID

Learning Outcomes

After reading this article, you will be able to:

- Explain the CIA concept of the "black bag job."

- Explain the CIA's Technical Operation Collection and how it carries out assignments.

- Explain the rivalry and present relationship between the CIA and NSA.

During a coffee break at an intelligence conference held in The Netherlands a few years back, a senior Scandinavian counterterrorism official regaled me with a story. One of his service's surveillance teams was conducting routine monitoring of a senior militant leader when they suddenly noticed through their high-powered surveillance cameras two men breaking into the militant's apartment. The target was at Friday evening prayers at the local mosque. But rather than ransack the apartment and steal the computer equipment and other valuables while he was away—as any right-minded burglar would normally have done—one of the men pulled out a disk and loaded some programs onto the resident's laptop computer while the other man kept watch at the window. The whole operation took less than two minutes, then the two trespassers fled the way they came, leaving no trace that they had ever been there.

It did not take long for the official to determine that the two men were, in fact, Central Intelligence Agency (CIA) operatives conducting what is known in the U.S. intelligence community as either a "black bag job" or a "surreptitious entry" operation. Back in the Cold War, such a mission might have involved cracking safes, stealing code books, or photographing the settings on cipher machines. Today, this kind of break-in is known inside the CIA and National Security Agency as an "off-net operation," a clandestine human intelligence mission whose specific purpose is to surreptitiously gain access to the computer systems and email accounts of targets of high interest to America's spies. As we've learned in recent weeks, the National Security Agency's ability to electronically eavesdrop

from afar is massive. But it is not infinite. There are times when the agency cannot gain access to the computers or gadgets they'd like to listen in on. And so they call in the CIA's black bag crew for help.

The CIA's clandestine service is now conducting these sorts of black bag operations on behalf of the NSA, but at a tempo not seen since the height of the Cold War. Moreover, these missions, as well as a series of parallel signals intelligence (SIGINT) collection operations conducted by the CIA's Office of Technical Collection, have proven to be instrumental in facilitating and improving the NSA's SIGINT collection efforts in the years since the 9/11 terrorist attacks.

Over the past decade specially-trained CIA clandestine operators have mounted over one hundred extremely sensitive black bag jobs designed to penetrate foreign government and military communications and computer systems, as well as the computer systems of some of the world's largest foreign multinational corporations. Spyware software has been secretly planted in computer servers; secure telephone lines have been bugged; fiber optic cables, data switching centers and telephone exchanges have been tapped; and computer backup tapes and disks have been stolen or surreptitiously copied in these operations.

In other words, the CIA has become instrumental in setting up the shadowy surveillance dragnet that has now been thrown into public view. Sources within the U.S. intelligence community confirm that since 9/11, CIA clandestine operations have given the NSA access to a number of new and critically important targets around the world, especially in China and elsewhere in East Asia, as well as the Middle East, the Near East, and South Asia. (I'm not aware of any such operations here on U.S. soil.) In one particularly significant operation conducted a few years back in a strife-ridden South Asian nation, a team of CIA technical operations officers installed a sophisticated tap on a switching center servicing several fiber-optic cable trunk lines, which has allowed NSA to intercept in real time some of the most sensitive internal communications traffic by that country's general staff and top military commanders for the past several years. In another more recent case, CIA case officers broke into a home in Western Europe and surreptitiously loaded Agency-developed spyware into the personal computer of a man suspected of being a major recruiter for individuals wishing to fight with the militant group al-Nusra Front in Syria, allowing CIA operatives to read all of his email traffic and monitor his Skype calls on his computer.

The fact that the NSA and CIA now work so closely together is fascinating on a number of levels. But it's particularly remarkable accomplishment, given the fact that the two agencies until fairly recently hated each others' guts.

Critical Thinking

1. How did the CIA and NSA, once fierce rivals, develop a reciprocal relationship at the present time?

2. How does "spy software" operate within "black bag jobs"?

3. Why do some women feel they have a "special genius" for spying?

Create Central

www.mhhe.com/createcentral

Internet References

The Verge
www.theverge.com/2013/7/17/4532788/cia-black-bag-squads-get-data-the-old-fashioned-way

CIA Conducts over 100 Black Bag Jobs in Past Decade: *US Magazine*
http://english.cntv.cn/program/newsupdate/20130724/104107.shtml

With Bags of Cash, C.I.A. Seeks Influence in Afghanistan
www.nytimes.com/2013/04/29/world/asia/cia-delivers-cash-to-afghan-leaders-office.html?_r=0

MATTHEW M. AID is an amateur researcher and historian who figured out that for at least six years, the CIA and the Air Force had been withdrawing thousands of records from the public shelves—and that Archives officials had helped cover up their efforts. Mr. Aid's profession is as a corporate investigator.

Aid, Matthew M. Reprinted in entirety by McGraw-Hill Education with permission from *Foreign Policy*, July 17, 2013. www.foreignpolicy.com. © 2013 Washingtonpost.Newsweek Interactive, LLC.

Article

Prepared by: Caroline Shaffer Westerhof,
California National University for Advanced Studies

A Cautious Win in Egypt's Power Struggle

Bob Bowker from the Australian National University offers his insight into the unfolding power struggle between the Egyptian military and the Muslim Brotherhood.

BOB BOWKER

Learning Outcomes

After reading this article, you will be able to:

- Examine the role of the military within the political order of Egypt.

- Examine the role and the future of the Muslim Brotherhood within the political order of Egypt.

- Explain the military and the Muslim backlash within Egypt today, which Dr. Bowker did not project in 2112.

The power struggle between the Egyptian military and the Muslim Brotherhood saw a shift in favour of the latter on August 12.

That's when the recently elected president, Mohammed Morsy, sacked the commander in chief of the Egyptian Armed Forces, Field Marshall Tantawi; his chief of staff, General Anan; and the chiefs of the navy, air and air defence forces.

Morsy also reversed a constitutional decree issued by the Supreme Council of the Armed Forces (SCAF) on June 18, shortly before his victory in the presidential election run-off, which significantly reduced the power of the presidency in regard to defence matters and formally placed SCAF in a dominant legislative position. He appointed a judge believed to be sympathetic to the Brotherhood as his vice-president.

Since the lower house of the elected parliament was dissolved by SCAF after the Supreme Constitutional Court ruled the parliamentary election law unconstitutional, Morsy now holds all executive and legislative powers of state.

Morsy could recall the Brotherhood-dominated People's Assembly, but he does not need to do so ahead of the elections, which will follow the emergence of a new constitution and its passage in a referendum. Those processes are expected to be completed before the end of this year, but if the Constituent Assembly tasked with drafting the constitution is dissolved

by the Administrative Judiciary Court, it will be Morsy who appoints a replacement, not SCAF.

Unless his moves are successfully challenged by the judicial system, Morsy has therefore taken a significant step towards asserting civilian control over the Egyptian military. He has set the framework for Egyptian politics in ways which the military will find difficult to change.

In making these moves, Morsy played his cards carefully. He appears to have seized an unexpected political opportunity which was created by popular frustration with the military leadership (and according to some reports, among the lower ranks of the officer corps) following an attack on an Egyptian post in the Sinai which saw the deaths of 16 policemen.

Shortly beforehand, he had replaced the editors of major state-owned newspapers with people viewed as compliant or sympathetic to the Muslim Brotherhood. A crackdown on other critical newspapers and broadcasters had also begun.

For its part, the ageing and incompetent Marshall Tantawi was hardly likely to be a rallying point for the military, and General Anan was disadvantaged by being seen as close to the United States. Morsy, however, did not challenge the very considerable depth of residual power enjoyed by the military beyond the political arena. Indeed, he appointed the removed service chiefs to civilian positions consistent with their seniority and experience—including as head of the Suez Canal Authority, as minister of state for military production, and as head of the Arab Organization for Industrialisation, the latter two of which are major revenue sources for the military.

Nor did Morsy give the military cause for concern about its immediate interests: Tantawi's departure was accorded a degree of formal dignity, and his replacement as defence minister, General Abdel-Fattah El-Sissy, had staunchly defended the abysmal human rights record of the military (including its 'virginity testing' of protesters) following the overthrow of the Mubarak regime. Anan's replacement as chief of staff, General Al-Assar, was a high-profile member of SCAF.

While it is clear that neither Morsy nor the military wanted to engage in a confrontation over the system in making or responding to these moves, the effect of the dismissals and appointments lies in its signalling to the military that civilian control over politics has begun. Morsy has initiated a process which will make those occupying senior military positions beholden to him, and those wishing to secure their careers will take note accordingly.

Whether Morsy will move to address corruption and other possible charges against the military for human rights abuses during the Mubarak era and in the revolutionary period remains to be seen. The whole issue of transitional justice and reconciliation has yet to be seriously addressed. At a minimum, however, he has now acquired a formidable bargaining card in that respect. It is also very unlikely that any future civilian government, Islamist or secular, would be willing to cede political power to the military, or to relinquish the power of a civilian president to determine senior military appointments.

While the political battlefield has been tilted in favour of the civilians as a result of the Brotherhood's moves, it is by no means certain that the Brotherhood has secured its long-term political dominance over the political scene as a whole.

The Brotherhood's performance in parliament was disappointing to many. Morsy won only narrowly against his secular opponent in the presidential election, largely because of divisions and abstentions among the voting public.

Popular frustration with the symptoms of a stagnant economy and failing electricity and other infrastructure will cost the Brotherhood at the polls. The bureaucracy remains resistant to reform, but seeking to address its failings and the influence of the military over the economy, business and regional government arrangements would be as challenging for an Islamist government as any other.

While the Brotherhood has presented itself as intent on achieving its social justice agenda through promoting business, and an immediate financial crisis appears to have been averted by receipt of substantial assistance from Qatar, its capacity to manage an economy beset by multiple structural problems remains open to question.

There are also serious doubts about the Brotherhood's capacity to attract and retain talent and experience in key areas such as the banking sector. The financial stringencies that any credible reform program will require will not sit easily with the Brotherhood's own rank and file, let alone with the Egyptian middle class and the wider public.

Egyptian political forces opposed to the Brotherhood face an unenviable choice between working with it in coalition, and reinforcing the Brotherhood's electoral prospects by helping it to achieve a measure of economic success, or seeking to regroup and contesting the forthcoming elections more successfully by attacking the government's record.

So far, the Brotherhood has not been able to draw in much talent from among Egypt's secular and liberal-minded political and intellectual elements: 18 of the 35 members of the newly appointed cabinet, and the prime minister himself, have connections to the disbanded National Democratic Party of the former regime.

The Brotherhood enjoys little popular trust. Some fear it will exploit its present political advantages to cement its grip on power through the constituent assembly and, if necessary, through repopulating the judiciary with judges of its choice. Its moves to limit press freedom are of obvious concern in that regard.

However, such an interpretation of the overall picture is unduly alarmist. The latest developments are part of an inevitable and necessary rebalancing of the relationship between the military and civil authorities, in which the Muslim Brotherhood has played its cards better than its opponent, but where the military is far from being a spent force.

Both sides still see more to be gained at this stage by avoiding a direct and open confrontation. Whether the Muslim Brotherhood emerges as the main beneficiary of that situation in the long-term, whether the checks and balances of a constitutional system will be allowed to function effectively in the medium term, and whether the calculations underlying the positions taken by the contending parties will remain unchanged in the short-term are all far from certain.

Critical Thinking

1. Can there be stabilization within the political order of Egypt?
2. How can democracy ever return to the political order within Egypt?
3. Why is the United States in a quandary with regard to its actions and relationship to Egypt?

Create Central

www.mhhe.com/createcentral

Internet References

Faculty of Arts Asia Institute—University of Melbourne
asiainstitute.unimelb.edu.au/

Mursi Ouster Rooted in Failure to Sprout Egypt Recovery—Bloomberg
www.bloomberg.com/news/2013-07-03/mursi-ouster-has-roots-in-unemployment.html

Egypt: An Islamist Insurrection?—*The Interpreter*
www.lowyinterpreter.org/post/2013/07/10/Egypt-An-Islamist-insurrection.aspx

A Cautious Win in Egypt's Power Struggle—*The Drum*
www.abc.net.au/unleashed/4200892.html

Bishop Suriel's Blog
bishopsuriel.blogspot.com

DR. BOB BOWKER was the Australian Ambassador to Egypt 2005–2008. He is presently a professor at the Australian National University.

Article   Prepared by: Caroline Shaffer Westerhof,
                                          California National University for Advanced Studies

Africa's Turn: A Conversation with Macky Sall

STUART REID

Learning Outcomes

After reading this article, you will be able to:

• Explain how Senegal has been a bastion of stability and democracy within the African continent.

• Explain the personality, power, and complexion of the nation-state Senegal under President Macky Sall.

• Explain why Senegal offers stability and growth to foreign investors.

Since it gained independence from France in 1960, the West African country of Senegal has been a bastion of stability and democracy on a continent that has seen relatively little of either. During the presidency of Abdoulaye Wade (2000–2012), however, the Senegalese exception seemed under threat. The elderly Wade grew increasingly authoritarian and corrupt, and he managed to run for a third term even though the constitution prohibited him from doing so. But in March 2012, Senegalese voters dealt Wade a decisive defeat, electing the reformist candidate Macky Sall instead. Trained in France as a geological engineer, Sall had served in a number of government posts under Wade, including prime minister, before publicly breaking with him in 2007. In opposition, Sall created a new political party; served a second term as mayor of his hometown, Fatick; and organized an anti-Wade coalition. Sall spoke with *Foreign Affairs* senior editor Stuart Reid in Dakar in June, days before U.S. President Barack Obama's arrival in Senegal for a state visit.

Since independence, most African countries have suffered from coups and civil wars. But Senegal has enjoyed over five decades of stability and multiparty competition. What's your secret?

It stems from a long historical process. Senegal's first revolution came at the same time as America's. In 1776, there was a revolution in the north of Senegal—what we call the Torodbe revolution—that set out new guidelines for governance. There

was colonization afterward. But even during the colonial era, beginning in 1848, people could vote for the colonial authorities. In 1914, we elected the first black member of the French National Assembly, Mr. Blaise Diagne, a Senegalese. So before independence, there was already electoral competition.

Another secret can be found in the Senegalese constitution. We have a semi-presidential regime, which means that the government is responsible not only to the president but also to the parliament. There is one chief executive, in contrast with some countries that have two—something that creates tensions that can end in coups. Senegal's flexible and robust constitution has protected us from coups for 53 years since independence.

We also have stable institutions. Only seven days elapsed between the election of March 25, 2012, and my swearing-in. In the meantime, the legal system issued a ruling, and democratic institutions prepared the transfer. The army and the police complied with the results of the election. A country that does not have stable institutions and a clear constitution cannot be successful.

Senegal is also something of a regional exception in that 90 percent of the population is Muslim, yet the state is secular.

Actually, 95 percent are Muslim. In Senegal, the state has the duty to protect people of all religions—Muslim, Christian, animist. People have the freedom to believe in what they want. That is a fundamental element of our constitution. This does not mean that the majority or the minority cannot express themselves; rather, the state is there to respect the freedom of each citizen to believe in what he or she wants to believe in.

Why did voters choose you instead of Wade? What did your victory represent?

My victory certainly meant that the Senegalese people chose change. The country was divided. The partisans of the former regime were committed to a path where the term of office was no longer limited, even though the constitution of 2001 was clear that no one could have more than two five-year terms. Then, the people came together to stand up against a proposed bill that would have allowed a president to be elected with 25 percent of the vote.

A great deal of hope is what put me in power. I'm quite aware of that. So my role is to strengthen this democratic choice. That's what I'm trying to do through the institutional reform commission that I set up, which must work to strengthen democracy and not to bring about a new regime.

You promised to crack down on corruption. What have you done, and what do you have left to do?

It's important that everyone, including those in government now, realize that the era of impunity is over. And we have done a lot in one year. I revived the anticorruption court, which was created by President Abdou Diouf in 1981 but eventually stopped functioning; it was there, but you couldn't nominate the attorneys and magistrates. I nominated magistrates who agreed to work according to the procedure of the court, which hasn't been changed. I have submitted a bill on budget transparency. From now on, the government has to make its accounts public on a quarterly basis. The law will also require budgetary officials to declare their assets publicly before they take office.

I also created OFNAC, which is an office to combat fraud. When there are allegations of corruption against current officials, that office has the power to conduct an investigation and refer the case directly to the justice system. These are new measures to increase transparency and good governance, which are important for guaranteeing investment.

Isn't it true that all politicians, including you, benefited from corruption under Wade?

As far as I am concerned, we benefited from privileges related to our position—prime minister or president of the national assembly—which is completely normal. It has nothing to do with embezzlement or corruption. When you can prove that your assets are in line with your income, there's no problem. That's not what is being challenged. What is being challenged is the accumulation of resources that has nothing to do with legal and justifiable sources of income, including mine when I was with President Wade.

Senegal's neighbor Mali has had a difficult year, with a coup d'état, the Tuareg rebellion, the Islamist takeover of the north, and French intervention. What can Senegal do to improve the prospects for Malian democracy?

First of all, we would like to recognize the role played by the international community, without which Mali would have lost its territorial integrity and independence. This is why we have commended the efforts made by the United Nations, which voted for a resolution that permitted France, along with African forces from ECOWAS [the Economic Community of West African States] and Chad, to stop the jihadist terrorists and reclaim Malian territory.

Today, we are in the final stages of consolidating the peace. The agreement that was just signed in Ouagadougou [Burkina Faso] will help organize elections for July 28 across the country—including in Kidal, a Tuareg stronghold. I believe that Senegal's role is to continue to side with Mali, to support it in its reconciliation policy as well as in its development policy. We share a long border, more than 400 kilometers [about 250 miles], which must be watched closely. Our fates are linked. What is happening in Mali could happen in any of our countries.

What role should countries such as Senegal play in regional security compared with outside actors such as the United States and France?

We cooperate with France, which is an ally and a friend. It is of course a former colonial power. But France understands the stakes in and the sociology of our countries. The United States also has a security policy in the region, and it is our partner through AFRICOM [the U.S. Africa Command] and everything that it does in terms of military cooperation with various countries.

It is clear that terrorism is a plague in our countries. It compounds our development problems. We have to ensure the security of our populations, the inviolability of our borders, and the stability of our states so that we can focus on such issues as development and poverty.

Senegal, like most members of ECOWAS, can be considered a pivotal country, because it has a military that can intervene at home just as it can abroad. Senegal has more than 2,000 soldiers in operations across Africa. We are present in Cote d'Ivoire, Guinea-Bissau, Darfur, the Democratic Republic of the Congo, and other countries. There could be better-thought-out cooperation that would enable Africa, in case of a challenge like the one we experienced recently in Mali, to have special forces capable of reacting first to stop the danger and neutralize the threat and, afterward, to cooperate economically and strategically.

So can Africa take care of its own problems now?

No. Africa cannot handle its own problems, because we are not yet at the point where we have the logistical capabilities to deploy troops in case of emergency. It's simply a matter of means, not a matter of men. Remember, when our troops intervened in Mali, they deployed over land. Today, Senegalese troops are in Gao, which is 2,400 kilometers [almost 1,500 miles] away. They had to travel there in convoys of trucks and four-by-four vehicles. That's a problem. So as long as the logistics are not sorted out, we will always be lagging behind. But we are handling matters with our community organizations, with our respective countries, and particularly with our partners, such as the United States, France, and the European Union, among others.

After much delay under the previous administration, the former dictator of Chad, Hissène Habré, will now be tried for crimes against humanity by a Senegalese court, not by a court in Europe. Does this represent a new model for African justice?

Yes. The world has changed, and in 2013, it's not acceptable for us to still be expelling African leaders to European countries. Africa should have the means to try people who have been accused of crimes. In the case of Mr. Habré, an African Union resolution demanded that Senegal, where he has lived in asylum for the past 20-plus years, organize his trial. Under my predecessor, the Senegalese government accepted this mandate. This mandate must be enforced, and that's what we're in the process of doing.

If Habré is convicted, will you go after his assets?

It is not our duty as a state to make a decision. It's the duty of the justice system to do what it has to do. We cannot interfere with his personal affairs or his assets. The justice system will shed some light on it and decide what must be done.

If Senegal is committed to justice for Habré, then why is your current prime minister Habré's former banker?

I did not appoint my prime minister because of the Habré case. Now, if it comes out that he is truly linked to the Habré case, or if he is charged with anything, then I will make a decision. But for the moment, there's no reason to doubt him or take measures against him so long as a ruling has not been made.

What did the election of Obama mean to Africans?

Africans took a lot of pride in the election of Obama, because it proved wrong those who believed in racist assumptions, that a black man could not live up to a white man. Of course, President Obama is the president of the United States, not the president of Africa, so he stands up for the interests of America. But his election broke down barriers.

Some say that Obama has done less than President George W. Bush and President Bill Clinton in terms of promoting trade with Africa or assisting with public health efforts there.

You cannot ask President Obama to do something that he can't do. He came to power in a time of historic difficulties in the United States. The economy was on the brink, there was a war in Afghanistan and a war in Iraq, there was the subprime mortgage crisis. All these crises led him to take care of his country first, to put an end to the wars in Iraq and Afghanistan.

I think he can be judged at the end of his tenure. None of his predecessors could do anything real during their first terms. It's in the second term that they enjoyed more freedom and could take the initiative. I do hope that he's going to do something that will be important. There's no doubt about it. That's the feeling I have.

Much of the budget of the Senegalese government, 20 percent, still comes from foreign aid. What can African countries do to wean themselves off international assistance?

Aid indeed represents 20 percent of our budget. But there was a time when it was 60 percent. We need that aid for development, but more than aid, we need investment. We are working today to establish public-private partnerships and attract private investment. That development will trigger productivity that will enable us to have a balanced budget and eventually no longer need aid, which is not easy to raise. African countries also have high levels of debt compared to elsewhere, and we cannot develop infrastructure without getting out of debt. Africa needs help.

Senegal's rate of economic growth is lower than those of its neighbors. Why does it remain so low?

Well, what accounts for Senegal's slow growth—in 2013, it will be 4.3 percent—is that we are handicapped by the energy sector, which is making the economy less competitive. We have initiated bold measures to provide for a sustainable response to the energy crisis. We also have another handicap: our agricultural sector, which should be the engine of growth, remains traditional, with low yields and the inefficient use of land. So

we have decided to modernize the agricultural system, while protecting the family nature of some holdings, with seed capital to increase yields and productivity through mechanization.

What about reducing the role of the state in the economy?

I'm a liberal, so I believe the economy is not something that the state creates. It is business, it is competitiveness, it is productivity that does that. But the state has a fundamental role: to secure an environment conducive to business. Thus, it is necessary to have the rule of law and make sure that private investment is protected. Above all, we have to fight against factors that limit investment—in particular, corruption and red tape. I have launched major initiatives to fight corruption and illegal enrichment, as well as to remove administrative constraints. Very soon, you will see our reforms aimed at speeding up the time it takes to start a business. Our single-window system gathers together in the same place—in APIX, which is the agency to promote investment—all the services that foreign or national investors need, to save time, in terms of procedures.

What about human capital? In Senegal, over 60 percent of women over the age of 15 are illiterate. Many people suffer from malaria or malnutrition. Sixty percent of the population lives on less than $2 a day. What are you doing about these problems?

Most of Senegal's population is young, as is characteristic of Africa. We have a high population growth rate, around 2.5 percent, so if the economic growth rate is not three times that, it is very difficult to create wealth. As a result of this very fast-growing population, we have youth unemployment. We need to educate young people, ensure their health, and make sure that they are required to attend school at least until they turn 16. There are more than 300,000 youths who enroll in primary school each year, so we need enough classrooms and teachers. Senegal made major progress in education before I even came to power, and we are continuing it, because we are deeply convinced that it is human capital that will make the difference. And then there are our major efforts in higher education, which we are continuing to pursue despite some difficulties. But we have no choice. We have to invest in vocational training in order to ensure the full development of our people through employment. And even if they do not get a job here, they can emigrate with their skills. Many countries need doctors, engineers, and technicians; Senegal can provide them.

Women's rights are correlated with economic growth; what are you doing regarding girls in school?

We have a law on gender parity for elected positions. It's really an extraordinary leap forward made by Senegal. We also have basic incentives so that young girls stay in school as long as possible. We are pleased to see the quality of training for girls in school; more and more, in secondary school and at university, they earn better grades than boys. Increasingly, women are getting trained in all areas. Initially, they studied literature and the law; now, they are in all fields—scientific, medical, everything. But we must persevere. In cities, there isn't a problem. But we want to see the same improvement in a rural areas, where there are still battles to be fought. But given our high rate of universal access to education, this is a fight we have almost won here in Senegal.

China has ramped up its investment in Africa. Some fear this is not good for the prospects of African democracy. Are they right?

Well, I can't see why the development of Chinese investment would constitute a danger for democracy. The cooperation with China is much more direct and faster than the cooperation we have with Western countries—the United States, European countries, and other bilateral donors. There are a lot of criteria on governance, on this and that, and a lot of procedures. That's one of the obstacles to effective cooperation: too many procedures. Each partner has its own list of these procedures, and so countries spend a lot of time dealing with procedures. I'm not saying that what China is doing is better, but at least it's faster. And we need speed.

Are you optimistic about the fate of Africa?

I am very optimistic, because I am aware that Africa today has every chance to catch up. Africa has a young population, natural resources, and, now, democracy. Africa is stable, democratic, and secure, and its natural resources are better managed thanks to transparency in the extractive industries. For investors, Africa provides a faster and more exciting return on investment, because everything remains to be done—infrastructure, energy, and development. Development has gone around the world, to Europe, to America, to Asia. It's Africa's turn now.

Critical Thinking

1. How has the state of Senegal remained secular in a country where 90% of the population is Muslim?

2. What makes Senegal president Macky Sall an icon of stability on a continent where such is not the norm?

3. What has been accomplished and achieved through the years since Senegal gained its independence in 1960?

Create Central

www.mhhe.com/createcentral

Internet References

Macky Sall News—Bloomberg
http://topics.bloomberg.com/macky-sall

Senegal Cheers Its President for Standing Up to Obama on Same-Sex Marriage—*New York Times*
www.nytimes.com/2013/06/29/world/africa/senegal-cheers-its-president-for-standing-up-to-obama-on-same-sex-marriage.html

World Leaders Forum
www.youtube.com/watch?v=IONU82c0yjA

Africa's Turn—*Foreign Affairs*
www.foreignaffairs.com/discussions/interviews/africas-turn

Macky Sall | euronews
www.euronews.com/tag/macky-sall/

STUART REID is Senior Editor, *Foreign Affairs*.

Article

Prepared by: Caroline Shaffer Westerhof,
California National University for Advanced Studies

U.S. Army Learns Lessons in N. Korea-like War Game

PAUL MCLEARY

Learning Outcomes

After reading this article, you will be able to:

- Explain the concept and theory behind "war games."

- Explain the types of deployment models that can make war games a success.

- Explain why war games are a benefit to the Army's Training and Doctrine Command.

Washington—It took 56 days for the U.S. to flow two divisions' worth of soldiers into the failed nuclear-armed state of "North Brownland" and as many as 90,000 troops to deal with the country's nuclear stockpiles, a major U.S. Army war game concluded this winter.

The Unified Quest war game conducted this year by Army planners posited the collapse of a nuclear-armed, xenophobic, criminal family regime that had lorded over a closed society and inconveniently lost control over its nukes as it fell. Army leaders stayed mum about the model for the game, but all indications—and maps seen during the game at the Army War College—point to North Korea.

While American forces who staged in a neighboring friendly country to the south eventually made it over the border into North Brownland, they encountered several problems for which they struggled to find solutions. One of the first was that a large number of nuclear sites were in populated areas, so they had to try to perform humanitarian assistance operations while conducting combined arms maneuver and operations.

One way of doing this was to "use humanitarian assistance as a form of maneuver," Maj. Gen. Bill Hix, director of the Army's Concept Development and Learning Directorate, told reporters. The Army dropped humanitarian supplies a short distance from populated areas, drawing the population away from the objective sites, he explained.

Many of the problems encountered were hashed out with Army leaders at a Senior Leader Seminar on March 19 at Fort McNair in Washington. The event—which included the Army chief of staff, Gen. Ray Odierno, and the vice chief, Gen. John Campbell, along with a collection of three- and four-star generals—was off the record, but under terms of the agreement that allowed a handful of reporters to cover the event, unattributed quotes can be reported.

One of the major complications was that "technical ISR was not capable of closing the gap" caused by not having human intelligence assets in the country for years before the fight, one participant said. Also, "our ability to get north was hindered by our operational inflexibility," particularly when it comes to dropping troops into austere, contested areas.

To move soldiers quickly, Marine Corps V-22 Ospreys quickly inserted Army units deep behind enemy lines, but leaders found that inserting troops far in front of the main force so quickly often caused them to be surrounded, after which they had to be withdrawn.

Overall, the friendly force ultimately "failed to achieve the operational agility" it needed to succeed, another participant complained, "largely due to the rigidity" of current deployment models. What's more, the joint force was "able to get the force there quickly, but it was the technical force" that proved more difficult to deploy.

Another participant agreed, adding "the key challenge was timely access to joint enablers" such as ISR and counter-weapons of mass destruction units, which were desperately needed by the general-purpose ground units.

While not all lessons learned from the exercise were fully hashed out in this unclassified setting, some officers involved expressed their views of how the past decade of war has influenced how the Army prepares to fight.

"We've had the luxury in the last several wars of a place called Kuwait" from which to launch troops and stage equipment, one officer said. "I think our skills have atrophied in the call you get in the middle of the night," and in forcible-entry operations from the air and sea. Skills haven't been kept fresh in doing things such as loading trains full of equipment, and in setting up new command posts, he said.

Another leader agreed. "We have been spoiled by a command-and-control network that has been established for a decade" in Afghanistan and Iraq, he said, adding that the Army has to get back to training to operate in an austere environment.

One lesson from Iraq and Afghanistan, reinforced by the Unified Quest game, was that "we're not going to fight a pure military war again," one four-star general opined. Instead, being successful in conflict will require a variety of solutions requiring cultural knowledge, political acumen and other intelligence activities. The problem is, according to another officer, that the service needs to better understand the cultures in which it will fight, since "we tend to focus on the clash, when we need to focus on the will" of the local population.

Gen. Robert Cone, director of the Army's Training and Doctrine Command, said the difficulties the Army faces in moving troops and materiel around the battlefield again reinforced that "we have significant inter-service dependencies on our ability to move" and that any future fight will be a joint fight.

When asked about the potential for conflict in North Korea specifically, Cone said that while he thinks the forces the U.S. has today in South Korea "are adequate . . . the question is what forces are adequate for the problem of loose nukes?"

Critical Thinking

1. What kind of war games, if any, could model "loose nukes"?
2. What are the benefits of conducting the Unified Quest War Games?
3. What are lessons learned in the development of current deployment models?

Create Central

www.mhhe.com/createcentral

Internet References

North Korea Puts Troops on War Footing and Warns of "Horrible Disaster"—*TIME World*
> http://world.time.com/2013/10/08/north-korea-puts-troops-on-war-footing-and-warns-of-horrible-disaster/

USA Thinks North Korea Will Collapse And Lose Control of Its Nukes—*Oceans Vibe News*
> www.2oceansvibe.com/2013/03/27/usa-thinks-north-korea-will-collapse-and-lose-control-of-its-nukes/

Decision Point: Understanding the US's Dilemma over North Korea—*New York Times*
> http://learning.blogs.nytimes.com/2013/03/19/decision-point-understanding-u-s-s-dilemma-over-north-korea/

War Game Exposes Gaps for U.S. Army—*Defense News*
> www.defensenews.com/article/20130331/DEFREG02/303310003/

US Army Learns Lessons in N. Korea-like War Game—*Defense News*
> www.defensenews.com/article/20130326/DEFREG02/303260020/

PAUL MCLEARY is Land Warfare reporter for *Defense News*.

Article

Prepared by: Caroline Shaffer Westerhof,
California National University for Advanced Studies

What Caused the Economic Crisis?

The 15 best explanations for the Great Recession.

JACOB WEISBERG

Learning Outcomes

After reading this article, you will be able to:

- Understand the balance between free market capitalism and social protection.

- Understand why regulatory failures exist.

- Understand the bureaucracy of globalization and monetary policy in the face of economic crises.

As the financial crisis of 2008–09 draws to a close, narratives of the meltdown are flooding bookstores, think tanks are cranking out white papers, and four different congressional committees, along with the official Financial Crisis Inquiry Commission, are investigating what went wrong. Well they might, as the most basic question about the meltdown remains unsettled: Why did it happen?

The only near consensus is on the question of what triggered the not-quite-a-depression. In 2007, the housing bubble burst, leading to a high rate of defaults on subprime mortgages. Exposure to bad mortgages doomed Bear Stearns in March 2008, then led to a banking crisis that fall. A global recession became inevitable once the government decided not to rescue Lehman Bros. from default in September 2008. Lehman's was the biggest bankruptcy in history, and it led promptly to a powerful economic contraction. Somewhere around here, agreement ends.

There are no strong candidates for what logicians call a sufficient condition—a single factor that would have caused the crisis in the absence of any others. There are, however, a number of plausible necessary conditions—factors without which the crisis would not have occurred. Most analysts find former Fed Chairman Alan Greenspan at fault, though for a variety of reasons. Conservative economists—ever worried about inflation—tend to fault Greenspan for keeping interest rates too low between 2003 and 2005 as the real estate and credit bubbles inflated. This is the view, for instance, of Stanford economist and former Reagan adviser John Taylor, who

argues that the Fed's easy money policies spurred a frenzy of irresponsible borrowing on the part of banks and consumers alike.

Liberal analysts, by contrast, are more likely to focus on the way Greenspan's aversion to regulation transformed pell-mell innovation in financial products and excessive bank leverage into lethal phenomena. The pithiest explanation I've seen comes from New York Times columnist and Nobel Laureate Paul Krugman, who noted in one interview: "Regulation didn't keep up with the system." In this view, the emergence of an unsupervised market in more and more exotic derivatives—credit-default swaps (CDSs), collateralized debt obligations (CDOs), CDSs on CDOs (the esoteric instruments that wrecked AIG)—allowed heedless financial institutions to put the whole financial system at risk. "Financial innovation + inadequate regulation = recipe for disaster" is also the favored explanation of Greenspan's successor, Ben Bernanke, who downplays low interest rates as a cause (perhaps because he supported them at the time) and attributes the crisis to regulatory failure.

A bit farther down on the list are various contributing factors, which didn't fundamentally cause the crisis but either enabled it or made it worse than it otherwise might have been. These include: global savings imbalances, which put upward pressure on U.S. asset prices and downward pressure on interest rates during the bubble years; conflicts of interest and massive misjudgments on the part of credit rating agencies Moody's and Standard and Poor's about the risks of mortgage-backed securities; the lack of transparency about the risks borne by banks, which used off-balance-sheet entities known as SIVs to hide what they were doing; excessive reliance on mathematical models like the VAR and the dread Gaussian copula function, which led to the underpricing of unpredictable forms of risk; a flawed model of executive compensation and implicit too-big-to-fail guarantees that encouraged traders and executives at financial firms to take on excessive risk; and the non-confidence-inspiring quality of former Treasury Secretary Hank Paulson's initial responses to the crisis.

Other analysts look to the underlying mindset that supported the meltdown. People like to say that the crisis was caused by shortsightedness, stupidity, and greed. But those are weak explanations, unless you think human nature somehow changed in the final decades of the 20th century to make people greedier or more foolish than they were previously. This isn't impossible, but it's hard to support. A subtler psychological argument is that the economy fell prey to recurring delusions about risk and bubbles, which economists Carmen Reinhart and Kenneth Rogoff describe in their book *This Time Is Different*. In another new book, *How Markets Fail*, New Yorker writer John Cassidy focuses on the fallacies of free-market fundamentalists (Greenspan again). Still other writers, like Nobel Prize winner Joseph Stiglitz in his new book, *Freefall*, point to the way globalization spread the toxicity from one country's mortgage market to the rest of the world. Not all such explanations fall according to ideological expectations. The polymathic conservative jurist Richard Posner, argues in his book *A Failure of Capitalism* that the free market itself is to blame for the recent troubles. What these "root causes" explanations have in common is that they don't lend themselves to practical solutions.

This survey leaves out various ideological and esoteric ideas about the cause of the crisis. Their reasons have shifted, but most libertarians and Wall Street Journal editorial page contributors continue to insist that government caused the whole ordeal. In *I.O.U.*, the only truly entertaining book of the many I've now read or browsed on the subject, British writer John Lanchester tosses out the theory that after the West won the Cold War, capitalism could go naked, because governments no longer had to worry about winning converts away from Communism. This is a fascinating idea about the crisis with no evidence whatsoever to support it.

Historians are still debating what caused the Great Depression, so it's not likely this argument will be settled anytime soon. But if we haven't at least learned that our financial markets need stronger regulatory supervision and better controls to prevent bad bets by big firms from going viral, we'll be back in the same place before you can say 30 times leverage.

Critical Thinking

1. What causes regulatory failure?
2. Is regulatory failure due to ineptitude in the bureaucracy, misunderstandings of people, or other circumstances?
3. How does the author expect that the individual "bureaucratic infrastructure across countries in the European Union. . . ." can "adopt labor market reforms . . ." to save the euro?

Create Central

www.mhhe.com/createcentral

Internet References

What Caused the Economic Crisis?—*Slate*
www.slate.com/articles/news_and_politics/the_big_idea/2010/01/what_caused_the_economic_crisis.html

Not Enough House Votes to Pass a Clean CR?—MSNBC
http://video.msnbc.msn.com/now/53209279#53209279

Blaming Rubin—*Reuters*
blogs.reuters.com/felix-salmon/2010/05/01/

What Caused the Financial Crisis?—Marginal Revolution
http://marginalrevolution.com/marginalrevolution/2008/10/what-caused-the.html

---

JACOB WEISBERG is chairman and editor-in-chief of The Slate Group.

Article

Prepared by: Caroline Shaffer Westerhof,
California National University for Advanced Studies

Rumors of Central Command's Decline are Wishful Thinking

RICHARD L. RUSSELL

Learning Outcomes

After reading this article, you will be able to:

- Examine the actions and issues of sequestration regarding the Central Command's "rumored" decline.

- Examine the role and actions of Central Command in the wake of the September 11, 2001, attacks on the World Trade Center and the Pentagon.

- Understand the lack of security intelligence in Central Command trying to put into place a secure environment conducive to the nurturing of a democratic government in Kabul.

Disclaimer: The views expressed are those of the author alone and do not reflect the policy or position of the U.S. government, the Department of Defense, the National Defense University, or Central Command.

Central Command's Marine four-star combatant commander James Mattis passed the command flag to Army four-star General Lloyd Austin in Tampa, Florida on 22 March. Mattis was widely known for his battlefield tenacity in the 2003 Iraq invasion and Austin is known for ably ending in 2011 American combat operations in Iraq leaving some wondering if Central Command's time in the American national security limelight after the drawdown in Afghanistan in 2014 will be at its end. And the hearing of sharpening of sequester budgetary knives up in Washington on Capitol Hill, in the White House, and across the Potomac River in the Pentagon aren't calming any rumors of Central Command's decline.

The sharpening is reminiscent of that heard in the early 1990s during the Clinton administration. International relations optimists wanted to reap huge "peace dividends" by slashing the defense budget because a "democratic peace" was going to characterize the post-Cold War world. The subsequent decades of international conflict should have sobered the democratic peace enthusiasts, but they are at it again. Today, they are arguing that the drawdowns of American forces in Iraq and soon in Afghanistan are now offering a window of opportunity to reap significant defense budget savings by slashing the armed forces and the U.S. Central Command in charge of military operations in the Middle East and South Asia. These policymakers and lawmakers ought to think again to avoid being "penny wise and pound foolish."

A bit of military history is in order for a wiser perspective on current and future defense strategy challenges. Central Command has come a long way since its humble beginnings and has had to mount a wide range of military interventions in the Middle East and South Asia over the last three decades. It grew from a rapid reaction force into a command during the Cold War to deter the Soviet Union from a feared military drive through Iran to the warm water ports of the Arabian Gulf for the projection of Soviet naval power. As the Cold War wound down, it shifted attention from keeping the Soviets out of the Gulf to balancing the Arab Gulf states against Iran, which threatened off and on to defeat Iraq during the Iran-Iraq war from 1980–1988. The simmering naval war with Iranian forces in the Gulf had not halted for two years before Central Command had to take the lead for a military campaign to liberate Kuwait from Iraqi forces. Central Command had to again jump from the pan into the fire after the tragic 11 September 2001 attacks which necessitated waging war against the Taliban and al Qaeda in Afghanistan and, by subsequent turn of events, marching on to Baghdad. Subsequently the command worked to provide stable security environments in both Afghanistan and Iraq for transitions to polities that looked more like democracy.

American policy makers, military men and women, and the American public writ large have been exhausted by the last decade of war in Central Command's area-of-responsibility. Many commentators clamor for the complete withdraw of American troops from Afghanistan after 2014 much like has been done in Iraq in 2011. President Obama himself appears ready to "wash his hands" of the region and his administration has been making great noises about shifting or pivoting America's strategic attention to Asia. If the Middle East and South Asia in Central Command's purview is seen by many as the lands of death, destruction, and misery, the lands of Asia under Pacific Command's watch, in the minds of many, are the lands of plenty, opportunity, and optimism.

But the reports of Central Command's decline and demise are grossly exaggerated. No matter how much Americans would like to turn our backs on problems and conflicts of the Middle East and South Asia, the more we do the more will we be stabbed in our backs. The grim reality is that Middle East and South Asia will a the cross roads of many of the world's ills at odds with American strategic interests to regrettably give Central Command more than its fair share of security burdens year—and even decades—after our 2014 drawdown in Afghanistan.

The Command's Pick-Up Warfare Game Past

Most people have long since forgotten, but the rationale for an American military command for the Middle East and South Asia stemmed from the Cold War rivalry with the Soviet Union. The Carter administration was especially alarmed by the 1979 Soviet invasion of Afghanistan. It worried that the Soviets, if left undeterred, could take a similar gamble and invade Iran to gain access for the Soviet Navy to the warm water ports of the Arabian Gulf. The Carter administration also was gravely concerned that the Iranian revolution had deprived American security policy of one of its great nation-state regional security pillars, making the Gulf all the more vulnerable to Soviet aggression.

The Carter administration undertook two important steps to deter the Soviets from Iran and the Gulf. It announced what came to be known as the Carter Doctrine, stating that, "An attempt by any outside force to gain control of the Persian Gulf region will be regarded as an assault on the vital interests of the United States of America, and such an assault will be repelled by any means necessary, including military force." The doctrine mentioned by all means necessary, which seemed to include the threat of American nuclear weapons. The Carter administration complemented the nuclear threat with conventional force projection capabilities with the establishment in 1980 of the Rapid Deployment Joint Task Force.[1] After the hostage rescue debacle in Iran, the United States turned in earnest to bolster both special operations and traditional military and force projection capabilities into the Middle East and Southwest Asia with the creation of the Central Command.[2]

The American military's sluggish bureaucratic inertia kept Central Command as "an odd man out" even though the command was waging low intensity conflict throughout the 1980s. All the honor, prestige, and promotions seemed to go to American general and flag officers assigned to European Command and NATO, even though a cold peace prevailed in Europe while their peers were in command of shooting conflicts with Iranian forces in the Middle East. Iran was aiding and abetting Hezbollah surrogate bombings and hostage taking of Americans in Lebanon with impunity while mounting naval guerrilla warfare against oil tankers in the Arabian Gulf being escorted by American and allied ships during the Iran-Iraq war. The Iranians harassed international oil shipping and American and coalition forces by laying mine fields and mounting hit-and-run attacks with Revolutionary Guard naval forces.

The American military built and deployed in the European theater to deter and fight the Soviet and Warsaw Pact militaries came in handy for Central Command in 1990 when Saddam Hussein ordered Iraq military forces to invade Kuwait. The forces and doctrine developed for waging war in temperate European theater proved applicable for fighting in the deserts in and around Kuwait. The Americans surged more than 500,000 troops to Saudi Arabia as the jumping off point for liberating Kuwait. The qualitatively better-trained and equipped American military outclassed the numerically superior and largely Soviet-supplied Iraqi military.

The American-led coalition's decisive battlefield besting of the Iraqi military gave birth to heralds of a "revolution in military affairs." They praised battlefield performances dominated by air power and informed by computers, communications, and intelligence. That enthusiasm dwindled in the years after the war after the awakening of ethnic conflict in the Balkans in the 1990s. Many downgraded expectations for battlefield technology and spoke of the "evolution in military affairs." Central Command spent the 1990s broadening and deepening its military support nodes in the Gulf beyond Saudi Arabia and Bahrain as it policed Saddam's Iraq and its largely non-compliance with the terms of the 1991 ceasefire and through Saddam's ejection of United Nations weapons inspectors from his country in 1998.

From Simmering to Hot Wars

Central Command was back front and center in American defense policy strategy in the wake of the 11 September 2001 al Qaeda attacks on the U.S. homeland that killed more than 3,000 people. If anyone had predicted anytime before that fateful year that the United States would one day dispatch up to 160,000 troops to Afghanistan, they would have been declared insane. But that is where American soldiers found themselves overthrowing the Taliban regime, destroying al Qaeda's leadership and infrastructure, and struggling to put into place a security environment conducive to the nurturing of a democratic government in Kabul.

The American military struggled for years, grappling with Afghanistan's security landscape. The military has imprudently turned-over the generals leading the war effort too rapidly, averaging about one per year. Commanding generals barely had enough time to get their bearings before they were dispatched to their next assignment. The American war effort in Afghanistan too was a struggle within the army between the "big army" advocates who focused on using "kinetics" to kill enemies and the "small army" adherents struggling to nudge an institution indoctrinated for fighting similarly organized and equipped militaries to mount a counter-insurgency campaign. The latter focused less on kinetics and more on providing security for the Afghan civilian population.

The struggle for the "hearts and minds" of the Afghan people—as well as for the American army's leadership—played out too in the parallel war in Iraq launched in 2003. President George W. Bush harnessed the political capital he gained in a politically unified United States in the ruins of the 9/11 attacks to order Central Command to oust Saddam Hussein's regime in Baghdad. Bush was shocked, as was the American public, that despite the pre-war American intelligence warnings about Iraq's reconstitution of its biological, chemical, and nuclear weapons programs, all of them were subsequently discovered to have remained in a shambles since the 1991 war. If the United States had launched the war guided by abysmal intelligence, at least the United States and the United Kingdom which bore the brunt of ground combat had given the Iraqi people a window of opportunity to seek a better future for themselves than they had under Saddam's heinous reign.

Talk of the Command's Future Decline Grossly Exaggerated

More than a decade of war in Central Command's strategic neighborhood has taken its toll on the United States. The wars in Afghanistan and Iraq have lasted longer than the American involvement in the World Wars, Korea, or Vietnam. We tragically have lost more than six thousand men and women in uniform, and thousands have been wounded. The men and women remaining in service are suffering as evident by broken military families burdened by seemingly endless combat tours and alarming suicide rates. We have spent hundreds of billions of dollars on the wars and have worn out our military hardware, to include tanks, infantry fighting vehicles, trucks, fixed-wing aircraft, helicopters, ships, and the like. The United States, its leadership and people, are looking to Central Command's area-of-responsibility and are collectively sighing: "Enough."

President Obama does not say it in public, but one certainly could read it "between the lines" when his administration announces its determination to strategically pivot to Asia. The United States is weary from the chronic problems and pessimism of the Middle East and South Asia and wants to geographically turn around to face and embrace the seemingly endless economic opportunities and optimism offered by the "Asian Tigers" and rising China. This worldview focus on Asia will come into sharper focus as the United States in years ahead starts making some dramatic and drastic strategic and military tradeoffs in order to make budgetary ends and means match in the Pentagon.

Nevertheless, the idea that the United States could simply walk away from the Middle East and South Asia for the sake of interests in Asia is simply an illusion. The United States is going to have to be prepared to wage the full spectrum of war in Central Command's area-of-responsibility whether it likes it or not. Central Command has had to militarily intervene in the Middle East and South Asia over the course of decades with direct action special operations, counter-terrorist operations, naval escort and mine clearing, surface-to-surface naval combat, air reconnaissance and policing no-fly zones, retaliatory and punitive aircraft and cruise missile strikes, hostage rescue missions, establishing sanctuary and safe haven for humanitarian assistance delivery, and for waging high intensity state-to-state warfare.

Central Command has performed these broad ranging and diversified types of operations in the past and undoubtedly, and regrettably, will have to dip into the full spectrum of warfare toolkit in the future. It cannot be stressed enough, however, that a consistent trend has emerged throughout our three decades of conflict in the Middle East and South Asia. We have never have been able to predict what kind of fight the next one will be. Consequently, Central Command will have to plan and prepare contingency plans for the full spectrum of military intervention and war.

Far too much of the world's energy wealth—and power derived from it—are married to the most acute security problems on the globe in Central Command's region. These threats stem from Islamic militancy exercised by terrorist and insurgent groups the likes of al Qaeda and the Taliban, as well as by the leaderships emerging in the post-Arab spring regimes—influenced or controlled by Salafists, Hamas, Hezbollah, or the Muslim Brotherhood. Other threats will stem from ethnic and religious conflict, and the proliferation of chemical, biological, and nuclear weapons. If the United States and its Central Command will continue to be embattled by these threats, Israel increasingly will find itself under outright siege. All of these problems, moreover, are growing in scope and magnitude at a time when the world is seemingly getting smaller with globalization and the revolutions in global travel, computers, and communications. To put it bluntly, what happens in Vegas may stay in Vegas. But what happens in the Middle East and South Asia spreads to the world.

Notes

1. Lawrence Freedman, *A Choice of Enemies: America Confronts the Middle East* (New York: PublicAffairs, 2008), 103–104.

2. For an excellent scholar-practitioner's account of the creation of Central Command, see William E. Odom, "The Cold War Origins of the U.S. Central Command," *Journal of Cold War Studies,* Vol. 8, No. 2 (Spring 2006).

Critical Thinking

1. Challenge the concept that current and future defense interventions are winding down.
2. What was the basis for the Carter doctrine?
3. How do the military and the administration look upon the importance of Central Command when we live today in a world that is "seemingly getting smaller with globalization, global travel, revolutions in computer technology and communications"?

Create Central

www.mhhe.com/createcentral

Internet References

U.S. Central Command
http://centcom.ahp.us.army.mil/en/about-centcom/posture-statement

Rumors of Central Command's Decline are Wishful Thinking—Small Wars Journal

http://smallwarsjournal.com/jrnl/art/rumors-of-central-command%E2%80%99s-decline-are-wishful-thinking

Former Commander of U.S. Central Command Cautions against U.S. Military Involvement in Syria without an Endgame—CNN

http://security.blogs.cnn.com/2013/07/21/former-commander-of-us-central-command-cautions-against-u-s-military-involvement-in-syria-without-an-endgame/

U.S. Military Assistance for Africa: A Better Solution—The Heritage Foundation

www.heritage.org/research/reports/2003/10/us-military-assistance-for-africa-a-better-solution

U.S. Military Bases: a Global Footprint—Geopolitical Monitor

www.geopoliticalmonitor.com/us-military-bases-a-global-footprint-3138/liked/

DR. RICHARD L. RUSSELL is Professor of National Security Affairs at the Near East and South Asia Center for Strategic Studies.

Article

Prepared by: Caroline Shaffer Westerhof,
California National University for Advanced Studies

Will Tunisia Follow Egypt?

HAFEZ GHANEM

Learning Outcomes

After reading this article, you will be able to:

- Understand the polarization between secularists and Isamlists in Tunisia.

- Explain the concept of the "Arab Spring" in relation to Tunisia.

- Understand the present discontent among Tunisians in the country.

There are two important similarities between Tunisia and Egypt. First, Tunisian society is polarized between secularists and Islamists. Tunisian secularists are even more vocal than their Egyptian counterparts. They are influenced by the French concept of *laïcité,* which implies a stronger separation between church and state than in the Anglo-Saxon tradition. They complain about the "Islamization" of the civil service and argue that Ennahda's long-term objective is to turn Tunisia into an Islamic state.

Second, the Islamist-led government in Tunisia has so far failed to deliver on the revolution's economic demands. About 78 percent of Tunisians are dissatisfied with the general direction that their country is taking, 83 percent feel that current economic conditions are bad, and 42 percent believe that the country was better off under the former dictator. Discontent in Tunisia appears to be even greater than in Egypt (see table 1). On a more positive note, the Tunisian government has recently reached an agreement with the International Monetary Fund, and some 75 percent of Tunisians expect their economy to improve.

About 81 percent of Tunisians feel that corruption has increased either a lot or a little after the revolution.

Tunisians also believe that their government has failed to control corruption, which was a major revolutionary demand. About 81 percent of Tunisians feel that corruption has increased either a lot or a little after the revolution. This is higher than in Egypt, where 64 percent of those surveyed felt the same way (see table 2).

On the other hand, there are three major differences between Tunisia and Egypt. First, unlike the Muslim Brothers, Ennahda has not been governing alone. It is leading a coalition with two secular parties and therefore may not carry all the blame for negative economic results. The Egyptian secularist claim that the Muslim Brotherhood monopolized power and that President Morsi was an autocrat could not be easily transferred to Tunisia.

Second, the process of constitution writing in Tunisia has been long and has included a real debate between Islamist and secular members of the constituent assembly; both sides have been making concessions and accepting compromises. This is different from the Egyptian case, wherein the constitution was written in a hurry by an Islamist-dominated commission and approved through a referendum in which the turnout was less than 33 percent. Tunisians are eager for this process to conclude. Therefore, it is hard to see them supporting the creation

Table 1 Responses to Questions about Economic Conditions (percent of the population)

	Tunisia	Egypt
Dissatisfied with the direction the country is taking	78 percent	62 percent
Think that the current economic conditions are bad	83 percent	76 percent
Feel that the country is worse off after the departure of dictator	42 percent	30 percent

Source: Pew Research Center's Global Attitudes Project. Tunisian data is from July 2012 and Egyptian data is from May 2013.

Table 2   Perceptions about Changes in Corruption over the Last Two Years (percent of population)

	Tunisia	Egypt
Feel corruption has increased a lot	61 percent	37 percent
Feel corruption has increased a little	20 percent	27 percent
Feel corruption has stayed the same	14 percent	21 percent
Feel corruption has decreased a little	5 percent	11 percent
Feel corruption has decreased a lot	2 percent	5 percent

Source: Transparency International, Global Corruption Barometer, 2013

of another assembly or commission which would start writing a new constitution from scratch (as is demanded by Tamarod).

Third, and perhaps most importantly, the Tunisian military is different than the Egyptian one, in that it does not have a history of political involvement. It is unlikely that the military in Tunisia will side with Tamarod and force the overthrow of the constituent assembly and the government.

The chances of Tamarod succeeding in turning Tunisia into another Egypt appear slim, at least for the time being. Things could change if the constituent assembly continues to delay agreement on a new constitution and a road map for elections and a stable government. This job was supposed to be completed some nine months ago, and Tunisians are starting to show signs of impatience.

Critical Thinking

1. Why do you believe there is more discontent today in Tunisia than is expressed and demonstrated in Egypt? Explain.

2. Can the Tunisian military overturn the government as has been done in Egypt? Explain.

3. Is the present Tunisian constitution sustainable? Explain.

Create Central

www.mhhe.com/createcentral

Internet References

Politicizing Security Sector Reform in Egypt—Real Clear Politics
www.realclearpolitics.com/articles/2013/03/04/politicizing_security_sector_reform_in_egypt_117258.html

Tunisia Opposition Calls for Mass Protests—Aljazeera
www.aljazeera.com/news/africa/2013/10/tunisia-opposition-call-mass-protests-2013101423567680416.html

HAFEZ GHANEM is a senior fellow in the Brookings Institution Global Economy and Development program, leading the Arab Economies project.

Prepared by: Caroline Shaffer Westerhof,
California National University for Advanced Studies

Article

We Shall Return

Don't be too sure there won't be another U.S. war in the Middle East.

RICHARD L. RUSSELL

Learning Outcomes

After reading this article, you will be able to:

- Explain the future of conflict and the implications for the Army.
- Explain Secretary of Defense Robert Gates' term, "next-war-it is."
- Explain how the Army can, and whether it will, adapt its practices and culture to 21st century strategic realities.

S hortly before he left office in February 2011, Defense Secretary Robert Gates told West Point cadets that "in my opinion, any future defense secretary who advised the president to again send a big American land army into Asia or into the Middle East or Africa should 'have his head examined,' as General MacArthur so delicately put it." The remark no doubt reflected Secretary Gates's fatigue and frustration from the enormous intellectual and emotional burdens associated with overseeing the wars in Iraq and Afghanistan.

One suspects, however, that in a more reflective moment, Gates would have acknowledged that "never say never" is a wise rule of thumb in planning for military contingencies, especially in the region that makes up Central Command's area of responsibility. Few, for example, predicted the 1979 Soviet invasion of Afghanistan. Gates himself—who was a senior CIA official during the covert war supporting the Afghan resistance—surely did not anticipate then that the United States would have to return to Afghanistan two decades later to oust a Taliban regime that was harboring terrorists. Before 1990, moreover, no one predicted that Iraq, having just ended a bitter eight-year war with Iran, would swing its battered forces south to invade Kuwait.

So if it's conventional wisdom that the United States will not, or should not, intervene militarily in the Middle East or South Asia after it draws down forces in Iraq and Afghanistan, it's also likely dead wrong. What is true, however, is that political and military trajectories in the Middle East and South Asia are likely to increasingly challenge U.S. contingency access in the coming decade. The ability for the United States to surge large-scale forces into the region, as it did in the 1990 and 2003 wars against Iraq, will grow increasingly circumscribed. The United States will have to adapt to this new strategic landscape by developing more nimble, highly-mobile, stealthy, and networked forces, and by abandoning the traditional practice of slowly and steadily building up conventional forces at regional logistic hubs prior to launching war.

Perhaps the most significant factor that portends against further intervention in the Middle East and South Asia is increased political resistance—and outright opposition—from the countries in the region. That resistance is likely to come from the new regimes emerging from the Arab uprisings, as well as a number of Gulf monarchies.

Indeed, the political trends in the region are unlikely to conform to the rosy predictions of democratic peace theorists, whose musings have implicitly informed the security policies of both Republican and Democratic administrations for decades. Old authoritarian regimes seem to be passing the way of the dodo bird, but the new regimes taking shape are heavily influenced by militant Islamic ideology that will make them less likely to engage in security or military cooperation with the United States.

Democracy optimists argue that these ideological regimes, once entrenched in power, will have to moderate their zeal in order to govern. Pragmatism will ultimately trump ideology. That line of reasoning, however, is based on the assumption that the policy decisions of such regimes can be explained by rational choice economic theory. In other words, if they want to attract international capital and participate in the world economy, they are going to have to break with their ideological affinities. But that reasoning ignores a hard fact of international politics: that time and again, political and ideological prerogatives trump economic rationality. It made little economic sense, for example, for Pakistan to pursue a nuclear weapons program in the 1970s, just as it makes little economic sense for Iran to do so today. Clearly, both Pakistan and Iran made major policy decisions based on political-military priorities rather than economic calculations.

As for the surviving monarchies in the Middle East, they too will likely be less accommodating to American military forces than they have been in the past. To be sure, much of the Arab support for past American military operations—like both Iraq wars—was hidden from the public eye. Arab states often loudly and publicly denounced "unilateral American" military action in the region at the same time as they supported it in backroom dealings, quietly authorizing facilities support and air, land, and sea access.

But if Arab Gulf states were quietly supportive in the past, their opposition to American military force is likely to grow in the future. They read the aftermath of the Arab uprisings much differently than did American and European policymakers. The Gulf monarchies were shocked that the United States "abandoned" Egyptian President Hosni Mubarak in his time of need in early 2011. Their leaders expected the United States to push for Mubarak and the Egyptian military to crack down on public protests in Cairo. After all, American policymakers during the Carter administration had at least given this policy option consideration during the Iranian revolution in 1979.

Already, several Gulf states have begun to translate their displeasure into policy independence from Washington. In 2011, for example, a coalition of Gulf states led by Saudi Arabia intervened in Bahrain to quell domestic unrest in the island country. They did so under the banner of the Gulf Cooperation Council (GCC), which for years had been a feckless military force. Largely unnoticed in Western commentary was that the GCC, for the first time in its history, mounted a relatively effective military intervention.

Bahrain today is for all intents and purposes a province of Saudi Arabia, even if it is not polite to say so in diplomatic circles. Since the Iranian revolution, Bahrain—like the United Arab Emirates, Kuwait, Oman, and Qatar—has pursued close ties with the United States, in significant measure to counterbalance Iran and Saudi Arabia. With Washington at their back, they were able to stake out security policies that were at least nominally independent from Saudi Arabia. When Saudi Arabia wanted American forces removed from the kingdom, for example, Qatar was eager to compensate by hosting a more robust American command presence in the region.

The Arab uprisings and subsequent GCC intervention in Bahrain have turned the tables, making Saudi security backing a necessity for the smaller Gulf monarchies. From their perspective, American forces are clearly more capable than Saudi forces, but given the alignment of their interests, Riyadh is a more reliable security partner. Gulf leaders and military commanders in the coming decade will be focused on how to avoid following in Mubarak's footsteps. Part of minimizing that risk will involve decreasing security dependency on the United States. Gulf leaders have to worry that if push comes to shove, the Americans will throw them under a bus just like they did to Mubarak.

★ ★ ★

If the political dynamics in the Middle East and South Asia do not favor further American military intervention in the future, neither do the emerging military trends. The proliferation of supersonic cruise missiles and mines in the region will make for nasty forced entries into narrow maritime confines like the Suez Canal, the Red Sea, and the Persian Gulf.

But the likely proliferation of nuclear weapons—and ballistic missile delivery systems—will pose even more formidable challenges to conventional military surges in the region. In the future, the United States will not be able to take for granted unchallenged surges of naval, air, and ground forces into regional theaters via logistics hubs. These hubs—like the American naval presence in Bahrain—are large, readily identifiable, and will be increasingly vulnerable to future targeting by nuclear weaponry.

Iran's nuclear weapons, assuming it gets them, will pose a direct threat to American military surge capabilities. Although American policymakers and military commanders might feel confident that they could surge forces into the Gulf despite Iranian nuclear threats because of the American nuclear deterrent, Gulf security partners might be more nervous and less willing to cooperate. As a result, they might not grant access to U.S. air, naval, and ground forces out of fear of angering Iran.

American observers who doubt that Gulf states would make such calculations should recall how Kuwait responded in the lead-up to Iraq's invasion in 1990. When faced with a build-up of Iraqi forces along its border, Kuwait decided not to mobilize its military out of fear that the move would provoke Saddam Hussein. The incentives for Gulf states to make similar strategic calculations in the future will be greater when Iran has an inventory of nuclear weapons to match its growing ballistic missile capabilities.

The Gulf states, moreover, will likely reason that the U.S. capability to threaten or use force against a nuclear Iran will be significantly diminished. Even without nuclear weapons, Gulf states have seen, in their view, a long history of American reluctance to threaten or use force against Iran. For example, the United States took no direct military action against Iran after it aided and abetted Hezbollah bombings against Americans in Lebanon in the 1980s, after Iran supported the bombing of Khobar Towers in Saudi Arabia in 1996, or even after Iran supported the deadly campaign of improvised explosive devices (IEDs) against U.S. troops in Iraq. Gulf states will no doubt judge that if the United States was unable and unwilling to attack Tehran under these circumstances, then it is certainly not going to attack Iran in the future, when it will be able to retaliate with nuclear weapons.

American policymakers may counter that Iran would never be foolish enough to threaten or use nuclear weapons against the United States, given its robust nuclear deterrence posture. But the threat or use of nuclear weapons might not look so foolish from Iran's perspective. One of the great strategic lessons drawn from the long history of conflict in the Middle East is this: Do not go to war without nuclear weapons, as Saddam Hussein did when he invaded Kuwait. The corollary is: Do not allow the United States to methodically build up forces in the Gulf prior to invading, as Saddam did both in the run-up to the 1991 re-conquest of Kuwait and in 2003, before the drive to topple the regime in Baghdad.

Drawing upon these lessons, Iran will likely do everything in its power to deny the United States the ability to surge conventional forces into the region—and that might include threatening to target U.S. forces with nuclear weapons. Iran might accept the risk that preemptive use of nuclear weapons could bring on American nuclear retaliation, because failure to do so would mean certain destruction for the regime. The United States would be able to build up conventional forces in the region and oust Iran's leaders just as it did in Baghdad.

This line of strategic reasoning runs counter to conventional wisdom in the West, but we actually know little or nothing about what Iranian decision-makers think about nuclear weapons or deterrence theory. Since the Iranian revolution in 1979, opportunities for the exchange of professional views between Western and Iranian scholars, policymakers, and military leaders on these critically important issues have been extremely limited. Therefore, it's not unreasonable to assume that the Iranians, like American policymakers in the early stages of developing their nuclear triad doctrine, will think of nuclear weapons as merely "big artillery." Unfortunately, the United States and its security partners lack formal and informal exchanges with the Iranians akin to the Cold War discussions and arms control negotiations between the Americans and Soviets, which allowed both parties to develop mutual understandings of the other's perception of nuclear weapons. These understandings were essential for crisis management in the Cold War strategic relationship after the Cuban missile crisis.

Meanwhile, the Gulf states, led by Saudi Arabia, are likely to look for their own nuclear deterrents. Much like France wanted its own nuclear *force de frappe* during the Cold War, the Gulf states will want their own nuclear weapons to deter Iran. Saudi Arabia and the smaller Gulf states will worry that the United States would be deterred from coming to their defense in future regional crises by Iran's nuclear weapons.

Saudi Arabia and other Arab states are likely to see nuclear weapons as a quick fix for all of their security woes. Although they have been on a shopping spree in the past decade, buying expensive and sophisticated Western military technology, they have had a tough time absorbing the new technology and fully utilizing and integrating weapons systems. To be sure, in a rough net assessment, Saudi Arabia and its allies in the Gulf have significantly greater conventional capabilities than Iran. But if Iran goes nuclear, they will want to follow suit.

Americans may be weary of conflict in the Middle East and South Asia, but strategic prudence demands that we contemplate future military interventions in the Central Command theater. A scan of the horizon reveals that both political and military trends in the region pose formidable obstacles to conventional force surges into the region.

But there is another wrinkle in this story that U.S. policymakers must contend with as they plan for the future. As Gulf monarchies seek to reduce their dependence on American military power, they will increasingly look to China for security assurances. China does not have a political agenda devoted to promoting democratization, and it maintains political and diplomatic ties with both Arab states and Iran. China's military activity in the region is modest but increasing, as evidenced by its recent peacekeeping dispatches to the region and naval port visits in the Gulf. Beijing is likely to send more naval forces to the Gulf to increase its presence there and enhance its ability to protect the sea lanes which bring oil to China's thirsty

economy. China is keenly aware that the United States has naval supremacy in the Gulf, but will be working to erode that strategic edge in the future.

Faced with these realities, there is a need for new thinking and innovative conceptualizations of surges into Centcom's area of responsibility. Theater campaign planners will have to think about contingencies in which the United States cannot slowly and methodically build up forces in the region and then kick off campaigns after most troops, arms, and equipment are in place. Future U.S. force build-ups in the region will be far too vulnerable to preemptive nuclear strikes. As a result, planners will have to devise campaign plans in which the insertion of U.S. military forces begins with an immediate rolling and flowing start. The United States will have to work from smaller troop footprints and be prepared to start fighting even as follow-on forces are on the way. Ideally, these forces would flow from multiple staging positions to reduce vulnerability to nuclear attack. The politics of the region, however, will work against securing a multitude of staging areas from which to deploy.

The region under the purview of Centcom has always been riddled with political violence that has posed formidable challenges to military operations. But in plotting a course over the horizon, the political and military obstacles for American military surges into the region are poised to grow even larger. As a result, theater contingency planners will have fewer good options for projecting American military power into the region—and they'll have to do more with the bad and the ugly.

Critical Thinking

1. How must the military service change to empower its leaders in the 21st century?
2. How has the Army, as an institution, been transformed by war?
3. Critique the meaning of the quote from the Revolutionary War that Secretary of Defense Gates often refers to: In a letter Abigail Adams wrote to her son, John Quincy Adams, "these are times in which a genius would wish to live. It is not in the still calm of life or in the repose of a pacific station that great characters are formed . . . great necessities call out great virtues."

Create Central

www.mhhe.com/createcentral

Internet References

U.S. Department of Defense—Speech
www.defense.gov/speeches/speech.aspx?speechid51539

Interview with Former Defense Secretary Robert Gates—CNN
transcripts.cnn.com/TRANSCRIPTS/1306/26/ampr.01.html

Robert M. Gates—*New York Times*
http://topics.nytimes.com/top/reference/timestopics/people/g/robert_m_gates/

Richard L. Russell, Ph.D., is Professor of National Security Affairs at Near East and South Asia Center for Strategic Studies, National Defense University, and Political, Military Analyst, Central Intelligence Agency.

Russell, Richard L. Reprinted in entirety by McGraw-Hill with permission from *Foreign Policy*, February 5, 2013. www.foreignpolicy.com. © 2013 Washingtonpost.Newsweek Interactive, LLC.

Unit 7

UNIT

Prepared by: Caroline Shaffer Westerhof,
California National University for Advanced Studies

Global Trends: Institutional Change, Progress, and Threat

The systematic treatment of the political behaviors of citizens, interest groups, parties, the executive, legislature, and unelected officers in government, such as the military, lobbyists, and others reflects other dimensions of policy and decision making within regimes. The discussions make clear the relevance of institutions and institution building in providing formal venues to regulate and regularize political behaviors so that they are clear-cut, comprehensible, constant, and, thus, predictable. But, if institutions affect political behaviors, it is also indisputable that political behaviors shape institutions. In this unit, we examine the "what, how, and why" of institutional changes. In the process, we consider the extent to which political behaviors shape institutions in general, and democratization in particular.

What are institutional changes? Institutional changes refer to the creation or alteration of political organizations, conventions, or participation. They include modifications in political or legal processes, bureaucracy and technology, enhanced by all types of electronics, including cyberspace. They may be radical or gradual; they may reflect democratic governments, as well as authoritarian. They may involve the creation of new political organizations, or they may involve the liberalizing trends in some Asian state institutions, and they may seek to project the future. It is more realistic "to project" what may or may not happen than "to predict." The science of projection is easier to develop than the database of predictions.

How do institutional changes occur? Institutional changes are brought on by a combination of the following: domestic demand, such as by citizens, interest groups, and the government; or new pressures from new climate-related disasters and globalization. Institutional changes generated by domestic demand often hinge on changes in values and attitudes, and the state of the economy. Can we project the future when we study climate destruction and an economy based on poverty? Does one destroy the other or can the destruction be corrected?

Can there ever be a definitive discussion of the events in the Middle East? Is it one's perspective versus another's? In surveying political behaviors and institutions across a wide net of countries we realize that this full circle returns to this: Institutional changes occur in response to demands for better or more representative venues within which citizens and government may interact. While onlookers may fault institutions or even countries for failing to be more accountable, representative, or just, it is primarily the demands of domestic constituents—the citizens—that will usher in and support changes. Supporting nation-states and non-supporting play a role in the manipulation of political power in such nation-states as Lebanon, Egypt, and Syria. We have not simultaneously witnessed such Middle East chaos on so many fronts, as in the present.

Representation and accountability are sorely lacking at the present time in many nations within the Middle East. It is not necessarily the spirit that will "move systems." Understanding comparative politics generates a greater awareness of actions leading to changes in organizational structures, or more turbulence, or why the actors are and must change. We are each part of multi-stakeholder behavioral patterns, economic rebalancing, and changes in governmental structures; there is explicit acknowledgment and awareness that the processes toward a global, regional and nation-state solution are far outpaced by the unknown of world problems, present and in the future. As a result, the first step—even if it is an "insufficient" one—is to try to understand what is presently happening and the undercurrents of the present and continuing changing actors. Thus it is crucial that all elements and actors in the institutions, including outlets, academics, military, governmental and nongovernmental organizations, work together to share information.

Any faith that providing more information and disseminating it widely will usher in better or more representative political and social environs by galvanizing the citizens misreads and misunderstands that there is as much information on the Internet that is deliberately planted and monitored. Similarly, if we expect that international or regional agencies are able to step in to provide a hand, and that the descriptions of global political development and actions that span across the boundaries of countries, then we, as responsible global citizens, should be informed about institution building and policy choices through understanding and knowledge. We continue to survey democratic theory and how citizens' behavior and institutional performance relate to democratization, and other political systems, typical and atypical. In doing so, we are better able to outline for the international community what it means to nurture and support citizen demands, without imposing our own preferences and impatience, in the interests of promoting stability and development within countries, intra-nations, and in inter-nation relations.

Article   Prepared by: Caroline Shaffer Westerhof,
                                   California National University for Advanced Studies

Economy Slows "Due to Rebalancing"

CHEN JIA, HE WEI, AND HE YINI

Learning Outcomes

After reading this article, you will be able to:

- Understand the slower economic growth in China and economic restructuring.

- Understand measures that will react to liquidity outflows.

- Understand the reality of GDP growth rates in China and why the country coud be increasingly vulnerable to a chaotic adjustment.

China's economy grew by 7.6 percent year-on-year in the first half, a marked slowdown in comparison with near double-digit growth recorded just two years ago.

A government spokesman said that reducing the growth rate is necessary for rebalancing the economy. The nation is capable of keeping growth momentum steady for the rest of the year, even though the economic environment is expected to remain grim and complicated, he added.

The government's yearly GDP growth target for 2013, set earlier this year, is 7.5 percent.

Sheng Laiyun, spokesman for the National Bureau of Statistics, said that despite the slowdown, China's growth is still higher than that in other major economies.

The nation saw economic growth fall to 7.5 percent in the second quarter, from 7.7 percent in the first and 7.9 percent in the fourth quarter of 2012.

Investment was the biggest growth driver in the first half of the year, contributing 4.1 percentage points to the 7.6 percent rate, while consumption contributed 3.4 percentage points and net exports 0.1 percentage point, the bureau said.

Industrial output in the first six months grew by 9.3 percent from a year earlier, compared with a 10.5 percent increase in the first half of 2012.

Annual growth of fixed-asset investments in the first half lost some steam, rising 20.1 percent year-on-year, down from 20.9 percent.

Meanwhile, consumer goods retail sales rose by 12.7 percent, 1.7 percentage points lower than in the first two quarters of 2012.

The slowdown was caused by the weak global economic recovery and measures taken by the new leadership, Sheng said.

Jonathan Holslag, a research fellow at the Brussels Institute of Contemporary China Studies, said the figures send a very strong signal that the central government is trying to rebalance the economy.

"The growth rate is still optimistic considering the scale of China's economy and is still contributing a lot to the global economy," Holslag said.

But he said this year will be very challenging as the country restructures the economy against a backdrop of global hardship. Holslag stressed that the risks the government faces come from the banking sector and the stock market.

Slowdown to Continue

Wang Jun, a senior economist at the China Center for International Economic Exchanges, a government think tank in Beijing, said China still faces pressure from downside risks in the second half.

"It may push the government to take measures ... to further expand domestic demand. Otherwise, difficulties may arise from tight local government financing and increasing unemployment," Wang said.

He denied that a large stimulus package will be needed, as the new leadership might tolerate a growth rate of no less than 7 percent.

After the statistics bureau released the first-half growth figures, JPMorgan Chase downgraded its forecast for the year's growth to 7.4 percent from 7.6 percent, saying manufacturing investment and overseas demand remain weak.

"A slowdown of GDP growth to 7.5 percent will not trigger a change in policy," said Zhu Haibin, chief economist in China with the US bank.

"The new government made it clear that it is willing to tolerate slower growth for better quality of growth. Economic restructuring is the priority task going ahead."

On July 15, Nomura Securities said it will keep its GDP growth forecast for this year at 7.5 percent, but lower it to 6.9 percent for 2014.

"We expect growth to bottom in the second quarter of 2014 at 6.5 percent," said Zhang Zhiwei, the company's chief economist in China.

An adjusted growth target of 7 percent may emerge in 2014, setting the country on a temporary but turbulent journey toward a more balanced economy, according to Michael McDonough, senior economist at Bloomberg LP.

But for the next six months, the government may still accelerate investment projects and cut interest rates, among other efforts to defend a 7.5 percent GDP growth target, he noted.

This year, China's macroeconomic data have consistently come in below analysts' forecasts, leading to a series of growth downgrades, he said. For instance, the government's 2013 GDP goal is 7.5 percent, well below January's consensus forecast of 8.1 percent.

It is interesting to note that historically the government's target has acted more as a floor than a legitimate estimate. But this year that is very likely to change, McDonough said.

"They won't set next year's target below 7 percent, but I do think a general trend is going to be a continued slowdown. Slower growth will be a good thing, though it will inevitably cause some short-term pain. But in order to rebalance, you need to lessen the reliance on investment," he said.

The 4 trillion yuan ($651 billion) stimulus package enacted following the 2008 financial crisis boosted growth, but essentially led to a surge in credit expansion and generated extensive industrial overcapacity, which McDonough said was responsible for much of the current slowdown.

The overcapacity was especially obvious in the manufacturing sector, where the Producer Price Index, a main gauge of inflation at the wholesale level, has dropped for 16 consecutive months, indicating tepid domestic demand.

Another case in point was the surging amount of social financing after the 2008 input. An increasing portion of these loans, which targeted lower-valued projects, may struggle to stay afloat in an environment of slowing growth.

Annual new yuan loan-issuance between 2008 and 2012 was on average more than 140 percent above the 2007 level.

Private Sector Encouraged

McDonough noticed a change in the response to the slowdown compared with five years ago.

"While the government still has room to increase investment in certain infrastructure projects that may boost urbanization, a goal the new leadership has highly valued, officials are showing a restrained response and instead are attempting to encourage more private-sector involvement," he noted.

He said urbanization-driven infrastructure investment is going to be a value-added, smart use of money to bring people to cities and would produce a decent return in the long run, whereas the stimulus program only resulted in industry bubbles.

While these types of investment may accelerate in the second half of the year, the aim will probably be to achieve the government's official target, rather than what investors might perceive as market-friendly 8 percent growth, McDonough added.

While officials have publicly recognized that China's economy needs to lessen its dependence on investment, there has yet to be tangible change on that front.

Investment's share of GDP rocketed to 48.3 percent in 2011, while household consumption shrank to just 35.4 percent, compared with 50 percent in 1989.

McDonough said that the rising contribution of investment has meant that slower growth is almost a "necessity" if China is to shift toward consumption and the private sector as a major growth engine.

"An economic slowdown is like a forest fire (that gets rid of the underbrush) in a forest. It's terrible at first, but then it cleans out the excesses of the current system, and everyone will be better off when the economy starts over from a sound base," Jim Rogers, an international investment guru, said in an exclusive interview with *China Daily*.

"It's happening in China at the moment as the government stays tight to cool things down. But I think it's a good thing."

The government said in a guideline issued on July 5 that it would continue belt-tightening and scale back the supply of funds in the market to a reasonable level to contain a debt-fueled economic boom.

The guideline came after a liquidity crunch, which triggered a dive in the stock market and pushed interbank rates to record highs, had eased. But economic concerns linger.

"The Chinese government does have a plan to stay tight to calm things down. Some people are going to suffer, and that's what's happening. But that will be good for China in the end," Rogers said.

"Even if some sectors of the Chinese economy have a hard landing and some people go bankrupt, people (doing business) in other sectors, such as agriculture, culture, pollution control, etc, will not be affected at all, because these fields will enjoy great prosperity in the years to come."

These fields, Rogers said, will be new sweet spots for investment in China.

He said all countries that rise have periodic setbacks along the way.

Critical Thinking

1. Why is the growth rate that really matters considered to be the average household income?

2. Why are ordinary Chinese most concerned about real disposable income, rather than per capita share of country's GDP?

3. What would affect the risk of a credit crisis in China?

Create Central

www.mhhe.com/createcentral

Internet References

National Forex

http://nationalforex.com/2013/07/15/

Chinese Economic Slowdown and Its Implications—The Frontier Post

www.thefrontierpost.com/article/41247

China's Economic Growth and Rebalancing—European Central Bank

www.ecb.europa.eu/pub/pdf/scpops/ecbocp142.pdf

China's Economic Rebalancing and the Impact on the Australian Economy—The Daily Reckoning

www.dailyreckoning.com.au/chinas-economic-rebalancing-and-the-impact-on-the-australian-economy/2013/07/04/

CHEN JIA is chief correspondent of *China Daily USA* in San Francisco and covers topics including business, technology, politics, and education.

Article   Prepared by: Caroline Shaffer Westerhof,
California National University for Advanced Studies

Democracy in Cyberspace: What Information Technology Can and Cannot Do

Ian Bremmer

Learning Outcomes

After reading this article, you will be able to:

- Examine the reality of how information technology has demolished time and distance.

- Identify the spread and the concept of the "freedom virus."

- Examine how the Internet is promoting pluralism and human rights around the world.

"Information technology has demolished time and distance," Walter Wriston, the former ceo of what is now Citigroup wrote in 1997. "Instead of validating Orwell's vision of Big Brother watching the citizen, [it] enables the citizen to watch Big Brother. And so the virus of freedom, for which there is no antidote, is spread by electronic networks to the four corners of the earth." Former Presidents Ronald Reagan, Bill Clinton, and George W. Bush have articulated a similar vision, and with similarly grandiose rhetoric. All have argued that the long-term survival of authoritarian states depends on their ability to control the flow of ideas and information within and across their borders. As advances in communications technology—cellular telephones, text messaging, the Internet, social networking—allow an ever-widening circle of people to easily and inexpensively share ideas and aspirations, technology will break down barriers between peoples and nations. In this view, the spread of the "freedom virus" makes it harder and costlier for autocrats to isolate their people from the rest of the world and gives ordinary citizens tools to build alternative sources of power. The democratization of communications, the theory goes, will bring about the democratization of the world.

There seems to be plenty of evidence to support these ideas. In the Philippines in 2001, protesters sent text messages to organize the demonstrations that forced President Joseph Estrada from office. In the lead-up to the 2004 presidential election in Ukraine, supporters of Viktor Yushchenko, then the leader of the opposition, used text messaging to organize the massive protests that became the Orange Revolution. In Lebanon in 2005, activists coordinated via e-mail and text messaging to bring one million demonstrators into the streets to demand that the Syrian government end nearly three decades of military presence in Lebanon by withdrawing its 14,000 troops. (Syria complied a month later, under considerable international pressure.) Over the past few years, in Colombia, Myanmar (also known as Burma), and Zimbabwe, demonstrators have used cell phones and Facebook to coordinate protests and transmit photographs and videos of government crackdowns. The flood of words and images circulated by protesters following Iran's bitterly disputed 2009 presidential election—quickly dubbed the "Twitter revolution"—seemed to reinforce the view that Tehran has more to fear from "citizen media" than from the U.S. ships patrolling the Persian Gulf.

But a closer look at these examples suggests a more complicated reality. Only in democracies—the Philippines, Ukraine, Lebanon, and Colombia—did these communications weapons accomplish an immediate objective. In Myanmar, Zimbabwe, and Iran, they managed to embarrass the government but not to remove it from power. As Wriston acknowledged, the information revolution is a long-term process, cyberspace is a complex place, and technological advances are no substitute for human wisdom. Innovations in modern communications may help erode authoritarian power over time. But for the moment, their impact on international politics is not so easy to predict.

There are many reasons why the optimistic view of the relationship among communications, information, and democracy has taken root in the United States. First, these communications tools embody twenty-first-century innovation, and Americans have long believed in the power of invention to promote peace and create prosperity. And with good reason. Admirers of Reagan argue that the United States' ability to invest in strategic missile defense sent the Soviet leadership into a crisis confidence from which it never recovered. The light bulb, the automobile, and airplane have changed the world, greater personal autonomy to many Americans. Similarly, Americans believe that the millions of people around the world who use the Internet, an American invention, will eventually adopt American political beliefs, much like many of those who wear American jeans, watch American movies, and dance to American music have. Champions of the Internet's power to promote pluralism and human rights point to bloggers in China, Russia, and the Arab world who are calling for democracy and the rule of law for their countries, sometimes in English.

But of the hundreds of millions who blog in their own languages—there are more than 75 million in China alone—the vast majority have other priorities. Many more of them focus on pop culture rather than on political philosophy, on pocketbook issues rather than political power, and on national pride rather than cosmopolitan pretensions. In other words, the tools of modern communications satisfy as wide a range of ambitions and appetites as their twentieth-century ancestors did, and many of these ambitions and appetites do not have anything to do with democracy.

Net Neutrality

A careful look at the current impact of modern communications on the political development of authoritarian states should give pause to those who hail these technologies as instruments of democratization. Techno-optimists appear to ignore the fact that these tools are value neutral; there is nothing inherently pro-democratic about them. To use them is to exercise a form of freedom, but it is not necessarily a freedom that promotes the freedom of others.

In enabling choice, the introduction of the Internet into an authoritarian country shares something fundamental with the advent of elections. Some have argued that promoting elections in one country in the Middle East will generate demand for elections elsewhere. A free Iraq is going to help inspire others to demand what I believe is a universal right of men and women," Bush said in July 2006; elections in Iraq would prompt the citizens of Iraq's neighbors to ask why Iraqis were now free to choose their leaders whereas they were not. Similarly, some have argued that the freedom that comes with the Internet will inevitably democratize China. Once Chinese people read about the freedoms of others, the thinking goes, they will want the same for themselves. The tools of modern communications will reveal to Chinese citizens the political freedoms they do not yet have and provide the means to demand them.

But the limited history of elections in the Middle East shows that people do not always vote for pluralism. Sometimes, they vote for security or absolutism, sometimes to express outrage or defend local interests. The same pattern holds true for the Internet and other forms of modern communications. These technologies provide access to information of all kinds, information that entertains the full range of human appetites—from titillation to rationalization, from hope to anger. They provide the user with an audience but do not determine what he will say. They are a megaphone, and have a multiplier effect, but they serve both those who want to speed up the crossborder flow of information and those who want to divert or manipulate it.

Cyberspace can be a very dark place. In *You Are Not a Gadget*, Jaron Lanier argues that the anonymity provided by the Internet can promote a "culture of sadism," feeding an appetite for drive-by attacks and mob justice. In China, the Internet has given voice to wounded national pride, anti-Western and anti-Japanese resentment over injuries both real and imagined, and hostility toward Tibetans, Muslim Uighurs, and other minority groups. It has also become a kind of public square for improvised violence. In an article for *The New York Times Magazine* earlier this year, Tom Downey described the "human-flesh search" phenomenon in China, "a form of online vigilante justice in which Internet users hunt down and punish people who have attracted their wrath." The targets of these searches, a kind of "crowdsourced detective work," as Downey put it, can be corrupt officials or enemies of the state, or simply people who have made other people angry.

These problems are hardly unique to China. In Russia, skinheads have filmed murderous attacks on dark-skinned immigrants from the Caucasus and Central Asia and posted the footage online. Also in Russia—and in the United States and Europe—hate groups and militants of various kinds use the Internet to recruit new members and disseminate propaganda. Of course, beyond all this fear and loathing, many more people around the world use the Internet as a global shopping mall and a source of entertainment. The Internet makes it easier for users with political interests to find and engage with others who believe what they believe, but there is little reliable evidence that it also opens their minds to ideas and information that challenge their worldviews. The medium fuels many passions—consumerism and conspiracy theories, resentment and fanaticism—but it promotes calls for democracy only where there is already a demand for democracy. If technology has helped citizens pressure authoritarian governments in several countries, it is not because the technology created a demand for change. That demand must come from public anger at authoritarianism itself.

Stateside

Citizens are not the only ones active in cyberspace. The state is online, too, promoting its own ideas and limiting what an average user can see and do. Innovations in communications technology provide people with new sources of information and new opportunities to share ideas, but they also empower governments to manipulate the conversation and to monitor what people are saying.

The collapse of Soviet communism a generation ago taught authoritarian leaders around the world that they could not simply mandate lasting economic growth and that they would have to embrace capitalism if they hoped to create the jobs and the higher standards of living that would ensure their long-term political survival. But to embrace capitalism is to allow for dangerous new freedoms. And so in order to generate strong growth while maintaining political control, some autocrats have turned to state capitalism, a system that helps them dominate market activity through the use of national oil companies, other state-owned enterprises, privately owned but politically loyal national champions, state-run banks, and sovereign wealth funds.

Following precisely the same logic, authoritarian governments are now trying to ensure that the increasingly free flow of ideas and information through cyberspace fuels their economies without threatening their political power. In June, the Chinese government released its first formal statement on the rights and responsibilities of Internet users. The document "guarantee[d] the citizens' freedom of speech on the Internet as well as the public's right to know, to participate, to be heard, and to oversee [the government] in accordance with the law." But it also stipulated that "within Chinese territory, the Internet is under the jurisdiction of Chinese sovereignty." That caveat legitimates China's "great firewall," a system of filters and re-routers, detours and dead ends designed to keep Chinese Internet users on the stateapproved online path.

The Chinese leadership also uses more low-tech means to safeguard its interests online. The average Chinese Web surfer cannot be sure that every idea or opinion he encounters in cyberspace genuinely reflects the views of its author. The government has created the 50 Cent Party, an army of online commentators that it pays for each blog entry or message-board post promoting the Chinese Communist Party's line on sensitive subjects. This is a simple, inexpensive way for governments to disseminate and disguise official views. Authoritarian states do not use technology simply to block the free flow of unwelcome ideas. They also use it to promote ideas of their own.

Nonaligned Movement

The techno-optimists who hope that modern communications tools will democratize authoritarian states are also hoping that they will help align the interests of nondemocracies with those of democracies. But the opposite is happening. Efforts by police states to control or co-opt these tools are inevitably creating commercial conflicts that then create political conflicts between governments.

In January, Google publicly complained that private Gmail accounts had been breached in attacks originating in China—attacks that Chinese officials appeared to tolerate or even to have launched themselves. In protest, Google announced that it would no longer censor the results of users' searches in mainland China, which it had reluctantly agreed to do when it entered the Chinese market in 2006. Beijing refused to back down, and Google automatically redirected searches by Chinese users to the uncensored Hong Kong version of the site. But much to the relief of mainland users, mostly students and researchers who prefer Google's capabilities to its main domestic rival, Baidu, Chinese officials eventually announced the renewal of Google's operating license. (It is possible that they backtracked because they believed that they could control Google or use it to monitor the online activities of political dissidents.)

As Chinese technology companies begin to compete on a par with Western ones and the Chinese government uses legal and financial means to more actively promote domestic firms that see censorship as a routine cost of doing business, there will be less demand for Google's products in China. In August 2010, the state-run Xinhua News Agency and China Mobile, the country's largest cell-phone carrier, announced plans to jointly build a state-owned search—engine and media company. In response to these developments, U.S. technology companies

will undoubtedly turn to U.S. lawmakers for help in creating and maintaining a level commercial playing field in China. Far from aligning American and Chinese political values and bringing the citizens of the two countries closer together, conflicts over the flow of information through cyberspace will further complicate the already troubled U.S. Chinese relationship.

Signs of strife are already visible. When Google first went public with its complaints about cyberattacks and censorship, Beijing looked past the company, which it sees as a high-tech arm of the U.S. government, and addressed its response directly to Washington. A Chinese Communist Party tabloid ran an editorial under the headline "The World Does Not Welcome the White House's Google"; it argued, "Whenever the U.S. government demands it, Google can easily become a convenient tool for promoting the U.S. government's political will and values abroad." In response, U.S. Secretary of State Hillary Clinton urged companies such as Google not to cooperate with "politically motivated censorship," further emphasizing the difference, not the convergence, of political values in the United States and China.

Revealing similar fears about the future of its political control, the United Arab Emirates and Saudi Arabia took action earlier this year against Research in Motion (RIM), the Canadian company that makes the BlackBerry, for equipping its devices with encryption technology that authorities cannot decode. Arguing that terrorists and spies could use BlackBerries to communicate within the uae without fear of being detected, Emirati officials announced in August that they would soon suspend BlackBerry service unless RIM provided state officials with some means of monitoring BlackBerry messaging. Within two days, Saudi Arabia announced a similar shutdown, although Riyadh and RIM have since reached a compromise that requires RIM to install a relay server on territory, which allows Saudi officials monitor messages sent from and within country. The UAE will probably also a deal with RIM: there are half a millon BlackBerry users in the UAE (about percent of the population), and the country wants to remain the Arab world's primary commercial and tourist hub. Yet far from promoting Western values in non-Western police states, the BlackBerry has sparked a new round of debate over the willingness of Western technology companies to protect their market shares by making concessions that help authoritarian governments spy on their citizens.

In fairness to these governments, the world's leading democracies are no less concerned about potential terrorist threats posed by unmonitored messaging. The Indian government has also threatened to ban BlackBerries unless RIM gives it access to certain data, and counterterrorism officials in the United States and Europe are considering the option as well. Via efforts to amend the Electronic Communications Privacy Act, the Obama administration has already taken steps to help the FBI gain access to "electronic communication transactional records"—recipients' addresses, logs of users' online activities, browser histories—without a court order if investigators suspect terrorism or espionage. Politicians and technology companies such as Google and RIM will be fighting these battles for years to come.

Of course, authoritarian governments, unlike democracies, also worry that individuals who are neither terrorists nor spies will use new communications tools to challenge their political legitimacy. China, Iran, Myanmar, North Korea, Saudi Arabia, and other authoritarian states cannot halt the proliferation of weapons of modern communications, but they can try to monitor and manipulate them for their own purposes. That struggle will continue as well, limiting the ability of new technologies to empower the political opposition within these countries and creating more conflicts over political values between democratic and authoritarian states.

Feedback Loops

The Internet may have changed the world, but now the world is changing the Internet. For 30 years, new communications technologies have driven globalization, the defining trend of the times. The companies that created these products made longterm plans based on the wants and needs of consumers, not governments. Their profits rose as they connected billions of customers with one another; borders became increasingly less important.

But now, the pace of technological change and the threat of terrorism are forcing policymakers to expand their definitions of national security and to rethink their definitions of "critical infrastructure." As a result, governments are turning to high-tech communications firms to help shore up emerging security vulnerabilities, and high-tech communications firms have begun to think more like defense contractors—companies whose success depends on secrecy, exclusivity, political contacts, and security clearances.

As a result, political borders, which the rise of information technology once seemed set to dissolve, are taking on a new importance: if greater openness creates new opportunities, it also creates new worries. Unable to match U.S. defense spending, China and Russia have become adept at information warfare. The Pentagon reported last August that China continues to develop its ability to steal U.S. military secrets electronically and to deny its adversaries "access to information essential to conduct combat operations." In 2007, a massive cyberattack launched from inside Russia damaged digital infrastructure in neighboring Estonia. The United States' vulnerabilities range from its nuclear power plants and electrical grids to the information systems of government agencies and major U.S. companies. Despite their political and commercial rivalries, the United States, China, Russia, India, and many other states also share a vulnerability to cyberattacks, and they have pledged to work together to build a joint cybersecurity strategy But when it comes to espionage, governments can never fully trust one another. And of course the Obama administration does not want to share technologies that would make it easier for security officials in Beijing or Moscow to track the online activities of political dissidents.

Other problems will exacerbate international tensions. Technology firms in the United States and Europe, mindful of Google's recent troubles in China, will increasingly turn to their governments for help with their own security needs. As cyberthreats become ever more sophisticated, these companies will collaborate more actively with national security agencies on developing new technologies. This will pull more technology companies into the orbit of the military-industrial complex. That, in turn, will make them even more suspect to authoritarian regimes and likelier targets for hackers and spies of all kinds. Borders are about to become much more important.

The result will be a world that has not one Internet but a set of interlinked intranets closely monitored by various governments. The Internet is not about to disappear, but the prediction that a single Internet could accommodate both the West and the evolving demands of authoritarian states was never realistic. American and European users will access the same Internet as before, but the Chinese government has already made clear its intention to declare sovereignty over an Internet of its own. Other authoritarian states have every incentive to follow its lead.

There are far too many variables at work to predict with confidence the full, longterm impact of modern tools of communications on the political development of authoritarian states. But it seems safe to expect that their effects will vary as widely as the motives of the people and the states that use them.

Critical Thinking

1. How has the Internet developed a "multiplier" effect?
2. Can the Internet threaten authoritarian governments with loss of political power?
3. How is the globalization of the world changing the use and misuse of the Internet?

Create Central

www.mhhe.com/createcentral

Internet References

Ian Bremmer
www.ianbremmer.com/book/every-nation-itself-winners-and-losers-g-zero-world
Challenges of Democratization
www.brandonkendhammer.com/democratization_Spring2013/schedule
Who's in Charge of the World? No One—Reuters
blogs.reuters.com/ian-bremmer/2012/04/30
Ian Bremmer—World Policy Institute
www.worldpolicy.org/ian-bremmer

IAN BREMMER is president of the Eurasia Group and is a geopolitical analyst.

From *Foreign Affairs*, vol. 89, issue 6, November/December 2010, pp. 86–94. Copyright © 2010 by Council on Foreign Relations, Inc. Reprinted by permission of Foreign Affairs. www.ForeignAffairs.com

Article   Prepared by: Caroline Shaffer Westerhof,
                                        California National University for Advanced Studies

The Coming Wave

LARRY DIAMOND

Learning Outcomes

After reading this article, you will be able to:

- Explain why democracies have gained ground in areas of
  the world except the Middle East.

- Explain the liberalizing trends that Larry Diamond notes
  in some Asian state institutions, besides Japan and South
  Korea.

- Explain how the political aftermath of the Arab Spring of
  2011 continues to shape world politics.

If there is going to be a big new lift to global democratic
prospects in this decade, the region from which it will ema-
nate is most likely to be East Asia.

With the eruption of mass movements for democratic change
throughout the Arab world in 2011, hopeful analysts of global
democratic prospects have focused attention on the Middle
East. Three Arab autocracies (Tunisia, Egypt, and Libya) have
fallen in the past year. At least two more (Yemen and Syria)
also seem destined for demise soon, and pressures for real democratic change figure to mount in Morocco, Jordan, the Palestinian Authority, and perhaps Kuwait, and to persist in Bahrain.
Yet among these and other countries in the Middle East (including Iraq and Iran), only Tunisia has a good chance of becoming
a democracy in the relatively near future. Aspirations for more
democratic and accountable government run deep throughout
the Middle East, and for years to come the region will be a
lively and contested terrain of possibilities for regime evolution. But if a new regional wave of transitions to democracy
unfolds in the next five to ten years, it is more likely to come
from East Asia—a region that has been strangely neglected in
recent thinking about the near-term prospects for expansion of
democracy. And East Asia is also better positioned to increase
the number of liberal and sustainable democracies.

Unlike the Arab world, East Asia already has a critical mass
of democracies. Forty percent of East Asian states (seven of the
seventeen) are democracies, a proportion slightly higher than in
South Asia or sub-Saharan Africa, though dramatically lower
than in Latin America or Central and Eastern Europe, where
most states are democracies. As a result of the third wave of
global democratization, East Asia has gone from being the

cradle and locus of "developmental authoritarianism," with
Japan as its lone democracy—and a longstanding one-party-
dominant system at that—to at least a mixed and progressing
set of systems. Today, Japan, South Korea, and Taiwan are all
consolidated liberal democracies. East Timor, Indonesia, Mongolia, and the Philippines are at least electoral democracies
with some resilience.

Moreover, as I will explain, there are now significant prospects for democratic change in a number of the region's remaining authoritarian regimes. Thailand is progressing back toward
democracy; Malaysia and Singapore show signs of entering a
period of democratic transition; Burma, to the surprise of many,
is liberalizing politically for the first time in twenty years; and
China faces a looming crisis of authoritarianism that will generate a new opportunity for democratic transition in the next
two decades and possibly much sooner. Moreover, all this has
been happening during a five-year period when democracy has
been in recession globally.

There are three democracies in East Asia today that rank
among the stable liberal democracies of the industrialized
world: Japan, South Korea, and Taiwan. They are not without
stiff economic and political challenges and large numbers of
disenchanted citizens who in surveys express only tepid support for democracy. Yet in each of these countries, overwhelming majorities of citizens reject authoritarian regime options
while voicing reasonably robust support for broadly liberal values such as the rule of law, freedom of expression, and judicial
independence.[1] Comparative data on political rights, civil liberties, and the quality of governance confirm that these are liberal democracies. They could become better, more liberal ones,
however, by deepening the rule of law and civil liberties and
improving mechanisms of accountability and transparency to
control corruption and political favoritism.

East Asia's merely electoral democracies have further to
go toward deepening and consolidating democracy, of course.
Mongolia scores relatively well in Freedom House ratings of
political rights and civil liberties, but in this phenomenally
mineral-rich country the judiciary remains underdeveloped,
the rule of law is weak, and corruption remains a grave problem widely recognized by the public. Indonesia's democratic
performance over the past decade has been much better than
what many experts on that country might have expected.
The Philippines has returned to democracy with the 2010

election, in which Benigno Aquino III won the presidency. Yet semi-feudal elites retain a strong hold on the politics of many Philippine provinces and constituencies, and their presence in the country's Congress has so far largely blocked basic reform. In the World Bank's annual governance ratings, Indonesia and the Philippines rank in the bottom quartile of all countries in corruption control and not much better (the bottom third) in rule of law. In 2010, among big (mainly G-20) emerging-market democracies such as Argentina, Bangladesh, Brazil, India, Mexico, South Africa, and Turkey, only Bangladesh did worse on these two governance indicators.[2]

In each of these three electoral democracies—Mongolia, Indonesia, and the Philippines—at least three-quarters of citizens agree that "Democracy may have its problems, but it is still the best form of government." In each, likewise, only about half the public is satisfied with the way democracy is working, but majorities believe that democracy remains capable of solving the country's problems. One possible reason for this faith in democracy is suggested by the wide majorities in each country (up to 76 percent in Mongolia and 80 percent in the Philippines) who say that they believe the people retain the power to change the government through elections.[3]

Prospects for Further Democratization

It is by now widely appreciated that Singapore is by any standard a massive anomaly. As we see in the Table (next page), Singapore is far richer today than any major third-wave countries were when they made their transitions to democracy (this includes Spain and Greece, which do not appear in the Table). Singapore is the most economically developed nondemocracy in the history of the world. But Singapore is changing, and this change will probably accelerate when the founding generation of leaders, particularly Lee Kuan Yew (who turned 88 last September), passes from the scene. In the May 2011 parliamentary elections, the ruling People's Action Party (PAP) recorded its weakest electoral performance since independence in 1965, winning "only" 60 percent of the vote. Although the PAP still won (yet again) well over 90 percent of parliamentary seats thanks to a highly rigged electoral system, the opposition Workers' Party broke through for the first time to win a five-seat group constituency, and a total of six seats overall—a record for the Singaporean opposition. While a postelection survey failed to reveal a general increase in support for greater political pluralism since the last elections (in 2006), the expressed preference for a more competitive political system did increase dramatically in the youngest age cohort (those from 21 to 29), shooting up from 30 to 44 percent.[4] If Singapore remains in the grip of a half-century-long single-party hegemony, that hegemony now seems to be entering a more vulnerable phase, as opposition parties find new energy and backing, as young people flock to social media to express themselves more openly, as independent media crop up online to provide a fuller range of news and opinions, and as the ruling party feels compelled to ease censorship and other controls. Singapore, in other words, has already joined the ranks of the world's "competitive authoritarian" regimes—the

class of autocracies among which democratic transitions are most likely to happen.[5]

Singapore's exceptionalism is widely known. Less well known is that Malaysia now also has a higher per capita income than most third-wave countries did when they made their transitions to democracy. In fact, among the prominent cases in the Table, only Taiwan had a higher per capita income than Malaysia when it completed its democratic transition. Moreover, Malaysia's score on the UNDP's Human Development Index—which, in measuring not only per capita income but also levels of health and education, is arguably a truer measure of development—is now significantly higher than the levels in Brazil, Chile, Mexico, and even Hungary, Poland, and Ukraine when they made their respective transitions to democracy. From the standpoint of modernization theory, then, Malaysia is also ripe for a democratic transition.

For more than a decade, Malaysia's competitive authoritarian regime has faced a much more serious challenge than anything Singapore has so far seen. As the opposition has gained in unity, credibility, and mobilizing power, the long-ruling United Malays National Organization (UMNO) feels under increasing threat. Much of what is driving change in Malaysia is not only exhaustion with half a century of rule by one party (formally through a ruling coalition), but also a much better educated and more pluralistic society, with the attendant growth in independent organizations and the intense and innovative use of social media (including one of the most influential online newspapers in the world, *Malaysiakini*).

Alarmed by the upheavals that began sweeping the Arab world at the end of 2010, Malaysia's Prime Minister Najib Razak pledged to appoint a broad committee to review the country's electoral system and recommend reforms, and then vowed to repeal the draconian Internal Security Act. Many opposition and civil society leaders, however, saw these promises as empty, citing Razak's push to enact stiff new security laws in place of the old ones. After winning control of five of the thirteen states in 2008, opposition forces are poised to do better in the next elections, which could come in 2012. The new opposition alliance, Pakatan Rakyat, is gaining momentum, and the regime's renewed effort to destroy former deputy prime minister Anwar Ibrahim with trumped-up charges of homosexual misconduct seems even less credible than when the ploy was first tried some years ago. To be sure, Malaysia's authoritarian establishment still has a lot of resources, but Razak's proposed reforms now seem "too little too late," as "cynicism still pervades the country."[6] A transition to democracy could happen any time in the coming years, through the familiar instrument that has brought it about in other competitive authoritarian regimes: the electoral process.

Thailand is less developed than Malaysia, but also has far more democratic experience and now, once again, more freedom and pluralism. Although Thais remain deeply polarized between a camp that backs ousted premier Thaksin Shinawatra and one that clusters around the institution of the monarchy, national elections are highly competitive and seem to meet the "free and fair" standard of electoral democracy. With the decisive opposition victory of the new Pheu Thai Party (led by

Thaksin's sister Yingluck Shinawatra) in the May 2011 parliamentary elections, the political force that the military deposed in the 2006 coup has returned, and Thailand has apparently become once again an electoral democracy. Yet it faces a rocky road ahead, as the stabilizing presence of long-reigning King Bhumibol (b. 1927) draws toward a close. If the end result is a weaker monarchy (and military), this might ultimately help to ease the country's intense polarization and create a more mature and securely institutionalized politics. At least the military seems to have learned from the political turbulence and polarization of the last decade that its own direct intervention will not solve the country's political problems. Though it clearly preferred the incumbent Democrat Party, the military made a point of declaring its neutrality in the recent election. If the 2006 military coup does prove to be the last in Thailand's history, democracy will put down firmer roots over the coming decade as modernization further raises incomes and education. Already, Thailand has a per capita income and human-development score roughly equivalent to those of Poland when it made its transition to democracy around 1990 (see Table).

It is not only Southeast Asia's wealthier countries that are experiencing the winds of democratic change. As Burma's iconic democratic leader Aung San Suu Kyi has recently acknowledged, that country's political opening, launched in 2008 amid widespread skepticism with many voters abstaining from a constitutional referendum, suddenly seems quite serious. Labor unions have been legalized, Internet censorship has been eased, and a number of political prisoners have been freed. Now, Suu Kyi's National League for Democracy (which won the aborted 1990 elections) is preparing to register for and run in parliamentary by-elections to be held probably later in 2012. As has happened with other authoritarian regimes that opted to liberalize politically, Burma's authoritarian rulers seem to have been influenced by democratic developments elsewhere in the world, as well as by the prospective economic benefits—chiefly flowing from closer integration with the global economy—that political liberalization might bring. As an advisor to Burma's President Thein Sein noted in December 2011, "The president was convinced about the global situation; he saw where the global stream was heading."[7]

The Coming Change in China

Annual per capita income in China is still little more than half what it is in Malaysia, but it has been rising rapidly and now approaches the level that South Korea could boast at the time of

Table—Development Levels and Democratic Transitions

Country	Year of Transition	GDP per Capita, PPP$ (2009 international dollars)	HDI Score (year of transition)
Turkey	1984	6,316	—
Brazil	1985	7,596	0.687
Philippines	1986	2,250	—
South Korea	1988	9,086	—
Pakistan	1988	1,722	—
Hungary	1990	12,979	0.692
Poland	1990	8,376	0.683
Chile	1990	6,896	0.675
Bangladesh	1991	748	0.186
Thailand	1992	4,732	0.685
South Africa	1994	7,235	0.716
Taiwan	1996	19,938	—
Indonesia	1999	2,666	0.681
Mexico	2000	12,662	0.698
Ghana	2000	1,653	0.431
Ukraine	2005	6,037	0.696
Asia (Current)			
Singapore	—	56,522	0.866
Malaysia	—	14,670	0.761
Thailand	—	8,505	0.682
China	—	7,519	0.687
Vietnam	—	3,134	0.593
Laos	—	2,436	0.524
Burma	—	1,256	0.483

Source: for HDI: http://hdr.undp.org/en/data/trends; for GDP per capita: www.imf.org/external/pubs.
Note: GDP per capita and HDI (Human Development Index) scores in the bottom index are for the years 2010 and 2011, respectively. All GDP per capita figures have been transformed into the value of constant 2009 dollars using the GDP deflator.

its democratic transition in 1987–88. In fact, by IMF projections, China could surpass that level (about US$9,000 in 2009 Purchasing Power Parity [PPP] dollars) by next year. In 1996, Henry Rowen predicted on the basis of data and projections regarding economic development that China would become what Freedom House would call a Partly Free country by 2015, and a Free one (with political-rights and civil-liberties scores as good as those of India or Indonesia today) by 2025.[8] More recently, Rowen affirmed that analysis, estimating that even if China's growth in GDP per capita slowed to 5 percent annually starting in 2015, it would have by 2025 a per capita income roughly equivalent to that of Argentina's in 2007 (about $15,000 in current PPP dollars—which is roughly where Malaysia is today).[9] And if China's growth in per capita income were to slow immediately to 6 percent annually, it would still reach $13,000 in current PPP dollars before 2020—the level of Hungary in 1990 and Mexico in 2000 when they transitioned to democracy.

It is not only modernization—the spread of democratic values and capacities in tandem with rising incomes and information—that is feeding the escalating pressure for democratic change in China. As Yun-han Chu notes in his contribution to this set of essays, the growing density of ties between mainland China and Taiwan—including direct access (through travel and satellite television) to political news from the highly competitive and even raucous democracy that is Taiwan—is serving as an additional stimulant to the growth of democratic norms and aspirations in China. The irony of Communist China's relentless push for closer integration with Taiwan is that it may well begin to generate political convergence—but not in the way that the Communist leaders imagined.

Rowen's projections were a bit mechanical in assuming that economic growth would necessarily drive *gradual* political change toward democracy in China. Instead, it seems increasingly likely that political change in China will be sudden and disruptive. The Communist Party leadership still shows no sign of embarking on a path of serious political liberalization that might gradually lead to electoral democracy, as their counterparts in Taiwan's then-dominant Nationalist Party did several decades ago. Instead, the rulers in Beijing are gripped by a fear of ending up like the USSR's Mikhail Gorbachev, who launched a process of political opening in hopes of improving and refurbishing Soviet Communist rule only to see it crumble and the Soviet Union itself fall onto the ash heap of history. Torn by intense divisions within their own ranks and weakened by the draining away of power and energy from the center to the provinces and a congeries of increasingly divergent lower-level authorities, China's political leaders seem as frozen and feckless on the grand question of long-term political reform as they are brisk and decisive in making daily decisions on spending and investments.

As Francis Fukuyama notes in the essay that follows, the one flaw in the otherwise impressive institutionalization of Chinese Communist rule is its lack of adaptability. For a regime whose specialty is producing rapid economic change, such rigidity is a potentially fatal defect. With every month or year that ticks by while corruption, routine abuses of power, and stifling constraints on expression go unchecked, citizens' frustration mounts. Already, protests erupt with ominous frequency across tens of thousands of Chinese localities every year, while subversive and democratic ideas, images, and allusions proliferate online, despite the best efforts of fifty-thousand Internet police to keep Chinese cyberspace free of "harmful content." As Minxin Pei has been arguing for some time and as he asserts again in his essay here, the strength of the authoritarian regime in China is increasingly an illusion, and its resilience may not last much longer. As frustration with corruption, collusion, criminality, and constraints on free expression rise, so do the possibilities for a sudden crisis to turn into a political catastrophe for the Chinese Communist Party (CCP).

Beyond the ongoing frustrations with censorship, insider dealing, abuse of power, environmental degradation, and other outrages that can only be protested by antisystem activity of one sort or another, there are, as Fukuyama notes, the big looming social and economic challenges that China faces as the consequences of its one-child policy make themselves felt in a rapidly aging (and disproportionately male) population. Jack Goldstone reports that China's labor force stopped growing in 2010 and has begun shrinking half a percent a year, which "will, by itself, knock 2.2 percentage points off China's annual economic growth potential." Urbanization, a key driver of productivity increases, is also slowing dramatically, and the growth of education "has clearly reached a limit," as the number of college graduates has expanded faster than the ability of the economy—even as it faces labor shortages in blue-collar industries—to generate good white-collar jobs.[10]

The Chinese economy will have to pay for rapidly rising wages and cope with industrial labor shortages even as it comes under pressure to finance pension, welfare, and healthcare benefits for the massive slice of the populace that is now moving toward retirement. Moreover, as it manages all this, China will need to address growing frustration among college graduates who cannot find jobs to match their expectations. If the suspected bubbles in the real-estate and financial markets burst as these twin generational challenges are gathering force, political stability in the world's most populous country may well become no more than a memory.

Increasingly, the CCP faces the classic contradiction that troubles all modernizing authoritarian regimes. The Party cannot rule without continuing to deliver rapid economic development and rising living standards—to fail at this would invite not gradual loss of power but a sudden and probably lethal crisis. To the extent that the CCP succeeds, however, it generates the very forces—an educated, demanding middle class and a stubbornly independent civil society—that will one day decisively mobilize to raise up a democracy and end CCP rule for good. The CCP, in other words, is damned if it does not, and damned if it does. The only basis for its political legitimacy and popular acceptance is its ability to generate steadily improving standards of living, but these will be its undoing.

For some time, I suspected that Henry Rowen's projections were a bit optimistic and that China's democratic moment, while foreseeable, was still 25 to 30 years away. Now, as the need for a more open, accountable, and law-based regime becomes as obvious as the current leaders' inability to bring one about, I suspect that the end of CCP rule will come much sooner, quite possibly within the next ten years. Unfortunately, a sudden collapse of the communist system could give rise, at least for a while, to a much more dangerous form of authoritarian rule, perhaps led by a nationalistic military looking for trouble abroad in order to unify the nation at home. But this would likely represent only a temporary solution, for the military is incapable of governing a rapidly modernizing, deeply networked, middle-class country facing complex economic and social challenges.

Whatever the specific scenario of change, this much is clear: China cannot keep moving forward to the per capita income, educational, and informational levels of a middle-income country without experiencing the pressures for democratic change that Korea and Taiwan did more than two decades ago. Those pressures are rising palpably now in Singapore and Malaysia. They will gather momentum in Vietnam as it follows in China's path of transformational (even if not quite as rapid) economic development. In Thailand, continuing modernization over the next decade will change society in ways that will make democracy easier to sustain. In short, within a generation or so, I think it is reasonable to expect that most of East Asia will be democratic. And no regional transformation will have more profound consequences for democratic prospects globally.

Notes

1. See, for example, Yun-han Chu et al., *How East Asians View Democracy* (New York: Columbia University Press, 2008), and various reports of the Asian Barometer, *www.asianbarometer.org.*

2. World Bank Group, Worldwide Governance Indicators, 2011, *http://info.world-bank.org/governance/wgi/index.asp.* Indonesia and the Philippines were rated in the 27th and 22nd percentiles, respectively, on control of corruption and the 31st and 24th percentiles, respectively, on rule of law. South Korea, by contrast, was in the 69th and 81st percentiles on these two measures.

3. Data is from Round III of the Asian Barometer.

4. Institute for Policy Studies (Singapore), "IPS Post-Election Survey 2011." My thanks to Tan Ern Ser for sharing a copy of the summary findings.

5. Stephan Ortmann, "Singapore: Authoritarian but Newly Competitive," *Journal of Democracy* 22 (October 2011): 153–64.

6. Ooi Kee Beng, "In Malaysia, Reforms Take a Staggered Path," *TodayOnline,* 3 December 2011, available at *www.todayonline.com/Commentary/EDC111203-0000021/In-Malaysia-reforms-take-a-staggered-path.*

7. "In Myanmar, Government Reforms Win Over Some Skeptics," *New York Times,* 30 November 2011.

8. Henry S. Rowen, "The Short March: China's Road to Democracy," *National Interest* 45 (Fall 1996): 61–70.

9. Henry S. Rowen, "When Will the Chinese People Be Free?" *Journal of Democracy* 18 (July 2007): 38–52.

10. Jack A. Goldstone, "Rise of the TIMBIs," *Foreign Policy,* 2 December 2011, available at *www.foreignpolicy.com/articles/2011/12/02/rise_of_the_timbis?page=0,1.*

Critical Thinking

1. Why are there no Arab democracies in the Middle East?

2. Could you compare the Arab Spring of 2011 to the tearing down of the Berlin Wall? Why or why not?

3. Has Thomas Jefferson's prophecy any reality with regard to the Arab Spring "I hope our wisdom will grow with our power, and teach us, that the less we use our power, the greater it will be"?

Create Central

www.mhhe.com/createcentral

Internet References

Stanford
http://fukuyama.stanford.edu/files/Patterns%20of%20History.pdf

Thinking about Hybrid Regimes—Project Muse
http://muse.jhu.edu/login?auth=0&type=summary&url=/journals/journal_of_democracy/v013/13.2diamond.html

Harvard
www.hks.harvard.edu/fs/pnorris/DPI403%20Fall09/DPI403_Powerpoint_Slides_Fall2010/3%20DPI403%20Applying%20the%20analytical%20framework.pdf

Larry Diamond Speaks on Governance and Democracy in Africa—United States Africa Command
www.africom.mil/Newsroom/Article/7522/larry-diamond-speaks-on-governance-and-democracy-i

Democracy's Third Wave
www.rickweil.com/s4421/Readings/Huntington.pdf

Larry Diamond—Stanford Center on Democracy, Development, and the Rule of Law
http://cddrl.stanford.edu/people/larry_diamond

LARRY DIAMOND is senior fellow at the Hoover Institution and the Freeman Spogli Institute for International Studies at Stanford University, director of Stanford's Center on Democracy, Development, and the Rule of Law, and coeditor of the *Journal of Democracy.* His forthcoming book, In *Search of Democracy*, will be published by Routledge later this year.

From *Journal of Democracy,* January 2012, pp. 5–13. Copyright © 2012 by National Endowment for Democracy and The Johns Hopkins University Press. Reprinted with permission of The Johns Hopkins University Press.

Article   Prepared by: Caroline Shaffer Westerhof,
                                        California National University for Advanced Studies

Iran Press Report: Reactions to Developments in Lebanon, Egypt, and Syria

MEHRUN ETEBARI

Learning Outcomes

After reading this article, you will be able to:

- Explain why some Middle East leaders felt that Morsi's fall from power became a losing strategy when he put trust in the Americans.

- Understand why Iran is compared to North Korea.

- Understand the fears of Prime Minister Netanyahu of Israel when he says if Iran were to reverse course and push for a nuclear bomb, Israel would have to retaliate.

In reaction to the week's bad news for Iran's close ally in Lebanon, there was all-around condemnation in the Iranian press this week for the European Union's decision to add Hezbollah's military wing to its list of terrorist groups. Mohammad Safari in the conservative *Siasat-e Rooz* argued that the move was likely to poison the atmosphere for future negotiations between Iran and the P5+1 over the nuclear program. He added that it was yet another example of the Western service of the Zionists: "The occupying regime [Israel] . . . has stood to this day only thanks to the West and the European nations, and if, one day, the West stops its support for the Zionists, that day will be the day of the definitive fall of the regime." Hossein Sheikholeslam in the reformist *Etemaad* agreed that the move was dishonorable, suggesting that much as European nations resisted against Nazi occupation in World War II, they are going against their historical principles in calling a group which is fighting Israel for its "occupation of Lebanon and Syria" terrorists.

The situation in Egypt has continued to draw reflection from Iranian commentators, many of whom focused their attention on where they thought deposed president Mohammad Morsi had gone wrong. Yadollah Javani in the hardline *Javan* said that Morsi's mistake had been trying to secure the Muslim Brotherhood's grip on power by reaching out to the United States,

Israel, and their allies, who could not be trusted. "After his victory, Morsi's first foreign trip was to Saudi Arabia . . . but after his fall from power, the Saudi king was the first person to congratulate the interim president who replaced Morsi," he wrote, adding that the coup had vindicated the anti-American nature of Iran's Islamic Revolution. He posed the rhetorical question, "If the American Embassy [in Tehran] had not been captured, would the Islamic Revolution still be around in its fourth decade?" In *Qods,* Mohammad-Mehdi Shirmohammadi agreed that Morsi had put his faith in the wrong partners, saying, "Instead of relying on the Egyptian nation he relied on the reactionary regimes and America," and argued that Turkish Prime Minister Recep Tayyip Erdogan should view Morsi's downfall as a cautionary tale and change his behavior. Meanwhile, Amir Mousavi added in a *Hamshahri* interview that the Muslim Brotherhood's rejection of cooperation with other parties and the retreat of Qatar from active support played roles in Morsi's fall.

Not all articles put the primary blame on Morsi and the Brotherhood. Despite Iranian problems with the Brotherhood, however, and despite the mistakes that Morsi made in government, Mohammad-Mehdi Mazaheri argued in *Hamshahri* that the Muslim Brotherhood being allowed an active role in politics is the only way Egypt can reclaim its democracy. In a more convoluted analysis, Hassan Hanizadeh claimed in *Tehran-e Emrooz* that instability in Egypt has been deliberately stoked by Washington as part of a conspiracy to create chaos that will prompt the partitioning of the nation between Christian and Muslim regions, with the Christian region used by America to provide greater security to Israel.

Commentators also discussed what they saw as weakness of countries that had been acting against the interests of Iran and the "resistance axis." In his interview, Amir Mousavi added that Turkish distraction with domestic protests, Qatar's retreat from the stage during the transfer of power to the new Emir, Sheikh Tamim bin Hamad, and the downfall of Morsi's presidency meant most of the regional actors who had been supporting the Syrian opposition were increasingly absent from the scene, leaving Saudi Arabia on its own there with little chance for success. This dynamic, wrote Seyyed Emad Hosseini in the reformist daily *Etemaad,* left one-time staunch Iranian ally Hamas, and its political leader Khaled Meshaal, in a tough situation. Citing the retreat of Hamas's new anti-Iranian supporters, he wrote that Meshaal has made a "180-degree turn" and is asking for Iranian support, and questions whether the resistance axis should welcome Hamas back. He suggests that Meshaal might be too ungracious to deserve it: "[Meshaal], meanwhile, has not explained why, in spite of the widespread support that the government of Bashar Assad had given his movement, he sharply criticized the Damascus government."

Critical Thinking

1. How has the condemnation of the European Union's decision to add Hezbollah's military wing to its list of terrorist groups affected Iran, Lebanon, and its neighbors?

2. What do commentators allege when they say, "Tehran is not Pyongyang"?

3. Why do commentators feel that it is a weakness of countries that had been acting against the interests of Iran and the "resistance axis"?

Create Central

www.mhhe.com/createcentral

Internet References

Iran—Press TV
www.presstv.ir

Iran Focus News and Analysis
www.iranfocus.com

Opinion Polls | The Arab American Institute
www.aaiusa.org/pages/opinion-polls

Prepare for the Worst—Brookings
www.brookings.edu/research/opinions/2013/07/25-middle-east-peace-talks-fall-apart-sachs

What to Read on Iran This Week: Looking Ahead to the Rouhani Presidency—Brookings
www.brookings.edu/blogs/iran-at-saban/posts/2013/08/02-what-to-read-on-iran-this-week

Mehrun Etebari is an Iran analyst in Washington, D.C., and Senior Research Assistant, Saban Center for Middle East Policy.

Prepared by: Caroline Shaffer Westerhof,
California National University for Advanced Studies

Article

A New Growth Paradigm

Vinod Thomas

Learning Outcomes

After reading this article, you will be able to:

- Understand how the Philippines' vulnerability to floods and storms is sapping the commitment of the government.

- Explain how the present weather disasters have hindered growth in the economy of the Philippines.

- Explain the microfinance programs in the Philippines.

The economy of the Philippines stands out for its relatively robust 6.6-percent growth in 2012 amid lackluster economic growth in most places around the world. The crucial question, however, is how the country can sustain this performance to generate far more jobs and reverse the rise in poverty seen in the past decade.

Domestic reforms are paramount to the Philippines' growth prospects, but cross-border factors matter, too, in our highly globalized world economy. Perhaps surprisingly for some, the danger of climate change arguably presents a greater threat than the current global economic malaise. If sustained growth is to take place, this challenge must be met. Specifically, we need to strengthen disaster resilience, care more for the urban environment, and confront climate change as part of the growth paradigm.

Climate-related disasters have crowded the headlines worldwide in recent years. East and Southeast Asia top the list of the regions affected. Floods and storms have cut significantly into annual growth rates in Australia, China, Indonesia, Korea, Thailand and Vietnam—a trend that is set to worsen. The Philippines, often the first major landfall for typhoons arising in the western Pacific, is among the most vulnerable.

Multiple factors, of course, explain these mounting disasters. First, many more people now live in harm's way, particularly in low-lying megacities like Manila. Second, soil erosion, deforestation, and just plain overcrowding leave people more vulnerable to natural hazards. And third, the hazards are growing more menacing.

Scientists are nevertheless cautious in linking any particular disaster to climate change, whether it is Typhoon "Pablo" in Mindanao or Hurricane "Sandy" on the US East Coast. In the same way, economists are reluctant to pin higher inflation in any given month on rising money supply. But, as with inflation, the broader associations are unmistakable.

For some, the front-and-center needs of the Filipino poor will apparently heighten a dilemma balanced on growth versus the environment. But the dilemma presents a false choice. Relying on a longstanding growth pattern that fuels economic momentum with environmental destruction will only aggravate climate change. And it is the poor who stand to lose most from the ravages of global warming.

So, as Einstein is said to have observed, we can't do the same things over and over again and expect different results. We must grow fast, but we also need to grow differently.

In essence, we need a new strategy that values all three forms of capital—physical, human and natural. Sound growth policies have long been understood as those that expand investments in physical and human capital. But unless we also invest in natural capital, all bets are off.

First, we should build disaster resilience into national growth strategies. Japan invests some 5 percent of GDP in this area: While paying a heavy price, it has avoided much worse economic damage and deaths from disaster because of this investment.

And high returns on such investment are evident even where the total spending is far less. In the Philippines, the effects of flooding in Manila after heavy monsoon rains in August 2012 contrasted strongly with the devastation in the city from Tropical Storm "Ondoy" in 2009.

The response to the most recent storm demonstrated the vast payoff from measures such as social media alerts, better relief operations, and early warning systems. It also highlighted the benefits of the hazard maps and upgraded rain and water-level monitoring systems promoted by Project NOAH (the Nationwide Operational Assessment of Hazards).

Second, planners need to raise the priority of urban management as a strategic thrust. The five cities considered most vulnerable to natural hazards are all in Asia: Dhaka, Manila, Bangkok, Yangon, and Jakarta. These urban centers are overcrowded and situated in ecologically fragile settings. The massive agglomeration notwithstanding, fewer than 50 percent of Asians live in cities, compared to 80 percent in Latin America. Further urbanization would seem inevitable. It is hard to overstate the high priority for careful physical planning, environmental care and judicious urban management.

Third, climate action needs to be part of the national plan. Economic growth will not be automatic if climate change is not dealt with. Adapting to the changing climate through better management of location decisions of people and businesses and protecting the natural environment assume urgency. But realistically, adaptation measures will not come nearly soon enough, so it is essential to mitigate climate change as well. No single country can make a difference in this respect. However, Asia, which is the most at risk, must be a powerful voice by switching to a low-carbon path and calling on others to do the same.

At the end of the day, we need to change our mindset on how growth is generated. Old-style growth at the expense of the environment will be self-defeating—a realization driven home by the stark reality of climate change.

Critical Thinking

1. Is the Philippines ever going to raise itself from poverty? Explain.

2. Can Vinod Thomas, the author, as a member of the Asian Development Bank, be instrumental in improving the economic growth in the Philippines? Explain.

3. What are the results, to-date, and what has been accomplished implementing the microfinance programs?

Create Central

www.mhhe.com/createcentral

Internet References

Vinod Thomas—Inquirer Opinion
http://opinion.inquirer.net/byline/vinod-thomas

Preparing Better for More Frequent Natural Disasters—Inquirer Opinion
http://opinion.inquirer.net/56761/preparing-better-for-more-frequent-natural-disasters

'More Funds Should Go to Disaster Preparedness'—ABS CBN News
www.abs-cbnnews.com/business/08/21/13/more-funds-should-go-disaster-preparedness

Bank Warns That Asian Growth Could Collapse—UCA News
www.ucanews.com/news/bank-warns-that-asian-growth-could-collapse/68640

VINOD THOMAS is the director general of independent evaluation at the Asian Development Bank and is responsible for the assessment of its many projects and programs in Asia and the Pacific.

Article

Prepared by: Caroline Shaffer Westerhof,
California National University for Advanced Studies

Towards a Renewed Global Partnership for Development

The global partnership for development that underpins the Millennium Development Goals (MDGs) was captured as a standalone goal (MDG8) in 2000. It has played a crucial role in the achievement of the MDGs by facilitating resources and an overall environment conducive to development. A report assessing MDG8 will be released in March and later followed by a chat on Facebook.

DEPARTMENT OF ECONOMIC AND SOCIAL AFFAIRS

Learning Outcomes

After reading this article, you will be able to:

- Understand the shared framework for the global development agenda, action, and cooperation as the world approaches 2015.

- Understand the work of the United Nations System Task Team.

- Identify the Global Partnership Thematic Think Pieces.

As the conversation gears towards the 2015 development agenda, there is great interest to learn from the experience of implementation of MDG8 and ways to strengthen the global partnership for development in the post-2015 era. In this sense, the Secretary-General's High-level Panel of Eminent Persons will place this important issue at the centre of its upcoming meeting in Indonesia at the end of March.

The UN System Task Team (UNTT) on the Post-2015 UN Development Agenda has prepared a report on global partnership which will be published in early March on the UNTT website. Titled 'Towards a renewed global partnership for development' the report presents an assessment of MDG8 and it reviews new challenges for the global economy as well as new trends in development cooperation. The report proposes possible contours, alternative formats and a robust accountability mechanism for a renewed global partnership for the post-2015 era.

Recognizing New Challenges

MDG8 served as an important advocacy tool to stress the important role of the international community in achieving the globally agreed development goals outlined in the MDG framework. Based in the context of 2000, when the MDGs were conceived, the focus of MDG8 is primarily in the areas of Official Development Assistance (ODA), debt relief, trade, technology and access to essential medicines. It also gave special attention to the needs of the least developed and most vulnerable countries.

Going forward, a renewed global partnership for development needs to recognize the challenges of the world we live in today and formulate adequate global efforts that corresponds with global challenges in the areas of climate change, rising inequalities, changing population dynamics, and remaining governance and human rights deficits. Fragile countries have seen the least progress in terms of MDG achievement and thus any attention to most vulnerable countries needs to include fragile states.

Sustainability at the Core

In the discussion about the characteristics of the post-2015 development agenda, there is broad consensus among all stakeholders that sustainability must be at the core of the new agenda. Larger financing needs can be anticipated which cannot be met by ODA alone. While ODA commitments will continue playing a key role supporting the development efforts of the poorest countries, the recent years have seen the rise of a more multipolar economy leading to a significant shift in global economic balance. Given the rise of middle-income countries, the face of poverty has changed significantly.

Today, 75 per cent of the poor live in middle-income countries and further progress to eradicate poverty will require greater policy coherence at global and national levels. Based on the emergence of new economic powers, South-South cooperation has increased and a large array of non-governmental actors (including the private sectors, philanthropy and civil society organizations) have engaged in various forms of global partnerships, often focusing on specific sectors, mainly in the areas of health, education and food security.

Reshaping Donor-Recipient Relationships

A renewed global partnership will need to move away from the traditional donor-recipient relationship that characterized MDG8 and consider a wider range of actors and mechanisms to make the most effective contribution to global development. Unlike MDG8, the new agenda should also build a robust accountability mechanism to address, on a continuous basis, possible shortcomings from commitments made as part of a renewed global partnership for development.

When speaking at an event recently, Secretary-General Ban Ki-moon also described the need for renewed global partnership. "The current global partnership for development needs to be rebalanced and redefined—taking into account emerging economies, South-South partnership, private sector engagement and innovative financing," he said.

Looking at the various challenges at hand and the need for consistent global responses with participation from multiple actors, the discussion about the characteristics of a renewed global partnership for development in the post-2015 era is rather complex. The report of the UN System Task Team provides an overview of the key challenges involved and makes recommendations on ways to address some of these questions with clear suggestions about the format and the contours of a renewed global partnership.

Critical Thinking

1. How has DESA achieved solutions in addressing the world's more pressing concerns?

2. Is DESA NEWS beneficial in understanding the United Nations' actions in the areas of economic and social development policy?

3. What have the Millennium Development Goals achieved to date moving toward the goal date of 2015?

Create Central

www.mhhe.com/createcentral

Internet References

DESA News Announces Release of Second UNTT Report—International Institute for Sustainable Development
    http://post2015.iisd.org/news/desa-news-announces-release-of-second-untt-report

United Nations
    www.un.org

IOM position on the Post-2015 United Nations Development agenda
    www.iom.int/files/live/sites/iom/files/What-We-Do/docs/IOM-Position-Paper-on-Post-2015.pdf

United National Department of Economic and Social Affairs
    www.un.org/en/development/desa/newsletter/desanews/2013/03.html

The United Nations Department of Economic and Social Affairs (DESA) works closely with governments and stakeholders to help countries around the world meet their economic, social and environmental goals. DESA News is an insider's look at the United Nations in the area of economic and social development policy.